Dirty Squatters

Phill Gee

Copyright © 2013-2016 Phill Gee
All rights reserved.

Edited by Debz Hobbs-Wyatt
Cover design by Sean-Franc Strang

ISBN: 0692841520
ISBN-13: 978-0692841525

ACKNOWLEDGMENTS & THANKS TO

Ben Ottridge, Zounds, Harry Enfield, Jaz Coleman, Dennis Bovell, Henri Charriere, LKJ (in Dub), Peter and the Test Tube Babies, Merrydown Cider, Rat Scabies, Watt Tyler, L.E.B., British Gas, The Big Breakfast, Michael Fish, the residents of Villa Road, The Prince Albert, The Rabies Party, Depeche Mode, Brixton Fire Brigade, Red Stripe, Baby Belling Cookers, The Sex Pistols, Fray Bentos, Pot Noodles, the hacksaw, CND, The Young Ones, Chubb Locks, The Squatters Advisory Centre (R.I.P.), The Tube, TOTP, Get Stuffed, Ronnie Biggs, Lightning Strike, Alan Bleasdale, The Ritzy Cinema, David Bowie, Glastonbury Festival (1987), The Squatters Handbook, Max Headroom, Gretsch Drums, Class War, Soft Cell, Crass, Loot, NME, Melody Maker, Viz, Crisis, The Big Issue, The Marquee Club, Jazz, Slippery, Brian, Kay, Sallie, Steve, Cindy, Grace, Camille, Chloe Fine Arts, Todd, Cathleen, Kirsten, Jon, Martha, Abi, Bill, Kristen, Dan, Sten, Frank, Mary, Joe, Mike, Donkey Paul, Dave Earl, Sean-Franc, Paul, Andrea and friends at The Joiners.

Dedicated to squatters new, old,
clean, dirty and anywhere.

Chapterettes

1 – Hackney Quick 3
2 – Squat Realities 9
3 – Outside Toilets, Inside 12
4 – 'Bedshitland' 14
5 – Knock, Knock 19
6 – The-Man-Who-Can-Scam 27
7 – Bedroom Parking 30
8 – Money, Merrydown and Motorcycles 34
9 – The Welsh Connection 41
10 – Jazz, the Squat Cat 46
11 – Santa Comes Early 48
12 – The Itchy Month 51
13 – The Squatters' Toolkit 55
14 – The Vodka Cupboard 62
15 – No Neck Day 67
16 – Pond Scum with Slugs 76
17 – Happy Hours and Whore Alleys 86
18 – Sink Plunging from Above 91
19 – Brixton Brew and Jam Jars 96
20 – Vote R.A.B.I.E.S. Party 99
21 – The Great Escape 102
22 – The Hurricane Season 112
23 – Villas and Mansions 117
24 – Sieges and Sirens with Eggs 127
25 – The Spirit of Community 135
26 – The Pigeon Room 138
27 – Bollock Bowls and Old Boilers 142
28 – Party Season 144

29 – The Rat Trap 151
30 – Medical Curiosities 154
31 – Wot's That Smell? 160
32 – The Ghosts of Brixton 163
33 – White Lightning Weekend 166
34 – Squatting, Dutch Style 173
35 – Maggie! Maggie! Maggie! Out! Out! Out! 182
36 – Secret Four 189
37 – Revolutionaries in Flight 193
38 – Mountain Men 198
39 – Trains, Thumbs and Autobahns 204
40 – Horsebox Hotel 211
41 – Der Deutsche Squat 215
42 – No Hats in Brixton 223
43 – Victim Value 227
44 – Fire and Underpants 232
45 – A Squat with a View 239
46 – The Pig's Head 246
47 – The Drum Shack 249
48 – End of an Era 253
Appendix 258

1 – Hackney Quick

In the late summer of 1983 I decided that it was now time to leave the leafy suburbs of my birthplace in Essex, and find a completely different life in London.

I loaded up with few personal belongings, as many clothes as I could carry on my back, and a small portable black and white TV, then made my way stoically to the train station in the early afternoon. I strolled the quiet, familiar streets and lanes I'd known so well from my childhood years with no idea of what I was about to embark upon on my journey into an unknown future.

I was twenty-one, a punk both in appearance and attitude and a drummer full of the dreams of a young person who needed to throw the fate dice and not really care where they landed. Besides that, Thatcher had just been returned to Downing Street with an increased majority and an even stronger grip on power, thus re-armed with a solid mandate which would allow her to continue with the destruction of British industry. I'd been made redundant from my most recent dead end job in my hometown so it was an appropriate time to make some life changes and move on, and hopefully, upwards…

I'd been invited some months before by a couple of friends to join them and live the squat life in Hackney, as they were aware that I wished to get out of my small town and move to the city. Also, being a drummer I needed to be closer geographically to my band who were based in London.

Events on the home front had taken a turn for the worse; the Tory gang had put my dad on the scrapheap after spending decades as a skilled Design Engineer, and their squeezing of small businesses had put an end my mother's area of expertise too. I was 'between jobs' and had to make the decision to get out before I rotted away from the inside out, or worse still, finished up claiming my own drinking tankard at my local pub all topped off with an increasing beer gut matched with mullet haircut.

After a somewhat reflective train and tube and journey into big London I leafed through my A-Z, then walked from Hackney Wick Station to the terraced Victorian street in E9, my new 'home'. I didn't harbour any fears or reservations about what I'd taken on; it was something that I needed to do and had made a lifestyle choice. I was somewhat obliged to stick to my plans as I stepped up to the red, battered front door.

Curt raised his eyebrows as I stood on the stone steps holding my bags and said TV.

'Hi, just wondering if you guys still have room for me?' I enquired.

'Of course' was his grinning answer.

If nothing else, at least the occupants of the Gascoyne Road squat now had themselves a television.

A cup of tea and a spliff was procured by Curt, then not long afterwards I was shown to 'my room'. Upon entry, it was immediately apparent that my 'basement apartment' was very warm and toasty, this due to the fact that the condemned gas fire down there could not be switched off, ever. There was a single bed, or rather a mattress on the floor in the corner and various bits of half busted nasty furniture no doubt recently thrown out by a neighbour or two. I was happy with my accommodation though my only real worry was that I might not wake up the next morning due to carbon monoxide poisoning from the never ending, totally free gas appliance chucking out continuous heat into the abode.

Curt and Roslyn were the couple who'd invited me to Hackney when they came to The Castle Pub (the only drinking venue suitable for both punks and bikers in my suburban hometown) one Friday evening with a carrier bag full of home grown weed. I really do mean a whole Tesco shopping bag crammed full of dusty buds, dried up leaves and twigs poking out through the weak plastic sides. Curt hadn't bothered with any 'preparation' he just pulled the plants from the back garden, hung them upside down in the hallway to dry, and then crammed into said bag before leaving for Essex.

That was a hilarious night, everyone was totally smashed, as we were rolling up fat spliffs of neat grass in the pub garden as the landlord periodically collected empty glasses and pretended not to notice the sweet smell of Hackney Wick in the air.

After looking around 'our house' and being introduced to the various occupants, the next thing to do was to find out where to look for a job, or failing that, where to sign on, the local food stores, and where to score a decent sized lump of Morocco export. The latter being sourced primarily and by the time Roslyn came back in the evening, Curt, Mark, 'Bullshit Bob' and I were chilled out on north African solid while enjoying the delights of amplified dub reggae in what could commonly be termed as the 'living room'.

Mark was a white Rasta, a quiet bloke also from Essex, and a bass player who also had a serious leaning towards reggae, I instantly liked him. There was another couple residing in the house, whom we rarely met. Then we come to another occupant of the Gascoyne squat, 'Bullshit Bob', he being a Crustafarian and seemingly to all observers a person who rarely washed. He was duly nicknamed 'Bullshit Bob' long before I arrived as he allegedly 'used to play drums in Siouxsie and the Banshees' and he'd also shagged Siouxsie. Yes indeed, that was definitely bullshit. Of course, he wasn't offensive by nature, it's just that his stories were just far too tall to believe, and invariably nobody did.

So, now I was a 'Dirty Squatter'? The general term of phrase used to describe 'homeless people' such as your narrator. The traditional view of those who occupied other people's homes uninvited is that these 'squatters' would break into your house when you were away on holiday, spray can the walls with fluffy hippy or gritty eighties symbolism, throw wild parties and consequently smash the whole place up with a total disregard for your property. When the genuine occupants returned home from their holiday in the sunshine they'd find a nightmare scenario awaiting them, a dozen unwashed people living in their wrecked house who have no intention of leaving. After all, this was only to be expected of class war anarchists, hobos, lowlifes, punk rockers and ageing hippies wasn't it?

    No, not the truth, people who squat decide to live in empty council flats or houses, or long unoccupied properties. The bad element is a tiny percentage, if not a myth. Many buildings are simply left to fall down often owned by 'The Wealthy' who are out of the country for many reasons, including tax evasion and will probably never return anyway. Sometimes a closed government building would be squatted, and ironically these places would often be Unemployment Benefit Offices in a previous life, and were usually red brick early 20th century in design. Occasionally somewhere really fancy would turn up, like an abandoned Embassy. Therefore, a loss by a foreign government of one form or another was someone else's gain, namely ours, the dirty squatters. A roof over one's head is apparently the democratic right of every citizen in any democracy, apparently?

    In defence of squatters everywhere, we are the people who prevent buildings (some of which are worth saving) from eventual collapse, simply by living in them. The vast majority of properties squatted in the UK were empty council flats and houses. Local governments in Britain had a lot to answer for; during the seventies and eighties countless thousands of empty and therefore potential homes in London were sealed up and rotting away while a huge number of people waited forever and a day on council housing lists. Squatters across the nation who would never consider sleeping on the streets used this bureaucratic failure in regards to public housing to our democratic advantage.

Therefore, the answer to our dilemma was all around us along the run down Victorian streets and the poorly designed, shabby housing estates hastily erected in the fifties and sixties. These council estates were sometimes a quick fix solution in an effort to relieve the chronic housing shortages of bombed cities in England still recovering from WW2.

By the early eighties I was among a growing number of the twenty something generation arriving in London to start new lives away from the constraints of our jobless, regional, no-hope-towns and cities up and down the country. The systematic destruction of the industrial heartland in northern Britain and Scotland was now altering many once strong communities into areas of grey uncertainties, social problems and mass unemployment.

A 'job for life' for Britain's youth was seen as a notion of a dying past, here and in the present day.

We were musicians, painters, writers, filmmakers, poets, punks, gays, trannies, arc welders, designers, artists, activists, beggars, eco warriors, buskers, bar hoppers, skilled (and unskilled) opportunists and people from all backgrounds and locales across the country. We were the disillusioned voice of Thatcher's Britain, making our way to London in search of our lives, our identities, our freedom of expression and to attend punk and politically motivated festivals where a few decent bands were playing. Sometimes if we were lucky it wouldn't actually be pissing down with rain during these open air anarcho type gigs.

It didn't matter where you came from, but you had left somewhere to be there.

I settled into my new life as best I could and knew how; I had to learn a lot in a short time and of course maintain my dignity by not crumbling under the pressure of a total lifestyle change. I could always manage to look after myself and eat properly, there was a fair amount of communal cooking and everyone took their turn. I generally got on with everyone and helped out when it came to 'light repairs' and 'house maintenance', more commonly known as botch jobs.

I learned that a squatter is occasionally required to fix things, and he (or she) can go a long way armed with a claw hammer, a screwdriver, a crowbar, a chisel, a fat spliff and a couple of cans of cheap lager. These tools can also be carried in a black or green canvas shoulder slung style army bag. It is a good idea to wrap the tools in a rag before you left home when out late into the night 'house hunting' as they'd often jangle and clang together in the bag as you went about your 'business', better known as breaking and entering.

I was happy to be in London at last, and although I knew very little of the real city and its people, I soon enough acclimatised to all the different cultures and diversity inside this amazing city.

2 – Squat Realities

Within a few short weeks of my arrival in the formerly gorgeous (but now rather grotty) borough of Hackney, an eviction notice slipped quietly through our letterbox one morning. This document (the first I'd seen) was the accepted hazard of squatting back then and to be expected in the post at any time. After a brief house meeting regarding this news, Curt, Mark and I walked across the tree lined common outside our place, and within twenty minutes we'd opened an even larger Victorian house in Meynell Road on the opposite side of the green. This residence was your typical 19th century 'basement to attic affair' with steps leading up to the double fronted entrance. This was formerly the sort of home once occupied by the wealthy upper middle classes in the height of the big, round queen's reign.

The first thing to check as we clumped about under the mild glare of torchlight was if the utilities were still connected. We discovered that the electricity supply (of sorts) was still working but unfortunately no gas and therefore no hot water. This meant that we'd be taking the once or twice a week trip to the Hackney Bathhouse to get cleaned up.

Though I suspected that Bullshit Bob would leave it considerably longer than that…

We dragged and carried our meagre belongings across the green that same day, chose our respective rooms and then 'decorated' the place with our crappy squat furniture, anarchist posters and slimy off cuts of mid 1970's carpet pieces and duly made the place our own. Once settled it was time to light the open fire and watch puerile rubbish on my portable, monochrome telly. Most of our time was spent this way that winter, with occasional outings to decidedly decrepit local pubs, cheesy smelling food shops and colourful squat parties in the area.

Mark and I decided to go on a short bus ride to procure a large bass speaker as he'd bought his bass guitar back after a short visit to Essex. My drum kit was now stored in the new squat and the two of us were harbouring thoughts about making 'dat heavy heavy dub soundz' and live like the true white Rastas we both were in our collective hearts and choice of musical genre. Having purchased a large speaker cone in Hackney Central, all we needed now was a box to mount the monster in. This problem was soon solved when we found a job lot of broken, white Formica covered kitchen units that had been thrown out in the street. We rounded up some tools and then nailed six approximately equally sized panels together into what looked like a large white dice. After cutting a crude circle in the middle of this 'bass bin' and filling it up with old cushions, we 'mounted' the speaker into one of the sides and now had something that looked to all like a psychedelic washing machine prop from a sixties movie.

This 'washing machine' really sounded great, with loads of bass response, it could easily keep up with the volume of my drums, which being a Gretsch kit, were loud. Thereafter, the two of us jammed out dub reggae tunes as the public watched us through our dirty upper floor windows from the bus stop, situated about fifty yards away in the wintry street below.

Within a few months I'd settled into this life, but it wasn't easy as I'd had it pretty good at home, what with my mother doing my washing and cooking all my life, I now had to learn how to cope independently. I had no regrets, no security, and no money except dole scum wages, but I was free, playing my drums whenever I wanted and was closer geographically to my current band who were based in Woolwich.

However, during this period I was smoking far too much hash, mostly though a chillum and seriously getting the nervous fear, mixed with feelings of general paranoia. It appeared that I was probably sinking into depression which wasn't helped by the fact that within no time at all we had to move yet again, as apparently there was a doctor's surgery in the building next door to our new squat.

Subsequent complaints about low life squatters with a love of dub reggae quickly moved the eviction process forward in the long wood panelled corridors of Hackney Council.

3 – Outside Toilets, Inside

As luck would have it, another empty house 'became available' and funnily enough it was right next door to the previous place we'd lived in back across the green. Once more, our possessions were again hauled back across the park and manhandled through the recently kicked in door.

However, the only amenities that were online in our new, gaudily painted shithole was the electricity, and one tap. The only toilet upstairs had been deliberately smashed as part of the council's policy to discourage squatting. The workmen would come in and break all the sinks and loos to bits before sealing the places up. The good news was that we did have hot water and a bath which balanced out the fact that we'd all have to shit into plastic bag and hurl our waste products into the overgrown, weed ridden back garden.

Hence therefore we were truly living up to our collective given nickname; 'Dirty Squatters'.

Curt and an extremely nauseous hippy he had recently befriended discovered an easy way to make quick money. This 'free income' was named 'Totting' which simply involved ripping all the copper piping and water tanks from the many empty properties in Hackney and flogging the lot to the local scrap merchants. They spent most nights out on the streets pushing a wheelbarrow and carrying their hidden tool bags as they pursued their new 'independent' dole scum startup business plan.

One night they came back with loads of copper cabling about 3" wide, encased in thick, hard black plastic insulation.

But in order to claim the booty at the scrap yard they'd have to remove this plastic covering to expose the copper prior to sale. Curt and accomplice decided to melt the coating from the copper over the fire in the living room which took a number of days whilst filling the house up with stinky and probably highly toxic orange fumes.

    One night as I lay on my bed listening to music through my headphones I was suddenly alerted by three policemen standing in my room. Curt and the dodgy hippy had been nicked in the middle of the night as they went about their scrap metal business. Once arrested on theft charges, the law allows the cops to come and check out your home address without a warrant to 'search for stolen goods'. The police didn't bother me much as it was my room in the house and not Curt's. So that was the abrupt end of the marginally profitable 'quick money scheme' for them I'm afraid.

I left Hackney upon arrival of yet another eviction notice and went to stay in the pleasant streets of Thornton Heath with a friend for a spell. I'd spent five months living the squat life, it wasn't altogether bad as I'd had the opportunity to learn a lot about life outside the comforts of suburbia, and more to the point a lot more about myself and my will to stay in London. But little did I know just what was in store for me on the housing front further down the road…

4 – 'Bedshitland'

After residing in the leafy suburbs of south west London for a few months, I decided it was time to move on. I wasn't keen on the insecurity of squatting for a while and soon enough found bedsit accommodation in nearby Streatham Hill via the ever handy Loot magazine.

'Bedshits' as they are commonly known, offer a cheap housing alternative for single people, and were especially popular in London during the seventies and eighties. This particular brand of human dwelling would commonly involve sharing hallways and bathrooms in a large, cheaply converted townhouse with eight to ten other people that you'd rarely, if ever, meet. The bedsitter occupants would each and singularly dwell within a cramped and reclusive self contained space that could very loosely be described as 'home'. These solitary and hermit like living conditions could lead to outbreaks of cabin fever, even in the hardiest of Arctic explorers in the long, chilly, inner city winter.

I shared the two bathrooms on my landing (these unfortunately being situated just outside my room) with at least four other people in this house, and believe me, these cheerless amenities were about as basic as one could possibly find anywhere in rented digs. No effort whatsoever had been made to brighten up these dank latrines; never would you see a lonely, wilting pot plant by the frosted window, which faced north anyway. Nor even a shabby pink floor mat to cover the worn out, treacherous-when-wet, pale yellow, peeling lino floor. These bland and purely functional bathrooms would be fitted with a 40 watt light bulb that swung without so much as a mouldy lampshade in the cobwebbed gloom above, this in turn grimly lit up the very minimum of your latrine facilities below.

The 'extras' as not included in the rent, included someone else's deep encrusted skid marks that would never flush away, a grubby unwashed hand towel that clung like a leech over a never heated rail, and a slimy light green shower curtain complete with brown patches of festering fungal matter. Not forgetting to mention of course, was the gas meter, which would of course be situated in a low and awkward to get at place directly under the sink. This facility duly extorted a 50p-per-shower charge to deliver a measly sprinkle of semi tepid water from an ugly clanking boiler jutting from the wall over the scum rimmed bath. This ancient plumbing monstrosity was the miserable view in front of your eyes whilst you showered quickly, devoid of warm satisfaction, in the pitiful silence, behind the aforementioned curtain.

So this it seemed, was 'Bedshitland'? A quiet spot where a serial killer can attend to his random murdering, without raising suspicions of the neighbours, even if the place was as quiet as the woods in winter. The house was an echo filled, soulless dwelling; a place where you'd hear an occupant's door suddenly closing in the distance the instant you opened yours. One soon learned to momentarily pause behind your door and listen for a few seconds to check for the 'all clear' before stepping out onto the landing, rushing downstairs and exiting the building promptly.

It was a characterless, dreary house, occupied by strange and seemingly lonely people that you seldom met and instantly forgot if you happened upon them occasionally on your way out. One could walk straight past your 'housemates' in the street, failing to remember their faces as you'd never socialize with them on any level in our lonely house anyway.

While some people are lucky enough to have cool neighbours in 'Bedshitland' with shared communal living rooms and kitchens as well, unfortunately, I like many, now lived in a poorly re-fitted townhouse that was plainly painted, décor less and at best, merely adequate. Of course one made an effort to dress your own room and create a reasonably comfortable abode, but the bathrooms however were not the places to spend any more time in than was absolutely necessary. Hence they were left untouched by any form of human creativity and were a droll addition to the overall spectre of the property. This form of private accommodation is not a congenial place to mix socially with the creepy people living opposite, below or above. In bedsitter world it was a pot luck lottery that decided who you ended up with as a neighbour across the hall. It appeared, at least in my instance, I'd drawn the losing numbers.

For the first two weeks after I moved into this place I didn't have possession of my TV, a radio or music centre. So for what seemed like an endless fortnight all I had to listen to in my new dreary accommodation were the screaming sounds of silence, a couple quarrelling beneath me and unknown people taking baths and ablutions on the other side of the wafer thin wall.

My bedsit room was charged at £26 a week and measured about eleven feet square from wall to wall with coin meters for both utilities. The sink, saggy single bed, plastic armchair, and humming half-sized fridge were all within a few paces of each other, across the sticky, patterned (pale blue) carpet. The only brightness this miserable abode had going for it were the three large sash windows that let in the morning sunshine and warmth in during the summer. But the howling wind just blew straight through and under the thin rattling window panes that following freezing winter, as I shivered next to my tiny gas fire, which used fifty pence pieces by the hour.

At last, after an endless and eternal fourteen days, Dave, an old friend from Essex turned up with my music centre, records and that ever-dependable portable telly. I was well glad to see him and have some much needed company, as I'd still not as yet met any of my neighbours residing around me. He stopped over that night and made his quick exit the next morning, giving the place a once overlook and probably thinking the same as I was regarding my new 'home'.

Now at last I could play some music and put an end to the ringing sounds of silence…

So, with relief, I put a record on, not loudly of course, just at room temperature to kill the punishing quietness, and then went about my business at about 1 o'clock on a Saturday afternoon. Within seconds the disconcerting sound of a broom being prodded on my floor came from an unknown occupant downstairs,

'Oh, is that loud?' I thought to myself momentarily, and duly turned the volume down to about level two. A few more seconds drifted past, and then another even louder bang bang came resonating up through the floor. Once again, being reasonable guy, I turned the volume down still further. However, by now one could almost hear more sound coming from the needle as it moved across the vinyl than what was emitting via the weedy fifteen watt speakers which were hardly cutting edge anyway.

'Is that quiet enough you miserable fucker?' I muttered to myself.

Someone was being selfish here and it wasn't me, I'd been listening to the nightly arguments from the couple downstairs for long enough to form a picture in my mind of a pair of control freaks who preferred that we all lived in oppressive, monastery quiet conditions.

I now wondered if it would've been a better option to have simply gone out and squatted again…

I tolerated my sad neighbours below but was now subject to their will. Although we'd never met, I knew them to be a couple in the final throws at the end of a miserable relationship; constantly rowing at ever higher levels, often starting in the middle of the night. I kept my patience as I listened to the inaudible exchanges between them night after night through the thinly carpeted floor.

One evening when an old friend was staying over, they kicked off again at three in the morning, waking us, and probably everyone else, up. That was it, enough of this shit; I got out of bed and stamped on the floor silencing them in their tracks. Then the woman of the outfit shouted something up at me, and I let them have it.

'So you don't like me playing my music huh?' I bellowed at them. 'Well I'm fucking sick of listening to yours, if you want to do something about it I'll meet you in the hallway now you miserable cunts!'

This was followed by silence, shocked silence. They'd bottled it and I had won a moral victory, both for myself and probably the other occupants of this lonely house. People don't like being woken up by sudden noise, and then have to take shit from those who are actually responsible for it.

5 – Knock, Knock

The next afternoon, being a Saturday, there came a very timid tap tap upon my door. As I swung the door open there in his full five foot six of skin and bone, was the male half of the couple downstairs.

I paused to allow him to say his bit first, which he duly did, apologising for what happened, and telling me how much he 'liked music' too (though I'd never heard them play any) and other congenial chit chat

But that aside, I was sick of living with the constant threat of the broomstick knocking on my floor, I felt it was now the time to lay down 'my law'.

'I'm going to be playing my music at reasonable levels, from now on, okay?'

'Okay' he ventured meekly in reply.

'And I don't want to hear any more brooms being banged on my floor either, is that okay?'

'Okay,' he answered with a degree of finality.

I then made the poor guy a cup of tea, and we entered into mild conversation. He left thirty minutes later feeling that he'd probably made his first friend in years. I never met 'her downstairs' she was an enigma to the end. The last time I saw 'him' he was crying outside a phone box in Streatham having been told his mother had just died. I naturally gave him my sympathy and I took him for a drink.

Soon after they moved out, and are now probably miserably married and living in total silence somewhere in deepest suburbia.

It also seemed that I'd turned a corner, as the rest of the occupants of that house were now quite congenial to me after that late night incident. The gay guy above me (with a liking for teenage boys) was now always friendly. Another neighbour just across the hall invited me into his 'flat' for a cup of tea one afternoon too. But it felt a bit unsettling as I stepped into his place, reaffirming my already poor impressions of Bedshitland.

This was due to the sad fact that although he'd lived there for the better part of eight years, but his place had that look as though he'd only moved in three weeks before. Apparently his marriage had fallen apart and obviously so had his life all those years ago, and it appeared he now belonged to that silent group of jinxed lovers, husbands and wives who then lived in a love strung time warp from that moment on, possibly for the remainder of their lives.

His meagre flat included a small separate kitchen, which by all accounts was just as dull and miserable as my place. But even in all those years he'd made no effort to instil any degree of his or 'a' personality on the place, it was worryingly soulless and unwelcoming. Not a watercolour adorned a wall, nor did an old family snap sit upon on the mantelpiece, so I made my excuses and exited the blandness before my eyes soon after I'd swallowed his piss weak tea.

Thankfully, a lively couple moved into the flat downstairs since vacated by the miserable duo, and we eventually struck up a valuable friendship in view of the other motley collection of weird neighbours. They were indeed a major relief after the pair preceding them, Jon was an excellent guitar strummer and a quality chess player, and we occasionally jammed together at Crockwell's rehearsal rooms in Camberwell. Chris, his partner, was a congenial Scottish lady who also liked music, conversation, and of course, a spliff as well. They were 'normal people' and not the types to bang on their ceiling with a fucking broomstick at the sound of music.

The three of us were soon transfixed as we watched the teary emotions of 'Live Aid' unfold in front of a good percentage of the world's population on that particular historic day. It was another one of those global events that one remembers exactly where they were on that momentous July Saturday afternoon in the summer of 1985.

The 80s boom time in Thatcher's Britain was in full swing; yuppies were the order of the day, dreadful clothes and even worse haircuts were all the rage in London and beyond. I was playing in a new band and gigging regularly. I bought a small van (for the drums) and also a Honda RS250 motorbike which I raced around on as a courier in the city and the west end. This being a popular, though rather dangerous, job for a young man in that era to which I crashed and destroyed four motorbikes (and nearly myself) in various accidents up and down the city streets of London in my efforts to earn 'Loadsamoney'.

I also purchased a Yamaha 100cc two stroke bike from my neighbour, the one with the grim room across the hall. It had been resting against the wall in the back garden (that nobody used) for a long time. He talked himself into virtually giving it away for thirty quid, the battery was dead of course, but he didn't realise that you don't need one to start a two stroke motorcycle. I disconnected it, wound the throttle back and it started on the second kick, it smoked a little but was generally sound. The cash was then somewhat guiltily handed over to the stunned seller, who couldn't believe it would ever start again. I went onto use (and abuse) that pitiful wreck for months on end as a courier; I clocked up thousands of miles and earned a lot of money sitting on that smoking bargain buy.

All good fun and money until one afternoon I trashed it when I ran over a tourist in Covent Garden. This accident was entirely his fault I'm sorry to say, being 'European' he looked the wrong way when he stepped off the pavement just as I was upon him. I hit him, knocked him down, ran over his legs, fell off and then slid along the road on my arse as I watched my cheap motorbike grind and scrape to a noisy halt in the middle of the road. Thankfully 'Euro-man' was relatively unharmed and luckily for him I wasn't sitting on anything bigger and heavier that day. So that was the end of yet another motorbike, although one cannot complain as that cheap transportation investment had served me very well indeed.

The mid eighties were the height of the dark days of Goth night clubbing; I wore raven black or platinum blonde hair and usually dressed in black, black, or black and like everyone else of the era looked pasty, wasted and ill most of the time. We were doing the rounds at the infamous Mud Club, and also an odd venue called Jean Pierre's, which played the latest Goth dance tunes every Friday night well into the small hours of Saturday morning. Camden Palace was always a great night out as well as free entry to 'Feet First' on a Tuesday evening if you helped to hand out flyers beforehand. Then there was notorious Kit Kat Club in Queensway. This was a cool club to go to for about a year during its heyday, until a hundred cops raided the place one swinging Saturday night and nicked a selection of drug dealers as the dance floor swung with those eighties' tunes. I remember exiting the toilet with a friend just in time to witness a blurry line of coppers jogging past us and arresting various vendors as directed by what were obviously policewomen who had been disguised as punks and punters as part of a well planned sting operation.

It was a fair cop I guess, as all the clubbers were made to wait in line in the echoing din of hundreds of voices you hear when the sound system has been switched off at the end of a club night. We were frisked one at a time and then turned out into the chill air of Bayswater Road, without a refund of course. Shame that as it was a top place to hang out on a Saturday night, always full of beautiful people, great music, cheap drugs, punky women, and on top of that we brought our own booze along, this being as much as you could possibly consume in a six to eight hour session.

Clubbers who arrived before eleven got a bar of KitKat chocolate upon entry before stocks ran out. Just what more could you ask for in a club in mid eighties London?

In a financial sense things had never been better, though there were often gaps in employment to which I signed on and claimed housing benefit. I had a good social life despite my horrible digs in Streatham, but I would go out as much as possible. I was playing in a dark, noisy band, owned a motorcycle and a van for carting my drums about in, and had plenty of girlfriend offers as it seemed that many women are apparently attracted to sweaty drummers, with transportation.

Being the nineteen eighties, when it came to bed bouncing fun (as often enjoyed accompanied with a total stranger) if you were both dressed in black it therefore stood to reason that you must've had something in common with one another, as formalities were sometimes overlooked in the rush to 'get to know each other'.

One Saturday morning, as a friend and I were dozing after the previous night's clubbing; Paddy, my landlord crept in and left three white envelopes on the seat next to the door. We were in a semi conscious state and didn't stir until Al woke up and said someone came in earlier and had left these letters for me. I realised exactly what they were from the size, shape and colour of them. These were housing benefit giro cheques and three of them all at once as well.

Having waited months on end for Lambeth Council to pay my housing benefit while I was unemployed it now looked like they'd finally paid the rent and in arrears too. I sprung up and ripped the first one open; 150 quid was the sum printed on it, the second was then eagerly opened and this was for another 200.

'Fucking great!' I thrilled as Al laughed along with me.

The third was for yet another 200 quid, so I was a pretty happy man now, hangover or not. It was quarter to twelve on a Saturday which meant I had fifteen minutes to sprint like an athlete to the post office before they closed at high noon. Sadly I didn't make it, despite running the twelve hundred metres in my fastest ever time. Therefore, I was still technically poor until Monday morning when the giros could be converted into hard cash in handy bundles of tens and twenties.

After a miserable and piss poor remainder of the weekend, Monday morning eventually arrived. I stood in the dole scum queue at Streatham Post Office gripping three government issued cheques in one hand and my driving license in the other, as those wads of cash were duly counted out before me. I then got straight on a bus to the west end and went shopping for a new hi-fi on Tottenham Court Road. I soon found what I was looking for at and somehow bundled it all back on the 159 bus to Bedshitland. Within an hour of my return, Paddy the landlord called at the door, knowing all too well that those envelopes delivered on Saturday morning were housing benefit giros. However, I'd been relatively up to date with my rent and the amounts were backdated a few months, I owed him some up to that point which was handed over straight away as he admired my new music centre currently being assembled before his eyes. He was happy enough with his payout and walked off rolling up the notes telling me not to blow the house down with the volume levels now being tested out by my grinning self.

Things were looking up, apart from now actually having something decent to play my record collection on, there were also many good bands to go and see all over town; as this is what people did a lot during this era. Bands were being formed and arriving on the indie, punk and Goth scenes in Britain by the week. We went to see strange people standing on stage, who were dressed weirdly, being creative with a message in their lyrics and they were actually playing instruments as well. The electronic era was still somewhat in its infancy; samplers and drum machines were pretty cheesy unless you could afford the top of the range equipment, and 'digital' was a word not yet in everyday use.

Brixton was just a short bus ride down the hill and more often than I can remember I made that long walk up it from the tube after a hard night's clubbing. However, by this time I was getting pretty sick of my lousy bed sitter and didn't want to spend another winter freezing half to death in Streatham, huddled by the tiny little metered gas fire at 50p an hour. It had been so cold during that winter of '85 that I'd taken to hooking up a bayonet fitting to the light socket in the hallway to run an electric bar fire (as found in a skip) in my room. This I thought I could get away with during the really cold spells as the hallways of the house weren't running on our interior room meters. But Paddy caught me out one stone cold Saturday morning and started moaning on about stealing his electricity, as if he wasn't making a mint from us and all the other droll bed sitters he owned in the Streatham area.

Enough was enough I thought and I was soon looking for an opportunity to get out of this miserable bedshitter existence. On top of that, I crashed my Honda twice in two days, once on the way to work in the morning, and again after my shift had finished on Southwark Bridge the following evening. This was the risk that runs hand in hand with that particular profession; you always hoped it wasn't going to be 'your turn today' when you kick started the bike up in the mornings. But having ridden around central London and at high speeds, dodging traffic and people for months, I end up falling off the thing twice in twenty-four hours, and not even while on the job. I'd had a few heart-stopping moments in the busy traffic, and you'd have to learn to become a skilled rider in order to stay alive. But one always knew in the back of your mind that the averages were going get you sooner or later.

Although I'd merely slipped off first thing in the morning on a greasy roundabout in the first incident, and was relatively unscathed; I rode into the back of a car the second day that had suddenly braked. I hit his bumper, went over the handlebars landed on my head as the bike followed through and landed in between my legs, giving me a right bollocking. I stumbled about at the roadside holding my knackers in the rush hour traffic, and on viewing the damage it appeared that my bike it seemed was a 20mph write off. Even at that low impact speed, I could see that the forks were bent, the headlamp was smashed and the clocks damaged too. The driver was cool about it, especially as his car was okay, bar a vertical tyre mark on his bumper. I spent a short time recovering at the kerb somewhat glad on reflection to have been wearing a helmet. I then rode my bent motorcycle home avoiding the bumps and potholes along the way so not to aggravate my now aching, swollen balls.

Just one slight lapse in concentration after a hard day in the saddle was all it took to wreck my Honda, and for me to end up unemployed yet again.

6 – The-Man-Who-Can-Scam

In the spring of '86, Dean, another old Essex friend, called on me out of the blue one afternoon while I was hanging out in my bedsit prison. He was looking for somewhere to live and had arrived exactly on time to save me from my dreadful housing dilemma.

Having spent two miserable winters in Bedshitland I was definitely up for squatting once again and this was an ideal opportunity to spend a few days looking for flats at our leisure while we still had somewhere to stay at night; that being my bedsit. We decided to seek help from the Squatters Advisory Service in Islington, but they could only offer places north of the river, including Hackney, which I really wasn't into. There was also the 121 Centre in Railton Road Brixton, a well established Squatter's one stop shop, and another place at the squatted fire station building in Old Kent Road.

We called on the 121 Centre first but unfortunately they were closed, and probably not for lunch, so we made the short bus journey to the fire station instead.

The bearded, slightly eccentric guy living there was really on the ball, clued up and very helpful. He had a great system and what seemed like an excellent relationship with at least some of the maintenance men employed by Southwark Council.

The way this all worked was as follows: the council workmen would lock up empty flats in the borough (thankfully without destroying the toilets first) then place the chipboard cover over the front door which in turn fitted over a steel plate that ran through the letterbox from the inside. Finally, the property was 'sealed' up with a 'bottom of the range' Squire padlock. The keys for these padlocks were then 'fixed', which simply meant that almost any slightly filed down Squire key for the same model would instantly release these old worn down padlocks.

The good men at the council would then pop into see the man at the fire station, drop off some 'fixed' keys and give the addresses of recently 'secured' flats. There must've been a few quid in it for them, or perhaps there were family ties involved too. Either way, 'the-man-who-can' loaned us a set of keys in exchange for a small cash deposit and gave us some good hints and some actual addresses of recently sealed flats in the surrounding Bermondsey area. He also supplied us with and a copy of the Legal Notice explaining our squatters rights in England and Wales, which you'd then pin up on an inside window near the front door after moving in.

So, off we went in the middle of the mildly sunny afternoon and before long we'd opened a number of 'apartments' in Bermondsey, some of which were as expected, smelly, scuzzy shitholes, filled with rotting bin bags stuffed with empty tins of squatter dog food and moulding Fray Bentos pie dishes.

But within a couple of hours we 'decided' on a ground floor flat on the Dunton Road Estate, Bermondsey that had (helpfully) recently been painted throughout in that council shade of 'off white'. The place was a dream, with two bedrooms, a fair sized living room, fitted kitchen units, and all the utilities were up and running, this being central heating and piping hot water. What more could a pair of punk squatters possibly need?

It did cross my mind that this flat had been cleaned and painted in preparation for new occupants who had long been waiting on housing via the council. I did feel a glimmer of guilt as Dean and I checked the rooms out. The other side of the story is that I'd been on Lambeth Council's housing list for years and being a healthy single man I knew I had zero chance of ever being offered accommodation by them or any other inner city council.

We stepped out back into the afternoon sunshine and quietly closed the place up, placing the picked padlock over the plate and 'locking it', while taking care to remain as invisible as possible to any potential spoilers that might happen upon us. Then we made the short walk back to the man at the fire station and told him we'd 'take it' and would be back with his dummy key tomorrow.

7 – Bedroom Parking

The next day, after hiring a van and under cover of the night, Dean and I quietly hauled our crappy furniture, bin bags of clothes, my drum kit, that telly and some kitchenware along with a few handy finds at the roadside on route to the bright red front door of our new flat in Stansfeld House, Dunton Road SE1.

We were housed, back to squatting, rent free, not legal, but under the circumstances the best and only choice.

I took the smaller room of the two, so that Dean could 'park' his recently purchased dodgy chopper conversion motorcycle in his bedroom…

The few possessions I owned in my tiny bedsit during the previous twenty months were distributed liberally around our new flat.

We soon settled in and acclimatised to the local area, I was between bands and my kit was cased up and spread about in the living room. We 'cooked' on an electric bar fire (as previously used to retrieve electricity from my now ex landlord) which we turned on its side, so not much more than toast and soup could be prepared in the kitchen at that time. Neither of us minded this minor inconvenience as we at least had a roof over our heads and hot baths whenever required.

We spent a lot of time that summer tinkering with Dean's motorbike, a Honda 400 subject to a cheap and nasty chopper conversion, in black, with the smallest pillion seat you'd ever want to park your arse upon. It didn't run very well and was somewhat tatty, but it looked badass all the same and had a nice throaty roar about it. With his pink hair (and eyebrows) knee high Doc Marten boots and the leather gear on, Dean looked the business on it, even though he was a new rider and didn't have a license either. I, however, had a motorcycle license so we insured it in my name, and he sat on the back when we were out on it together, and pretended to be me when riding it alone.

Dean bought it on a bit of a whim (much against the advice from friends) and it was the sort of vehicle that had a spooky feeling etched all over its oily black fittings.

Throughout that winter our friends from Essex could stay over in our comfy flat after the very long, wide eyed, speed fuelled Friday night clubbing in the west end, usually in a darkened, dry iced, all night Goth establishment. Regular visitors from my Streatham days would also pop round to roll a few spliffs and admire our new warm accommodation.

By now I'd met and played music with a number of new faces based in Emu Road Battersea. There was Stan (a bass player) and his brother Mike from north Wales, and another Mike, also a drummer and also Welsh. Then there was the Irish contingent, including Shamus, Pete and Jimmy the hippy, a guitar player I'd been jamming with in Camberwell and his crazy brother Dave an all round top geezer.

Then there was big Grant (the bass player in above outfit) who had quite a high pitched voice, said 'Actually' a lot and kind of reminded me of the Alf Roberts character who was unceremoniously thrown from the roof of a multi story car park by Michael Caine in the infamous seventies Brit gangster film 'Get Carter'.

There were various other musicians kicking around in Emu Road, a place once occupied by The Alarm, a Clash sounding type band from north Wales. There were four, twenty something blokes sharing the two bedroomed ground floor flat in Battersea, so it was kind of grimy before one even throws up a mind's eye image of four blokes in their twenties sharing digs… in the eighties.

Meanwhile, back in Bermondsey, Dean and I decided to throw a party just for the sake of it. After informing the Battersea contingent, club land people, and the usual suspects from Essex, we hurriedly spent our meagre cash on cheap lager and spliff, then sat back and waited for the crowd to show. It was a good party despite the fact that Dean's chopper (as still parked in his bedroom) and had been leaking petrol all evening. It was fortunate that we didn't torch the whole block that night, and the fumes were making us all as nauseous as backstreet glue sniffers.

One afternoon not long after the party, Dean was tinkering with the machine in his bedroom while I was sitting in the living room and could occasionally hear the sound of spanners being dropped, then the thing being kicked over and periodically starting up, only to conk out once again.

Then a strange stamping and frantic flapping type noise came emanating from Dean's 'garage'; I rose from the narcotics of afternoon television and casually strolled into his room only to be confronted by a potential nightmare. Dean the mechanic was holding the fuel pipe in his mouth, a lit cigarette in one hand while using his spare hand to try to pat out the flames licking from all over the bike frame and spreading quickly across the floor. I grabbed a t-shirt (one of his) and started to flap at the flames too. Thankfully, and with rapidly beating hearts we brought the near total disaster to a swift end.

'For fuck's sake, Dean!' I bellowed.

'What the fuck are you doing smoking with the fuel pipe unhooked?' I asked

'You stupid fucker!' I added

There was a momentary silence before we both burst into a bout of nervous laughter.

The following week, a Fire Officer from Southwark Council called at the flat while I was out. Our neighbour had complained about the petrol fumes and the noisy bike being started up in Dean's bedroom below. You cannot really blame the old lady upstairs for reporting us, what were we thinking?

We were given a once only stern warning and thereafter the Honda was chained up and parked outside the flat, just like 'normal bikers' do, I think. I plucked up the courage to go upstairs and knock on her door to apologise for the trouble we had put the lady to. She was cool about it, thankful for the apology and was one of those salt-of-the-earth, wizened, cockney old ladies, with a rasping cough, born in Bermondsey, had lived there all her life, been regularly bombed to bits by the Luftwaffe in WW2 and smoked about seven Regal Blue cigarettes an hour in her brown walled, tobacco stained flat.

She was a good old doll, and totally reasonable about our housing situation, so thereafter Dean and I turned our music down at night and learned to have a bit of respect for our aged neighbour.

8 – Money, Merrydown and Motorcycles

The summer arrived and by now Dean and I were well settled into our cosy flat in Stansfeld House. We'd patched up relationships with our neighbours and didn't have to worry about any more visits from fire prevention officers at Southwark Council.

There was a lot of unemployment in Britain in 1986, very little on offer at the job centres which meant that many people were on the dole in one capacity or another, including both Dean and myself. The UB office was usually crowded and somewhere in the overloaded, autocratic benefits system giro cheques often wouldn't either be processed or posted. This meant that every other week, one or the other of us would have to visit a miserable grey building near the Elephant & Castle and grimly wait for most of the day to receive a handwritten giro along with dozens of other unemployables.

This bureaucratic fuck up usually lead to scuffles and occasional fighting as the mob of pissed off dole scum all arrived together at the post office at around four o'clock to cash their 'Emergency Personal Issue' cheques, also known as 'Tramps' Payments'. Thankfully, Dean and I signed on for 'benefits' on alternative weeks, but nevertheless the UB office managed to accommodate us both by fucking up our claims on alternative weeks as well. Therefore, both of us would have to go through 'The System' on a twice monthly basis in order to procure a pathetic sum of unearned money from the state.

It usually took at least six hours to 'process your claim', so that was six hours to kill after you'd 'booked in' and seen an 'Advisor'. You'd have to get there before 11am in order to be paid later that afternoon, and always at exactly the same time as every other blagger, work avoider, squatter, pilferer, shoplifter, drunk and hobo. That's two long queues for the price three. One wouldn't dare to leave the building for any more than a few seconds, and this would only be to smoke a dog end with the front door held open by your foot just in case your name was suddenly called in the background over the weak, tinny public address system. If you missed your name being called, you then missed your chance 'to get paid', which would mean only one thing; you'd have to live through the whole miserable charade again tomorrow.

The 'Dole Scum Advisors' were stationed behind very thick, filthy, graffiti ridden, and butt end burned Perspex windows in tiny cubicles for their own personal protection. There were no fancy pink ticker tape machines or overhead number counters to remind you that you were gradually moving along the endless queue. This inadequate system when running at full capacity usually operated at two speeds; dead slow and dead, dead slow. So you'd want to make sure you were standing in the correct line for 'Processing' right from the start.

To pass the endless hours away and to help prevent the benefit claiming masses from actually communicating with each other and possibly forming into a credible riotous mob; caged television sets were mounted on the walls at a neck straining twelve feet high (to prevent random theft) which were then tuned in (badly) to screen nauseous mid morning 'light entertainment shows' followed by 'the news' and then onto 'meditative afternoon soaps' to keep we, the unemployed, adequately sedated.

However, the volume would usually be turned down too low to hear above the din of the collective work avoiders complaining about their lot. We could also keep our spirits up by listening to the amusing drivelling and random mutterings of the strong lager tin drinking crazies as they made the rounds to annoy each and every dole customer, as one and all grimly sat it out hour upon eighty minute hour.

Full scale civil unrest among the non employed was definitely an option here and always brewing close to the surface. However, there just wasn't enough furniture (that hadn't already been securely bolted to the floor) to smash and torch as part of the exciting and ever present possibility of mob mentality taking hold at any given moment.

Therefore, irritated 'Job Searchers' occasionally stepped up to bang on the hardened reinforced plastic kiosks with various questions to the staff such as 'How much longer will my claim take, mate?'

Or to sound off that other ever popular request: 'Where's my fucking money, you c**ts?!'

One eventually learned to have patience, and to take a good book with you to ease the tedious, lengthy wait. Oh the joys of Thatcher's 'employment policy' as the percentages of the not employed grew ever larger month upon month.

Dean and I took it in bi-weekly turns to endure this pitiful charade, armed with an interesting read and a determined willingness to 'get paid' one way or another, by four thirty pm. After our identities were checked and cash was finally slid from under the post office counter, whomever had lived through the endless day at the U.B.O. would then buy enough food, rolling tobacco, Merrydown cider and weekly consumer supplies to keep us both going until the following week when the other one had to lose another day of our lives care of the Unemployment Benefit Office, Blackfriars Road, London SE1.

On one particular occasion, yet again, Dean's giro unsurprisingly didn't arrive in the Friday post. We were as usual completely skint with absolutely zero in the cupboards. No fags, no food, no margarine and not even a pint of milk in the fridge. On top of all that, it was a May Bank Holiday weekend as well.

We jointly scraped all our copper shrapnel together and soon discovered that we really were penniless and therefore proper fucked for the long weekend.

By that evening Dean and I had to resort to the level of street winos and visit the local bus stops to dive-bomb for re-useable cigarette butts. Every semi homeless person knows that these areas are the best places to seek half smoked cigarettes, as people often light up just as their bus irritatingly swings into view.

Then we'd return home to eat the remainder of a loaf of bread (without margarine) washed down with tap water, as there weren't even any teabags left either. By Saturday afternoon the bread had gone and we were down to tap water and 'poverty smokes' only.

I tried (unsuccessfully) to stay asleep all weekend to help fight off the hunger pains now getting ever louder and more frequent in my empty belly.

That was a very long and miserable bank holiday weekend; we were awake for much of it discussing what sort of petty crime we could commit locally in order to eat. I dived out early on the Sunday morning and out of desperation stole bread and milk from someone's doorstep, we devoured that in moments and sat back to share a fag butt that had been recycled four times already. Come the bank holiday Monday I decided to take radical (and by now, starving) action. I visited the corner shop we used regularly and asked the man for enough food credit to last until 'giro day' tomorrow. He was pretty reluctant at first and had to be heavily persuaded to part with £3 worth of groceries, which he eventually did after my driving license was handed over as a security deposit.

Dean and I then gorged ourselves on soup and eggs and whatever else the grocer had supplied to keep us alive for another day longer.

Post the 'longest weekend, ever', Dean duly went to the giro shop, and after that usual half-day wait he received his handwritten 'tramps' cheque' then put some fuel in the Honda, paid off our debt at the corner shop, and bought all the goods needed to create a full English breakfast. This was then washed down with a cup of tea and rounded off with real Benson & Hedges filtered cigarettes.

That May Bank Holiday of '86 was without doubt the worst one I've ever had to live through, and there's been some shit ones down the years. I did learn one vital thing from that horrible experience, and that's a simple lesson about what is really important in this life; the sustenance of food in one's stomach. We were not quite starving to death, but to have constant hunger reminders even for a few days is an experience that I think many people should endure just once in their lives. It will simply show you that nothing whatsoever in this world matters but your stomach, you cannot think straight or concentrate on anything for more than two minutes at a time when your body is crying out for food you cannot sleep properly (if at all) or care about anything else but where the next meal is coming from.

    It is a lousy and a miserable situation to endure, but it also felt like a highly valuable human experience.

A few weeks later, another human tragedy came along to knock the stuffing out of me, and more so, Dean. It was a hot Friday afternoon in June, he was busy trying to get the bike to tick over evenly, and periodically riding it around the block to test it. This was broken up by regular fag breaks and long swigs of Merrydown cider, I would come out and help out a bit but I had other things to do and was not really in the mood for bike mechanics.

    By the late afternoon in the waning sunshine, Dean had done at least one bottle of Merrydown and was into the second, and decided to take a ride to The Castle Pub in Brentwood, about twenty miles away. I told him that he shouldn't go, as he was half pissed and riding a powerful motorbike in the heat of midsummer, and on top of that it was

Friday the 13th as well.

A bad combination all round, but he went anyway; I decided to stay in that night and go out the next.

Sometime around 1am next morning a knock came on the door, a copper was waiting to inform me that my flatmate Dean had crashed his motorbike in Essex and was in Harold Wood Hospital with a broken arm and leg. I immediately went to the nearest phone box and called some people in Essex to find out more. Someone mentioned that Dean had told the ambulance crew in his delirium that he was I, as previously agreed between us for insurance purposes. Therefore the Essex crowd and the police were not sure who'd been involved in the accident. It was another friend who finally identified Dean late that night when a nurse showed him a pair of knee length Doc Marten boots and his painted leather jacket.

In the meantime I arranged to visit him the next day with a few other friends, to cheer him up and take the piss out of him for crashing his bike.

The next morning I took the train out to Essex, met the others and we made our way to the hospital. On arrival we were shown along a typical long hospital corridor to Ward 12, a place where they store all the local young men who'd been involved in various horrific road accidents.

What met us as we confidently strolled up to Dean's bed was a shock indeed; he was a total mess, having spent five hours in an operating theatre being sewn and screwed back together, as well as being given a complete change of blood too.

There he was, a sorry looking sight, all bolted and pinned together and strapped up in traction, drugged out of his face and concussed as fuck. This all looked a lot more serious than a mere broken arm and broken leg, and as it turned out, it certainly was.

He very nearly died the night before; he'd left a part of his right leg behind on the road and very seriously and permanently damaged his right arm too. He'd bitten through his tongue with his bottom teeth (probably from the pain) and there was apparently a fracture to his neck as well, his leg and elbow had been pinned up and there were stitches everywhere. I looked sadly along his young smashed body as my eyes stopped at a plastic tag strapped to his left arm bearing my name upon it. At that moment I felt giddy and sick and my legs almost went from under me, I immediately requested that this identity error was corrected by a nurse, a reactionary consideration out of my own thoughts of self preservation. I was weak with nausea, anxiety and pity for my eighteen-year-old friend, whose life was changed forever before it had hardly started.

He couldn't talk nor move, and although he was semi conscious his eyes told us which planet (and medications) he was currently on. Our misplaced, jovial, cartoon style 'Get Well Soon' card that we'd jointly bought for him on route, which was full of piss taking jokes from us all, was quickly hidden from sight.

I can't say I didn't warn him the night before, he wasn't even legally allowed to ride the monster bike anyway, let alone getting even more pissed after spending the whole evening in the pub as well. It was a stupid and reckless thing he did despite the fact that apparently the accident wasn't his fault. But it is if your drunk and doing a fair speed along a stretch of a seemingly empty road.

I stayed at a friend's house in Essex that evening and spent a long, sleepless night crying for my friend. I got up early and walked the empty streets as a new dawn rose, reflecting upon the fact that from this moment on my friend Dean's life would be totally and permanently different.

In between the tears for my mate I also knew that my life was now somewhat uncertain too, at least in the present, as I was now looking at the risky prospect of squatting alone…

9 – The Welsh Connection

When I arrived back in Bermondsey after that heartbreaking weekend the first thing I found myself doing was gathering up all of Dean's motorbike spare parts and ditching the lot in a skip parked close by. I felt that I didn't want to be reminded of that cursed machine anymore. The bike was a total write off anyway. Dean would be in hospital for months and god knows how long recovering in the future, it also looked like he'd probably never fully physically recover from his near death experience.

I wanted no more memories of his awful fate living beside me anymore; everything to do with motorbikes was hurled straight into that metal container within an hour.

I regularly took the train to Essex during the weeks and months after the accident to visit Dean, now gradually adjusting to his terrible injuries in Ward 12. His leg was full of pins, plates and screws, but his arm was seemingly permanently disabled and useless having incurred extensive nerve damage and leaving him in severe pain around the clock. It was a small mercy that he wasn't paralysed and wheelchair bound or worse still, brain damaged. So in view of this, he was very lucky considering the multitude of other terrible injuries he could've endured.

One evening some weeks later, Stan and another Welsh guy Robbo called over, they were looking for somewhere to live. I knew Stan a bit by now, but not really Robbo who was also a musician, so I naturally assumed he was an okay guy too.

As I was now squatting on my own they'd picked the right moment to call on me. Besides, I was off to visit my family that weekend; therefore the new guys could have the keys and move in while I was away.

So what did my mum and dad think of my lifestyle and the squatting? They had always allowed my sister and I plenty of freedom to express ourselves. When I told them I wanted to become a drummer, shortly after my hair went spiky my mother's answer at the dinner table was 'Okay, where are you going to practice?'

Immediate answer from me 'In my bedroom.'

My dad just grinned and shook his head.

My parents were cool, they put up with those awful 'early learner drummer' beats, they just turned the volume on the telly up downstairs, and I stuffed pillows in the bass drum of course to deaden it down a bit. The next door neighbours hated me in particular and us in general, but they always did and were full members of the suburban curtain twitcher society anyway.

My mum had her concerns about my living conditions and the often change of addresses, but we wrote and she did come and stay with me a one of my squats a few times when on a trips to London.

After five days in the countryside, where my parents now lived, I returned to London and Stansfeld House. Immediately upon entering the flat, I was overwhelmed by the terrible stink of old socks, clothes strewn about everywhere, plates with festering mould growing on them and the general mess around the whole place. I opened some windows to let fresh air in as I began to think that maybe I'd have been better off living there on my own.

Three was definitely a crowd in a two bedroomed flat anyway; I soon found that Robbo boy was the culprit. He was a dirty, lazy, crisp munching and extremely boring fucker who sat on the sofa all day watching soap operas on my telly surrounded by his smelly socks and pretended to write songs on his equally scuzzy guitar.

Sorry, but he had to go!

We briefly argued about his sloth-like demeanour and I duly threw him, his crappy guitar and his stinking socks out after a couple more nights. He left without a struggle but never forgave me for it. But I for one wasn't prepared to live with or in that level of sloth, so he went to squat nearby with some people who would accommodate his sloppy habits and rancid sock collection.

Stan asked if it was okay about him staying. This was fine by me as far as I was concerned; he was cool and like myself, had reasonable living habits. Robbo had been an error in my judgement and was now out of the picture.

Then began a crazy period of squatting with Stan, he was working in the kitchens at Hammersmith College and soon enough we procured a Baby Belling cooker too. These popular mini cookers must've saved many squatters such as us from a shitty diet of sandwiches, soup, bananas and pot noodles. Ours was a 'top of the range' model of the famous Belling design with two rings, a small oven and even a grill too; this meant that 'real food' was now altogether possible. Even though I could cook adequately, Stan was vegetarian, and a trainee chef who would make great lasagnes for consumption in front of the telly on the massive white leather sofa we'd bundled home during another late night local bargain furniture hunt.

Speaking of which, the furniture search often threw up some good local tat, there were always tables, chairs and the odd decent settee to be found dumped in the streets. This was especially so of the white leather sofa we stumbled upon one night, it weighed a ton and had been rained on for a few days, but it soon dried out in the warmth of the flat, and was one of the better items of furniture squeezed through our red squat door during our stay in that particular abode.

Stan decided to dye his hair black one evening (as we all did in the eighties) and while waiting for it to go off he chilled out on our 'new' and most comfy leather sofa, skinned up a spliff and proceeded to fall asleep. During the lull into snore world he gradually slid down this white sofa thus leaving a black trail starting at the top and eventually leading down to the arm rest where is sleeping head eventually settled. The effect of this black mark looked a bit weird and people laughed when it was explained how the stain got there.

This sort of behaviour was commonplace in the long dark evenings in Stansfeld House; we'd get completely stoned and go drinking in Brixton usually in the ever popular Prince Albert Pub. There was no way we'd consider drinking locally in the Old Kent Road area, as the musty pubs in Bermondsey looked like they hadn't been upgraded since the sixties, and often occupied by the hardened criminal elements of south east London, and probably still are.

Our Brixton excursions were often followed by a Friday all-nighter at the famous The Ritzy Cinema. These were the days when you would score a £5 bag of weed in The Atlantic or The Coach & Horses on Coldharbour Lane, then queue up for the selection of mad films to watch one after the other for most of the night. After you'd purchased a coffee and a slice of the always popular carrot or spinach cake you were sorted until the morning daylight burned your eyeballs out around six hours later.

The motley collection of film fans could and would smoke spliff inside The Ritzy back then, so there was a constant misty cloud of sweet smelling grass or Moroccan hash wafting up to settle in the high ornamental rafters of the late Victorian auditorium. The 'stoned free' then settled back to enjoy filmic visual delights such as Eraserhead, Tin Drum, Repo Man, Freaks, Rumble fish and one of my all time favourite stoner films, Reefer Madness, which was definitely not intended to be a hilarious stoner comedy when commissioned by the US government in the 1930s.

We'd stagger out of that cinema in the small hours and make the lengthy walk back to Bermondsey along Coldharbour Lane and through Camberwell, keeping a fair pace all the way knowing that there was a warm flat, strong coffee and plenty of spliff left to get us ruined before crashing. We'd often finish off the night by listening to the serious vibes of 'Strictly Dub Wise' by Dennis Bovell in its full acoustic glory, on lovely scratchy black vinyl.

10 – Jazz, the Squat Cat

Sometime in the autumn of '86 Stan came in one evening announcing that he wanted to get a cat as he'd seen an ad posted in a local shop window. I was kind of against it initially; we were squatting and had enough to deal with let alone the added responsibility of owning an animal.

With that in mind, a squatter isn't usually fully recognisable as such unless he or she is attired in the proper 'near homeless' look, owned a squat cat and a mangy mutt dog attached onto a homemade, multi coloured, bit-of-rope type leash.

Stan and I, however, were 'cat people' and I was soon persuaded to accompany him to check out the various feline creatures being given away on an estate in lovely Bermondsey.

I followed Stan later that evening to a flat nearby and was invited into the family kitchen to look at a selection of tiny, cute, five-week-old bundles of fur, milling around and doing the kitten things that kittens do.

'How many do you have?' I asked

'Four,' was the reply from the lady of the house.

We looked around and could see only three staggering around on the floor,

'Where's the other one?' Stan and I both asked in unison.

On cue, a black kitty with a small white flash under the chin emerged from behind the fridge, patted over in our direction and was immediately picked by the pair of us.

We were informed that the kitten was a female; it looked at us in that way that kittys do, we said our thanks and transported her by hand to its new squat home.

After a brief 'cooling off' period of observation, we decided to name our cat 'Jazz' after Jaz Coleman of Killing Joke. Reason being was that she demonstrated a mad and unpredictable personality, such as the aforementioned doom mongering lead vocalist of the above band.

Sometime later (about a year) we discovered that 'she' was in fact a 'he' cat, and a randy little sod he was too, especially as our Jazz was a friendly, good looking cat that loved people's laps, and an occasional sniff of second hand spliff smoke as well.

But little did our Jazz know just what was in store for him during his long and eventful life…

11 – Santa Comes Early

We were frequenting the Soho Club scene after drinking sessions in The Cambridge Arms and other hip bars around Shaftesbury Avenue. There were gigs at The Astoria on Charing Cross Road, The Marquee in Wardour Street, Gossips and other underground, darkened venues to visit on weekday evenings. I was hanging out with Ian and Stan's brother, Mike, and some of the other Battersea people.

We were usually out gigging or clubbing over the weekends and friends often came back to stay at our place in Bermondsey. Now that the winter had arrived our squat was always a good option in the small hours as we had central heating, so the place was warm, sort of furnished but comfortable enough.

Midway through that December a deliveryman called one morning, and asked no questions as I accepted a large, heavy cardboard box at the front door.

'Thanks,' I said.

'Okay mate,' he replied and then got back in his transit van and drove away.

I stumbled along the hallway clutching the weighty 'Delivery' into the kitchen and of course out of curiosity immediately opened it. It turned out to be a Christmas Hamper full of all the usual yuletide delights including Tinned Hams, Pate, Brandy Butter, Nuts, Cake, Chocolate Log, fancy biscuits and a tin of something called Game Soup. This wasn't a cheap hamper, it was a quality one full of good stuff as I picked through the contents. 'Who does this belong to? Someone has made a delivery mistake here' and 'We can't be that lucky can we?' I checked the carton for more information and a name but only our address was to be found on the box. Although somewhat tempted at that moment to get stuck into the early Christmas present, I put everything back and waited for Stan and Ian to add weight to my conscience later on.

That evening, as the three of us sifted ever deeper into the box of goodies we decided it a good idea to ask the old gal upstairs to put the word about and see if someone on the estate was missing a hamper, especially if it belonged to a pensioner. The thought of us gorging ourselves on quail, cake and nuts on Christmas Day while some old biddy in a flat around the corner was hungry and miserable, made us put it all back and wait.

Had the box showed up the day before the previous May bank holiday it would've been a different story entirely for Dean and I on that particular weekend.

We waited two weeks for 'The Deliveryman' to call again and ask for his carton back, or for someone local to claim it. But neither happened and by Christmas eve the untouched carton was still parked invitingly on the kitchen floor. Stan was going away, so Ian and I now stood grinning over the tempting box sitting in the corner and persuaded ourselves that 'It was meant to be' or 'A mystery present for us' and other such self appraising bullshit when one is about to take something that doesn't belong to you.

Ian and I then cleared our consciences and prepared ourselves for hamper delights as we re-opened the box of goodies. Some of our friends called over during that particular festive season mostly to escape the usual family quarrelling and were happy to help us to consume the contents of the mystery yuletide present.

The following February, there was a knock at the door. It was a 'Delivery Man' but a different guy this time. He asked if a box had been delivered to this address many weeks ago.

I thought really hard for a couple of seconds and replied, 'No mate we're squatting here, and we've only just moved in' I directed his gaze to the Legal Notice on the window. With that he ticked something off his clipboard saying, 'Okay, thanks, bye' and then got back into his van and drove away.

In view of that, I hope we're not all condemned for eternity for scoffing on someone's Christmas Hamper. I'd hate to think of anyone missing out on a tin of Game Soup, whatever that is, was.

12 – The Itchy Month

During the spring of '87 Stan and I were offered some unused furniture and a spare mattress from the overflowing garage at a friend's house in Essex. I'd often stayed at their place during my visits to Dean, now an outpatient at the hospital and gradually recovering but still unable to contemplate moving back to Bermondsey. Stan and I had use of a van one weekend so we drove up to Essex to collect our free furniture. After piling a few small tables, lamps, the mattress and various other useful items into the van and returned to Stansfeld House to offload our 'new' fittings. We distributed the furniture about the flat I took the single mattress as my current one was a bit saggy and tired.

A couple of weeks later, while Stan and I were watching evening telly and getting stoned, we couldn't help but notice how itchy we both were. He and I were scratching like mad, in between the fingers, toes, under the armpits, down the thighs and along the back of our legs.

This condition continued relentlessly on for a week or so, usually much worse in the evenings, and eventually to the point where it was keeping us awake at night. We were red raw from the damn scratching, and this affliction wasn't showing any signs of going away on its own. This wouldn't do so Stan decided to visit the doctor; he booked an appointment and disappeared for an hour.

He returned sometime later armed with a perplexed look on his face carrying white bag of pharmacy goods and immediately informed me that we had caught a dose of 'Scabies'.

'What's that?' I asked

'Fleas,' he replied. 'Tramps get it,' he added.

The Doc had explained that Scabies is a microscopic bug that burrows under the skin and makes one itch like fuck. We were instructed to wash our clothes and bed linen, clean the flat out and let plenty of fresh air into the place.

In the pharmacy bag were some pills to relieve the itching and a large glass bottle of white lotion.

Stan handed the lotion bottle to me, then added, 'The doctor said we are to have a hot bath and then cover ourselves in the lotion, from the neck down.'

To which I respond with, 'So, you mean he wants us to have a bath together, then rub the lotion on each other's naked bodies? You and me, tonight?'

We laughed as we both spontaneously scratched at the same moment.

Stan went first while I scratched a while longer in front of the telly, and then it was my turn. After a hot bath I stood naked and clean in the steamy bathroom, gently opened the partially used bottle and proceeded to cover myself lightly with the clinical smelling toxic lotion. I went up my legs, down my arms, over my chest and between those raw fingers and toes.

As I waited for a moment to let my body absorb the fluid I was suddenly struck down by a searing red-hot feeling on my scrotum and arse. Within seconds I was yelping in pain as I tried to bathe my bollocks and arsehole over the sink to relieve that 'on fire' feeling. When the heat and 'flames' finally died down a bit I eased myself gingerly out of the bathroom to find Stan sitting in the front room holding a large spliff and an even larger grin.

'Did you remember to get plenty of that lotion on your arse and bollocks then?' he retorted.

We both burst out laughing and after a short discussion we agreed to keep our dossers disease a secret from everyone, especially as he was currently working in a college kitchen and would be sacked as a health hazard if it became known that he was a dirty squatter.

However, about a week later, the scratching began once more. This time I volunteered to go and see the doctor, who then wrote another prescription for toxic white lotion while I assured him that we'd washed all our clothes and bed linen and this second dose should do the trick. Once again it was arse and bollocks on fire time in the steamy bathroom for the both of us. By now we'd been monitoring our friend's reactions in the last couple of weeks when they'd popped over in the evenings to pay us a visit.

Many of them were seen to be scratching slightly from the corner of one's eye; we kept silent and hoped that they didn't catch the highly contractible hobo's affliction from us. If any of them did, they said nothing and probably went to visit their own doctor in quiet shame just as we had.

Yet again after a further week, we were back where we started, itching like fuck in the evenings. Stan made the journey to the doctor once more and was duly grilled deeply on the cleanliness of our flat. We had washed all of our clothes and the place wasn't a pigsty for heaven's sake, we were as perplexed as the good doctor. Then he stuck upon the real culprit when he asked if we'd brought any old furniture home from the streets, such as sofas or mattresses.

'Oh yeah,' Stan remembered.

'We did pick up some stuff and an old mattress from a friends garage recently,' he added.

The doctor sighed and told us to drag the culprit out into a field and burn it immediately, then wrote another prescription of bollock burning lotion and said that he didn't expect to see either of us scratchy squatters again.

Later that night, two young men with second degree burns on their arseholes and scrotums were seen dragging an old blue mattress across Dunton housing estate and forcing it into a large, round metal bin. Apparently this mattress in question had been sitting in our friends' garage for 'a few years'.

So let that be a warning to squatters everywhere who are offered second hand beds from helpful friends. Nobody we knew ever mentioned that they'd somehow got a dose of scabies from somewhere unknown, but if you're out there and kept quiet about it we'd like to hope that in your eagerness to rid yourselves of the filthy ailment, you'd also remembered not to cover your genitals and arsehole in that deadly white-hot potion, at least on the second occasion.

13 – The Squatters' Toolkit

Within a couple of months we had to move once again, although this time it wasn't the usual legal eviction process that was to end our time in Stansfeld House; it was due to our own stupidity by neglecting to pay the electricity bills which had been periodically arriving but continually ignored. We'd paid some of the charges owed, but seemingly not sufficient dues. One morning while I was making something to eat everything electrical around me suddenly went dead with that reassuring 'click'. When I stepped outside the flat and looked towards the basement lock-up room where the electricity supply came in and there was a man busily removing our meter with little sympathy for our dilemma. He threw the meter in the back of his L.E.B van and drove away.

So that was that, our fault entirely and the L.E.B would not accommodate us as far as reconnection knowing that we were squatting, so we were basically fucked. After a night or two in the dim candlelight as the food began to moulder in the mini fridge it was decided by Stan and I that we'd have to find somewhere else to live.

I went to call on our squat-man-that-can again in Old Kent Road to see what was 'on offer' that month; he gave me a few indicators and mentioned a guy with the title of 'Squatters Advisor' who would be on hand that night to help if we cared to call on him later. Stan and I then got ourselves ready for an evening of flat hunting as we gathered together the necessary equipment for our 'Squatters' Toolkit' in preparation of the coming nights' forays…

Itinerary of items generally required for a Squatter's Toolkit

<u>Dark clothes</u>: Always a good idea if you're breaking open flats late at night under cover of darkness, as you don't really want to stand out under the Moonlight like race track steward.

<u>Junior Hacksaw</u>: The essential tool needed for cutting through those tough padlock brackets. Preferably one with a sharp blade and a spare in the tool bag.

<u>Vice Grips</u>: Essential tool required to bend the 1/4 steel plate down in order to pass the (still locked) padlock through the gap that you've just sawn (noisily) through.

<u>Screwdriver</u>: Ideally an insulated, electrician's type; as used to test for a live supply, and to generally poke about with upon gaining (illegal) entry into said property.

<u>Small Crowbar</u>: To finally, once and for all, force open those extra stubborn front doors.

<u>Pocket Torch</u>: To dimly enlighten the horrors awaiting you in the dark recesses of what will most likely be an environment not suitable for human habitation.

<u>Candle</u>: See above, if the torch was unavailable that evening, or in the event of dead batteries.

<u>Lighter</u>: To light the candle and also that first celebratory spliff having now gained access into your 'potential new home'.

<u>Something Electrical</u>: Usually a light bulb and something to plug into various wall sockets for that definitive 'sorted or not sorted' electrical test.

<u>Optional Accessories when flat hunting during the day</u>: Black Donkey jacket (or similar), scuffed 'work boots', light blue jeans, Hi-Vis over-jacket, and a copy of a daily tabloid newspaper.

When one is daytime scouting for accommodation and attired as above, the newspaper gag is to dupe the locals into presuming that you're a regular council workman going about your general estate maintenance duties. However, in this instance it's good to be prepared with a convincing story if questioned by a tenant while in the process of hacking through a padlock bracket or levering a front door from its hinges on your chosen housing estate.

<u>Note</u>: *The above subterfuge option may not always be possible should you be sporting a wild multicoloured haircut, a ring through your nose, wearing a tatty, stud covered leather jacket, knee high lace up boots and a pair of red bondage trousers with the arse hanging out.*

Stan and I were now all 'tooled up' and ready for flat hunting at about nine o'clock on a weekday evening, we called on our designated a 'Professional Squatters Advisor' and the three of us slipped into the mild Bermondsey evening, as the metal tools occasionally clanked in the bag slung over my shoulder.

Our 'Squatters Advisor' by appearance wasn't your typical scuzzy, unwashed, anarcho-dreadhead, but a well spoken, public school type guy. He was a bit younger than us, very fat, politically a red, and talked mostly bollocks about everything he claimed to know about squatting.

On that note of confidence, Stan and I duly followed him like a couple of sheep into a grubby estate nearby and set about the grim task of locating our 'new flat'. After only a few minutes we found an empty place a couple of floors up in a small block, which seemed an encouraging start to our evening's work. However, after a few seconds of jarring, high pitched sawing that instantly overwhelmed the calm evening silence, our potential new neighbours started to emerge from their evening slumber in front of the telly to stare uncomfortably in our direction.

This undue attention was making us feel very nervous, so we hurriedly packed up our tools and exited quickly while meekly apologising and assuring the locals that 'We're only squatting empties, not breaking into people's homes, sorry'.

Our lardy 'Advisor' barked out some legal bullshit to the grumpy residents which didn't really help the situation, so we moved on to another estate close by.

Next up we located a ground floor flat conveniently situated at the end of a small block, which in squatting terms is often ideal. We got straight down to business and took turns to hack through that cold grey steel plate enclosing the dubious and weak looking padlock. Our sawing was once again exerting decibels of an ear splitting volume, resonating from building to building as the blade once more rasped away destroying the peaceful tranquillity of a council estate in the quiet of mid evening. Therefore, our best option here was to try to hack through it 'amputation style' (as quickly as possible) and get in before anyone became seriously vexed by our noisy presence.

The hacksaw blade held up and we succeeded in this endeavour before anyone challenged us and in we strode through the front door straight into a damp, dark, dirty, miserable flat. On first inspection, it wasn't a patch on what Stan and I had been used to and if chosen, was going to be a definite step down. Within a few minutes as we searched the dank rooms by torch and candlelight the sound of a police radio could be heard from the street outside, followed by the revolving blue light show and the opening of car doors. The three of us froze momentarily in the hope that they'd go away but it was soon obvious that someone local had called them, and here they were, cops when you didn't need them. Next, there came a knock at the slightly ajar door to which Stan and I nervously jumped, but not our 'Advisor'.

He immediately turned on his fat heels in the dim hallway and charged his huge bulk up to the front door and pushed it closed just as the coppers were entering, thus pushing them back out into the passageway as he commenced on a tirade of verbal jargon such as: 'Squatters right to occupy!' and other unhelpful phrases including 'It is illegal to enter this property, it is now occupied'.

Then adding with undoubting authority, 'You are liable to a fine not exceeding a thousand pounds if you force entry into this now occupied property!'

He loaded his wobbly twenty stone frame against the fragile door as the much thinner cops pushed from the other side demanding that we open the door or get seriously nicked in about thirty seconds. The whole charade was all becoming a bit Laurel and Hardy, as Stan and I realised that we were all going to be arrested, very soon.

The two of us decided after a minute of this bollocks to let the police have it their way, things would only get worse from here on in, and we told fat boy to move aside.

The red faced and slightly annoyed cops entered and gave the fat guy some verbal shit and told him to be quiet or he's nicked for breaking and entering in the usual 'copper speak'.

We told them what we were doing and the reason why we were opening a closed council flat, and the general 'not guilty' blah blah.

Then one cop replied saying, 'Yes we know, there's a lot of squatting going on in this area.'

The other cop then asked who 'The Leader' was to which the fat guy replied helpfully, 'None of us, we're all together.'

Although I was tempted to point in his direction, the nice guy in me decided to keep quiet.

The same cop looked down at my junior hacksaw laying by the front door and asked, 'Who owns the hacksaw?'

After a brief pause I said, 'It's mine.'

'I'm arresting you on the charge of Criminal Damage,' said the same copper smartly.

At this Stan quipped in, 'We'll all take responsibility; everyone took turns sawing the lock off.'

The now congenial copper explained that he understood our camaraderie but the law states that the police can only arrest one of us for this particular offence, and unfortunately as it was my junior hacksaw, I would be the one getting nicked tonight.

An unfair cop but I gave up without a struggle, Mr Policeman stooped to pick up my hacksaw 'as evidence' while Stan picked up the tool bag and I was then guided into the back of the posh squad car. I said a quick goodbye with a wave to the guys and stating, 'I'll see you later, back at the flat.'

I was then driven in semi comfort to Southwark Police Station by the now ever friendlier and understanding policemen. The copper driving said that if none of us had admitted owning the saw they would've had to let us go with a warning, which basically meant that I was tricked into admission, and therefore kind of conned into a confession.

At the police station I was duly charged with the above offence, photographed from three angles, fingerprinted and interviewed for about twenty minutes. I was then served a summons for a court appearance and offered a lift back to our candlelit home by the nice coppers who now had a nick under their belts for their night's work. They assured me of a minimal conviction and a small fine, if any, for the minor criminal misdemeanour.

'Nothing to worry about mate, the magistrate will understand your situation,' the driver added reassuringly as I exited the squad car and bid them goodnight.

About a week later I put some half decent clothes on and walked the short distance to Southwark Crown Court, where I waited in the dock with an assortment of local petty criminals until my name was eventually called.

The magistrate seemed relatively uninterested and didn't pay any attention to your narrator until the clerk mentioned that I'd been arrested while breaking into a flat on a nearby estate recently. At that he looked up from under his bifocals and then turned to the clerk and said, 'Was the young man trying to squat an empty flat?'

At this the policeman answered, 'Yes your honour, he was breaking into a closed flat and in his defence he mentioned that he was looking for somewhere to live.'

'So the flat was empty and unoccupied?' asked the magistrate.

'Yes,' answered the copper.

The magistrate then turned to me and said words to the effect of it being very wrong to break and enter regardless of one's situation and other quotations along those lines, to which I nodded in full agreement and answered in my defence, 'It was empty, I would only look at empty flats, and I wasn't looking to burgle, only for somewhere to live, your honour.'

With hardly a pause he informed me I would be bound over for twelve months for criminal damage; and that this offence would be taken into consideration should I end up before him or any other magistrate during the period of one full year.

'Do you understand what this means young man?' he asked, gazing at me from under his specs perched on the end of his considerable nose.

'Yes sir, your honour,' I replied.

'It is your responsibility to stay out of trouble for the next twelve months, is this clear young man?'

'Yes, your honour,' I reaffirmed.

So, with that all sorted out in four minutes flat, I left court with a mere warning and thankfully no lighter financially.

But the reality of our situation was the fact that we still had to find somewhere to live very soon, one way or another.

14 – The Vodka Cupboard

Stan and I really had no choice but to keep venturing out at night to find somewhere else to live. We were now kicking ourselves at our own stupidity by neglecting to pay enough of the periodic electricity bills at Stansfeld House, which although were not in either of our names they should've been attended to all the same.

We often wondered months down the line, how long we may have been able to live there had we not been so stupid? The neighbours were now all fine with us, and the old gal upstairs had even given me a get well card for Dean in hospital and had also informed Southwark Council that we were no longer a problem in that estate. We were idiots to push our luck so far, and now we were back at square one yet again, with the added worry of my getting nicked again on any given evening for breaking and entering.

This time however, we stayed on the Dunton Road Estate and decided not to employ the services of the previous lardy 'Squatters Advisor' again. After a couple more hours of climbing into various empties which were the usual non starters, we found a second floor flat on a corner of a block literally just across the road from our soon-not-to-be place.

With two upstairs bedrooms and the electricity sort of on, it looked like we were in business again, but the hot water tank wasn't working and looked much like something designed and manufactured during the height of the rocket age. Therefore, we'd have to survive without hot water until we 'fixed something up' although the gas supply was also on so we could at least boil up enough water on the crappy stove as parked in the drab kitchen to accommodate face washes, shaving and as and when necessary, a 'Gentleman's Wash'.

The aforementioned electricity supply was a very dodgy affair indeed. The meter had been ripped out and two thick white cables had been directly 'connected' into the mains supply entering from somewhere in the world outside. One lead fed the needs of our flat, the other we curiously followed across the floor, as it went out through a slightly open window, down the outside wall, and through a hole in a window frame into the flat directly below us. Obviously, the people living downstairs were squatting too and had plugged into 'our supply' as it was (before we arrived) unoccupied. This situation wasn't a problem for us of course as it looked like a 'professional squat job' and they were just as welcome to free electricity as we were looking forward too.

There were two men and a woman downstairs from Ireland, and although we had little contact with them, they sometimes had to (carefully) break into our flat when we were out to push the 'Reset Free Electricity Button' on the overloaded system when it occasionally popped. But being fellow homeless types they could always be trusted to shut our front door behind them. Our only reservation with this arrangement was that sitting on the floor in the dodgy electricity cupboard was a very large and half full bottle of blue label Smirnoff vodka, minus the lid. Although we wondered who it belonged to, Stan and I were never tempted to sample its delights, we just left the bottle sitting there alone and unwanted in that dark cupboard.

Our new abode was in desperate need of decorating; it was old and obviously hadn't been painted or subjected to 'home improvements' in many years. In fact the whole block was in a bad way, with a number of legal occupants living alongside squatters. These dwellings were probably somewhere down on the council's list for a refit at an undisclosed date far in the future, especially in view of the rising damp on one side of the entire building. As for that mauve, gloss painted ancient water boiler mounted on our living room wall, it was probably installed as new when the Beatles were still together, and was a long time broken and more than likely irreparable.

We soon chose our (upstairs) bedrooms and settled in without a care for the future, our relief in the first instance was having a roof over our heads again, and we'd worry about baths and all the rest at our leisure. The usual people came over to visit and admire (or rather grimace at) another 'new squat'.

Stan was now in a band and still working in Hammersmith College. But as I currently wasn't doing either, this meant that I did most of the fixing around the place which often involved periodically standing and staring at the nasty old boiler, willing it to as if by magic, start working once more. Jazz the cat sniffed the place out and got used to it soon enough, even though cats generally hate a change of address. He was a bit stuck for going out as we were now above ground level though he was still young and mostly housebound anyway.

One afternoon I decided to try to fix the water boiler, a task that I expected to last for ten minutes before giving up. I tinkered with the beast for an hour or so, and ended up tracing some very old wires all the way back to the supply, finding to my surprise that some leads were disconnected. I very nearly juiced myself when cutting a wire that I failed to realise was in fact still hooked up directly to the 'fuse box'. A large blue flash soon brought me to my senses as I swayed on a wobbly chair. After that nearly shocking moment, I methodically went through the general safety motions, which included a short prayer and a couple of deep breaths then installed some lengths of wire as ripped from another unused accessory.

I then gingerly hooked the lot back up to the national grid, stood well back in my rubber soled Doc Marten boots, and tripped the switch with one of my drumsticks. Suddenly, a little yellow light came on by the prehistoric appliance and something else happened, the sound of water being moved about through ancient pipes and other likewise encouraging noises were soon abundant all around.

I watched, listened and periodically felt pipes as cold water started to become lukewarm and gradually hot, as the Jurassic tank creaked and clanked back into life like the un-dead being woken after a long slumber. After an hour I cautiously ran the hot tap in the bath, it coughed and spluttered and shook on its mountings before a stream of very brown and obviously very old water came gushing forward. But more to the point, behind it soon came piping hot water flowing into the bath, which meant that a major obstacle to living in that flat had now been sorted. After all of the remaining rusty red water had been pushed through the system, and clean, hot H2O now teemed from the tap, there only remained one thing left to do…

After three long weeks without a decent wet down, and with a spliff hanging from the corner of my mouth, I eased my filthy body into the blissfully steaming hot bath, and duly basked in the success of a particularly satisfactory squat type electrical repair job.

Later that evening Stan arrived back home, pissed off, tired and stressed out from toiling in a baking hot kitchen, as I chilled on the leather sofa, mega clean and chilled out. I wasn't going to let him suffer too long as I told him to test the water in the cheesy bathroom. His eyebrows rose in hope as he made his way to the washing quarter, feeling the heated boiler as he passed by. Thereafter he was gone for an hour and more as the happy, splashy sounds of muffled singing could be heard emanating through the thick steam following under the door of our now 'fully operational' bathroom.

As we slumbered in front of the telly we now saw our rather grotty flat with a renewed sense of enthusiasm; the dowdy old place was suddenly transformed into a near palace now that we had access to a luxury commonly known as hot running water. We began to visualize a coat of paint around the place, posters on walls, record collections being pulled from their cases and other such homely ideas were duly discussed leisurely over a few beers for the remainder of the evening.

We settled into this 'great flat' with our crazy cat, everything was cool and life went on.

I began to feel that I wanted to be occupied more in life than to merely be spending my time moving from one pissy squat to another every few months. I needed to do something creative again. After all, that's what I came to London to pursue in the first place. I started to do the usual rounds, checking the Melody Maker, Loot & NME for bands seeking drummers. Phone calls were made from local, vandalised, piss smelling kiosks; demo tapes of previous bands were sent out and received in the mail. I listened patiently to the tunes delivered in the post and waited for the right C90 compact cassette to fall through our loosely fitted, alloy letterbox.

But I shouldn't have bothered anyway as guess what came in the mail along with the usual selection of poorly wrapped demo tapes?

15 – No Neck Day

Once again, just as we'd sorted the amenities out (that being hot running water and other associated fancies) we were kicked in the teeth yet again. That brown, windowed envelope with the red words stating effectively to 'Get out of our shitty flat' fell onto our doormat one weekday morning.

This tedious 'Legal Process' would be followed as always to the letter. Firstly the 'Please vacate this property' note arrived, followed six weeks later by the less cordial 'final demand; haven't you lot left yet?' in a slightly more threatening tone.

Not long after that the eviction process made its way through the local County Court, and an even more official, rubber stamped date to 'Absolutely, definitely leave our crappy property, now' would then be delivered by mister postie.

The vast majority of squatters didn't bother to make an appearance in court to contest an eviction, as the result was inevitably the same in each case; you're out, no squatters, fuck off and that's that. This legality was finally completed by a letter from a bailiff's agency who were contracted to vacate any remaining human beings, dogs, cats, exotic pets, squat belongings, scratched album collections and terrible 'found in the street' furnishings from the said property.

These notices were always written in the usual font, in the standardised style, and all part of 'Southwark Housing Services'.

Stan and I browsed the official letter from 'No-Neck-Thugs & Sons, Bailiffs Ltd to the County Court', made a brief mental note of the time and date 'to leave' a couple of weeks in the far and distant future. Then we simply went about our lives as usual.

One morning, about two long weeks later, at 7am on the dot, came a very loud and demanding knock knocking upon our door. Stan was up in a flash and down the stairs first asking who the hell it was, just as I was awakening from a peculiar squatter dream and then realised who it probably is.

No Neck & Sons did show up alright, at precisely the allotted hour, and we could see through the frosted window the silhouette of a large geezer balancing a 20lb sledgehammer over his shoulder and seconds away from putting the front door in with it.

Stan shouted back through the letterbox, 'Okay, we'll be out in a minute.'

'You've got five minutes mate, okay?' came the stern reply from Mr No-Neck, the dad bailiff man, as son-of-no-neck waited impatiently with his big hammer

We then started packing our belongings in record time, things were being stuffed into bin liners and boxes as instant decisions were made as to what stays and what goes. It was bloody frantic and total chaos of course, trying to dress and pack under those circumstances, one began to feel more worthless as a human being by the second. But alas despite our enforced rush, we didn't quite manage it in the tiny allotted time we had been given. The warnings came thick and fast via thug outside which were soon followed by a couple of loud bangs with the sledgehammer, and in went our light blue door.

Two members of the No-Neck Bailiff family stepped through the shards of timber, sledgehammer guy and what looked like a younger member of the Neck-less clan followed by a copper who immediately asked us where the electricity meter was. We said nothing as he followed his nose (and the cable from downstairs) to the vodka cupboard and gazed quizzically at the science fiction before him.

'Where's the meter lads?' he asked.

'Err, don't really know,' replied Stan.

'Was like that when we got here, I don't know anything about electricity officer,' I lied.

We left the cop looking at the chaos of wires that was our electricity supply as another young policeman led us out onto the balcony where a small crowd had gathered to watch the morning's entertainment unfold. We noticed that our neighbour two doors away had failed to leave his squat in time too, although the Irish lot downstairs were well away a few nights before. They obviously had the sense to realise that bailiffs really do turn up when they say they will and wisely left.

In the mounting confusion that followed, the cop radioed in to the station and was ordered to arrest Stan, myself and our neighbour for the crime of 'Theft of Electricity'. What a pissy way to start the day I thought, as we were bundled into squad cars while catching a last view of our meagre belongings being thrown out of our recently smashed front doors.

We were each allowed two bin liners of belongings which were placed in the boots of the cop cars, then off we went to the station.

Once again in the space of only a couple of months, I'd been nicked twice, fingerprinted, photographed and treated like a common criminal just because I was having 'housing problems'. We should've left the flat at the very latest the night before and saved ourselves a lot of aggro.

After being charged I was led downstairs to a white tiled cell, as was Stan and our also nicked neighbour. We were each allowed to bring one bag in the cell with us; I took the one stuffed full of my last minute packing while Stan at least ended up with his acoustic guitar to keep him in tuneful company in the cell next door.

As I sat back and contemplated my next move in life from the comforts of my warm and sterile jail, I realised that if I was done for this stupid charge I'd also get that previous criminal damage hacksaw business loaded on top too. But it wasn't really worth bothering about at this moment as there was nothing I could do about it anyway.

The twist to being arrested at that particular moment in my life was the fact that I was halfway through a thoroughly engrossing and entertaining book Papillon by Henri Charriere. A real life, men's own horror story about the French penal colonies of Guiana in the 1920s and 30s as written by Charriere who was nicknamed Papillon by his companions. This was grim story about adventure, escape, and the struggle to survive in the violent, disease infested swamps of tropical South America.

Despite the fact that he was a gangster and career criminal, and he admitted as much, he was handed a life sentence without parole in French Guiana for a murder he actually didn't commit, or so he said…

This injustice gave Henry Charriere a gritty resolve and the determination to escape that miserable prison colony under any circumstances, and he made it his life's mission to do just that.

I opened the book to the chapter I was currently up to; it became apparent that this book would now take on an almost surreal meaning as it was now being read in jail by your narrator.

I was almost there with him as he described spending two terrible years in solitary confinement in a tiny dark cell for his first failed escape attempt, which he took part in almost as soon as he arrived at the penal colony. Part of the punishment in solitary was that you never left the confinements of your cell for the whole of your sentence; the door was sealed behind you when you entered. Minimal light came from anywhere as the guards patrolled on catwalks above and between the cells. The only possibility of contact with another was when you stuck your head through a window of your cell door to have your head shaved once a month to keep the lice at bay. The food was insufficient to sustain you physically and more importantly, mentally during the endless sentence, unless a friend risked their own three month stretch in solitary to slip a coconut husk into the gruel they called food.

But the worst part of the whole miserable process was that everybody spent their entire sentence in total silence, that's two long, long years without speaking to a soul, a nightmarish and cruel punishment on top of solitary confinement. Many didn't survive the two years you'd be handed for your first escape attempt, let alone the five years you'd be given if captured on your second try.

Charriere explained in horrifying and graphic detail the misery of his life for twenty-four endless months, as his mind took him off into deep hallucinations while he learned to practically sleepwalk the four paces across his cell. He'd been informed that nobody had ever lived longer than three and a half years in those conditions, and that it was better to die trying to escape than to contemplate any time in solitary.

As I leafed through the pages of Charriere's incredible story the hours seemed to melt away in the comforts of my twentieth century cell. Lunch duly arrived and was actually edible too, I only really missed a cigarette break every hour or so, but that book kept me in good company with my new anti hero – Papillon.

Sometime that afternoon the door was abruptly opened and Stan was shown in carrying his guitar, a heavy bin liner and a wry smile. He settled onto the bunk opposite, as this was a twin cell or 'double' as they say. We discussed our situation and philosophised on the reasons why we didn't bloody move before we ended up in this shit, but that was all irrelevant now anyway. Not long after that, our cell door clanked open once more and in strode our squat neighbour also carrying his belongings in a saggy bin bag. It appeared that the station was filling up rapidly and they needed the single cells for the real south London criminal fraternity. The police constables who periodically looked in on us and served up dinner were a bit put out by the fact that a promotion seeking sergeant had ordered our arrests that morning on this stupid charge. The whole debacle was a complete waste of time and money, and the cops knew it too. It's not as if the L.E.B. couldn't afford to lose a few quid in revenue on account of some homeless people using a free supply for a couple of months, for fucks sake.

The three of us sat about getting gradually bored and more in need of a tobacco hit by the hour, as this was obviously being denied to us during our stay. At about 10pm we were taken up to the charge room, then each of us were handcuffed to a separate copper and lead outside to a waiting transit van and driven the short distance to Southwark Police Station for the night. It seemed that the other substation we were being held in was now full to capacity with local petty crime doers.

We spent the night sharing a two man cell with our neighbour who bedded down on the floor and was supplied with a spare crash mat to sleep on. After breakfast the following morning we were beginning to get nicotine withdrawal symptoms and becoming restless in the confines of the clinical tiled walls surrounding us. But what came next was a revelation indeed; we were queued up in single file outside the station along with the other mixed bag of crims residing at Southwark cop shop, and stuffed into one of those murderer transport vans with blacked out windows you see being chased by photographers on the news.

These vehicles must be absolute hell for those with claustrophobia; you are pressed through a narrow door and along a tiny passage to an even smaller cubicle. It's sitting room only I'm afraid, in a space about half the size of a public toilet cubicle, the partitioning in front of your face is about ten inches from your nose, while your legs can just about slip under the divide and you have about four inches either side of your shoulders to really enforce that nauseous, cramped feeling. The only relief is to be able look out of the tiny black slit window which in my instance was situated on the right, and watch normal people go about their morning business on the streets of freedom outside. Although the public cannot see into these boxes from the other side, you most certainly can see out very clearly which is somewhat uncomfortable and you do feel like a proper villain during the bumpy ride to court.

I could hear Stan from his cubicle in front shouting with laughter, 'It's a toilet! It's a toilet! Get me the fuck out of here!'

This was abruptly replied to by a cop guarding the slim corridor with an 'Okay, okay! Shut up you lot, and quieten down!'

Was this the worst vehicle I've ever ridden in? Yes, most certainly the winner without a doubt.

Not only did we have to endure the uncomfortable ride to court, but we also diverted to a couple of other local police stations to pick up even more criminality for the dock that morning. I felt travel sick and like a genuine gangster by the time we pulled into Southwark Crown Court forty minutes later.

Us three electricity burglars were taken downstairs (still handcuffed of course) and placed together in a very grizzly open plan type cell unit block that looked like animal holding cages at a circus to wait for a solicitor to be appointed to us and discuss our case. These grim cells must've accommodated countless people down the years awaiting their fate in the halls of justice above. They were covered in scratchy graffiti from floor to ceiling, in all shapes and sizes, some of which were very old doodles, and others obviously more recent. It was a busy, miserable holding area and a place to really put one off the idea of a life of crime.

Eventually our allotted solicitor emerged and told us all immediately to plead not guilty and to say in our defence that we had every intention of paying for the electricity we were using. It was basically down to the L.E.B. to prove this otherwise, but we didn't really care by now anyway, we were irritated and all we wanted was a fucking light for the fags we could finally now smoke.

All this legal talk was conducted through the thick door bars in the amplified, echoing void of that open celled block. Around us were a multitude of discussions and conversations all jumbled up in a cacophony of continuous sound as various legal representatives were in conference with their particular villainous clients.

By the time we were eventually sent upstairs and placed in the dock together, all three of us had the look of unwashed, tin drinking homeless losers, who'd had a bad night and been denied cigarettes. We smelt like shit, looked like crap, we hadn't had a shave in a couple days, and were all by now pretty pissed off and miserable.

We were as good as convicted before any of us stood up and said 'Not Guilty' as the clerk of the court set a date for 'trial by jury' in Crown Court and promptly discharged us when they were satisfied enough that we had addresses to go to which we could call 'home'.

Stan and I both volunteered the Battersea flat, where we could at least get a floor for a few days, then left the court with our bin liners in tow and made for the first pub we saw in Borough High Street. Our freedom after thirty hours in custody felt very good, as did that first pint. How people can endure years of prison is beyond me, but then again some deserve it, others are born into it, and some are better off for everyone's sake to be locked up. But to end up inside as a miscarriage of justice is a miserable karma indeed.

Stan and I visited a friendly solicitor in Camberwell on a number of occasions regarding this charge in preparation for our next imminent court appearance. We were still advised to plead not guilty which we did on our first showing back in Southwark Court after a few weeks. At this point the prosecution told the clerk of the court that they were still 'collecting evidence', to which the magistrate duly postponed 'the trial' for a further six weeks. When six weeks had passed, the prosecution once again still didn't have a case to offer, so once again it was postponed for another four weeks. When we showed up for the third time in Southwark Crown Court to plead our innocence, the prosecution yet again announced they had not prepared the evidence against us. At that, the now irritated magistrate bashed his gavel down and immediately dismissed the case. The three of us went to the pub laughing all the way. We guessed that trying to prove how a few squatters were thieving a precious electricity supply was a complete waste of public funds.

    I would bet that our case files were 'accidentally' force fed into a shredder by an experienced duty sergeant sometime in the run up to our 'trial' and seen as a case that simply couldn't be proven nor won anyway.

16 – Pond Scum with Slugs

Being homeless yet again I made my way to the guys in Emu Road as Stan had decided to go and stay with some friends in the lovely borough of 'Hounslow-under-the-air-traffic' way out west. Besides, there wasn't enough room for any more than four people at the house in Battersea.

The Battersea situation was another in the long line of squat stories, although it wasn't originally a squat it had been legally occupied by some friends I'd come to know through Stan and the bands he and I had played in. The guys that lived there had been forced out by the greedy landlord with the intention to sell the downstairs property on the now lucrative housing market. After they'd obediently moved out he simply locked the front door after them and left the place to rot on the cards at a local estate agents office.

Mike and Des decided to go back after a couple of months and squat the place as they were in a housing crisis of their own. They actually unlocked door with their original key one dark evening and simply 're-occupied' the flat. Ian made up the third person sharing a room with Mike, I moved in with Des in the other bedroom. It wasn't the best place I'd squatted but a roof over my head was the main priority and this was now accomplished.

The flat had been left in somewhat of a hurry by everyone who'd lived there previously and someone had placed all the cooking pots and pans in the bath and covered them with water. So for many weeks these utensils sat and festered in the bathroom. By the time we came to clear it all up in order to re-use the bathroom facilities, the now lime green coloured algae had reverted back to nature and become stagnant pond full of frogspawn, silverfish and other rare diversions of platonic and microscopic life forms.

Before we could actually use the bath Mike and I tasked ourselves with the rubber gloved job to rinse and wash the slimy green pond soup down the plughole, and scrub the green tide mark away. The half submerged aluminium pots and pans harbouring the building blocks of life went straight in the dustbin and new ones were purchased at the local pound store.

The notion that the universe must be positively teeming with life was an equation that definitely included house number 13 Emu Road, Battersea, London, England, Planet Earth. Speaking of life forms, we soon noticed that the kitchen and living room floor next door were covered in strange silvery tracks every morning. It was soon deduced that slugs were the other occupants of our home as they went about their slippery business in the night hours whilst we slept soundly in our bowing, decrepit 'landlord supplied' beds. If one was to get up in the night and use the kitchen on the other side of the living room, you'd often catch these creatures of the night also making their respective journeys very slowly across the floor.

One morning I noticed many silvery trails crisscrossing our grizzly living room floor which included passing right over the occupied light blue sleeping bag of a guest who'd stayed over and slept on the living room floor. I didn't mention it to him, I guess nobody else did either, as he stayed a more few nights on slime floor.

To say the least, despite having free accommodation in Battersea the place was pretty scruffy and a bit on the nasty side in the kitchen area as well. The occasional silverfish would be discovered lurking in the fridge and you'd often catch a glimpse of those dreaded cockroaches scampering back to the comforts of the darkness when you strode into the kitchen and switched on the light. Upon seeing these night visitors from the corner of one's eye, late evening stoner Marmite toast would no longer seem like such a delicious night time snack. After the first sighting of roach approach, nobody entered the kitchen without wearing something on their feet.

On the first weekend that I moved into Emu Road we all went up to the west end to go clubbing and to use this as an opportunity for me to settle in a bit more, as I didn't really know Mike that well and Des hardly at all. We ended up in The Mud Club where I then got completely totalled and was fast asleep upstairs by kicking out time. I was rudely shaken back to that half pissed / half asleep state by a very large bouncer who I then told to fuck off as I tried to slip back into my alcohol induced coma. He of course wasn't having any of it and I was then thrown roughly towards the fire exit while still airing drunken complaints. I was even more roughly shoved down the back exit stairs and punched in the guts for good measure and put into the street like a bin liner by the said thug.

    I soon sobered up after this humiliation and started to stagger on my way back via a night bus to the new squat in Battersea, while holding onto my bruised stomach. I arrived at Emu Road sometime later and realised that I still didn't have a key but was certain that someone would be home.

    I knocked smartly but there was no reply, I then banged a bit harder on the knocker, nothing. I called through the letterbox and waited some more, still nothing, but I could hear the sound of loud snoring so someone was definitely in. I bashed on the door knocker loud enough to wake the street up, but still an occupant didn't stir. By now I could hear movement in the street around me so I just made the swift decision to kick the door in.

    It swung open with ease at the first attempt and slammed against the crummy wall as I stumbled in and made straight for my bed, to the sound of deep, drunken snoring all around me.

Next morning I rose late with a hangover and wandered into slug living room to be confronted by three worried faces who'd obviously been talking in my absence.

'What happened to you last night mate?' was asked by one of our number.

I suddenly tweaked and realised exactly what was wrong and what these guys were concerned about.

I explained the beating I'd taken in The Mud Club and that I'd arrived back without a key and was banging on the door for ages to the sounds of snoring before I had to kick it in.

As they didn't really know much about me or my character and the fact that I'd only been there two days, I reassured them all that I most certainly don't make a habit of kicking the front door in every night when I come home, pissed out of my face.

At that the air was cleared and we all had a good laugh about it. Heavy sleepers I ask you? I could have chopped them all up in their miserable cots without even stirring the guy in the next bed two feet away.

We then jointly purchased a Chubb lock to which I duly fitted as reparations for damages caused, I then shared the keys out among us and that was sorted.

There was also a lot of art going on in slug house, Ian was deep into songwriting, Des was a solid bass player and gigging quite often with his band, whereas I was between bands and making those long across town trips to dark rehearsal rooms to 'audition' with usually unsuitable bands. The three of us did book a few jams at the ever reliable Crockwells rehearsal rooms where we bashed out some of Ian's songs and pass the hours as we honed our own particular musical persuasions.

Des was quite a funky, slap bass player and had his own unique style, Ian enjoyed the art of acoustic melodies, while I was heavily influenced by dub reggae and tribal rhythms. For me it was LKJ in Dub (Linton Kwesi Johnson the reggae poet and a Brixtonian) Scientist, Mad Professor, Scratch Perry, Dancehall Ska, The Congos, and one my all time favourites;

Dennis Bovell also known as Blackbeard.

There was a multitude of musical diversity at that time in the mid eighties to influence up and coming muso types such as ourselves. Bands usually dressed up in anything that went and anything they damn well wanted and made a serious effort to look different, really way out and more often, completely weird. The Virgin Prunes for instance looked pretty scary on stage when attired in dirty, torn wedding dresses and warped face make up when they gigged on the UK circuit, and that was just what the blokes in the band wore.
    Even though black was basically the colour during these times, men (me included) would experiment with eye liner, blusher and occasionally fishnet stockings worn under ripped (black) jeans in the winter. Dress sense and musical styles were a mismatched blend and they often overlapped between different genres throughout the dark era of Thatcherism.

For instance; The Stray Cats had a rockabilly and ageing teddy boy following, but plenty of punks and bleach haired psychobillies went to see them play on a the same bill as acts such as The Damned The UK Subs, or The Ruts. Then you'd get the new wave of punk bands featuring The Anti Nowhere League, Chron Gen, Discharge, Chelsea, The Addicts and the like who'd do the rounds on the punk all-dayer bills often at the Lyceum Ballroom in The strand. These bands were usually followed by the diehard Sid Vicious lovers who dressed in multi painted, studded leather jackets, knee high boots, green or pink Mohawk haircuts, bum flaps and other assorted rags.

Then from the darkest depths of the punk movement came the really dedicated squat anarchists in the form of Crass. This lot were total hardcore politicos with radical ideas that would simply never work in reality. One afternoon a group of their members discovered a large, disused, underground nuclear bunker in Kelveden Hatch in Essex. Some fool had forgotten to lock up this government complex during the paranoid days of MAD, CND and the Women of Greenham Common. Thus adding weight to the theory that 'we the people' will be left to instantaneously fry or, worse, in the event of a 'first strike' nuclear Armageddon type attack by 'The Russians'. Whereas, the 'chosen few' would be issued with backstage passes to their new underground sanctuary and maybe in time would possibly end up living like The Morlocks.

Given the choice, I'd probably go for the 'vaporised instantly' option rather than end up eating a former member of Thatcher's cabinet a couple of years down the line, broiled slowly over an upturned oil drum.

Crass even got a mention in Parliament during PM's Question Time after releasing 'How Does Feel to Be the Mother of a 1,000 Dead?' in 1982. A happy little tune aimed at Thatcher's Falklands War campaign during that year. They also wrote a few other light and quirky tunes including 'Nagasaki Nightmare' 'Bloody Revolutions' and 'H Block'. They were totally anti society as prescribed by the evil tongue of western democracy. They had their place in that era but weren't exactly the happiest bunch of hardcore anarchists, lyrically speaking.

In the wake of Crass came a load of other rather doom mongering crusty bands such as The Mob, Anthrax, Poison Girls, Conflict, Omega Tribe and Zounds. The latter produced a great album called 'The Curse Of Zounds' which included a brilliant track called 'Dirty Squatters'. The lyrics of this song are about as close as you can get to how it really was for the dedicated homeless, punk-muso fraternity back in those days. Therefore, I acknowledge fellow hardened squatters who wrote such an accurate description of our similar life paths in London during the nineteen eighties.

By the middle of the decade the Goth movement was well established, the pasty, mostly stick thin followers of death were listening to Sex Gang Children, Bauhaus, Play Dead, The Cure, Joy Division, The Birthday Party, Siouxsie, Fields Of The Nephilin, The Sisters Of Mercy, Cabaret Voltaire, Alien

Sex Fiend, The Cramps, Killing Joke and Southern Death Cult to name a few. This scene would also blend into the new wave movement so we'd appreciate other bands and genres who were producing thought provoking lyrics expressing the sign of those times.

    One cannot forget to mention the influence that Electro Pop bought to many areas in the music scene during that era as well. Basildon's finest export Depeche Mode were one of the prime movers in the early days of synthesized rock, along with Soft Cell, The Human League and Tubeway Army. Whacky makeup, diagonal hair, riding trousers, pointy suede boots and amphetamines were mandatory when following the foot tapping sounds of the 'New Life' when living in 'Bedshitland, My Only Home'.

The 1980s are often viewed cringingly as the decade of big frizzy hair, leg warmers, Bros, Thatcher, Reagan, Gorbachev, General Noriega, Black Monday, Negative Equity, floppy disk drives, Body Popping, *Blankety Blank*, *Moonlighting*, *GMTV*, Sigue Sigue Sputnik, stick thin Supermodels, The Sinclair C5, Trivial Pursuit, *The Big Breakfast*, *The Kids From Fame*, Mister fuckin' Motivator, *Cagney and Lacey*, shoulder pads, big glasses, big hair, M.A.D. the Filofax, De Lorean, pigtails, boys wearing eyeliner and blusher, *Dallas*, Live Aid, Pac-Man, B.T., really tight football shorts, brick sized mobile phones, C90 compilation cassette tapes, pointy suede boots, Michael Fish fucking up the weather forecast, the hole in the ozone layer, Dexys Midnight Runners, Yellow Pages Adverts (see 'Fly Fishing' by J.R. Hartley) Rubik's Cube, Arthur Scargill getting arrested, Dungeons & Dragons, *The Terminator*, Terry Wogan, The 'Tell Sid' British Gas sell off campaign, the war on drugs, Cruise missiles, cheap amphetamines, big plates, small dinners, *Miami Vice*, yuppies in Porsches… to name but a few.

Much of this is undeniably true of the era of course; we lived within but also outside of the eighties and were a driving force behind that decade, creative people who were moving forward despite our now sometimes embarrassing photograph collections of the era.

If comics were your thing, 2000AD, Crisis, Tripping Yarns and Viz were popular reads in that decade. The Big Issue was launched to help the homeless to help themselves, and some became poets. The radical's news rag 'Class War' kept the dedicated Anarchist regularly updated on Thatcher's crimes and sometimes had a crossword puzzle on the back page.

The Young Ones gave us a modern take on slapstick in student digs, The Comic Strip team created oddball characters and stories loosely basing them on apparently real ones. The late night three minute cooking show Get Stuffed gave essential culinary tips aimed at penniless students on a starvation diet. Blackadder served our need to take the historical piss out of ourselves, while Max Headroom offered a glitchy insight into a probable future where we'll reside in a sort of new world order of high tech and mass media, but unfortunately the cabling and connections will be shite.

From the north arrived the unmissable Alan Bleasdale's weekly fix of Boys from the Blackstuff: a harshly grim and often hilarious tale of unemployment, alienation and desperation in eighties Liverpool. It was a memorable portrayal into the lives of many in the northeast who had fuck all, as compared to the 'loadsamoney' culture of the 'haves' in the south of the country.

This was a highly political and artistic period in which people didn't really worry about staying within your own clan or keeping tight to one particular musical genre or fashion style. Everything and everyone was kind of mish mashed together without a sense of musical or fashion snobbery among the youth during that particular decade. It was exciting to just do your own thing, be your own person and operate our lives which at that point were free from the constant distraction of mobile phones and the information superhighway. We went to the pub to talk, not text.

Perhaps the reason for all this radical thinking and musical experimentation was that we were all in it together with a common cause; Thatcher and her company of wolves must be defeated.

After residing in slug and roach infested Emu Road for a number of months, things were getting a bit cramped, what with four men sharing a small two bedroomed flat. There was little in the way of personal privacy, let alone the chances of any of us bringing a lady back for that late night bed creaking fun, especially as we shared two to a room, so even deep snoring from the other occupant a couple of feet away wouldn't quite cut it.

Mike had a disaster in that particular area when he had the place to himself during Christmas season of pigswill. The rest of us were going away for a few days, so he excitedly invited a Swedish babe he'd met at a gig over to Emu Road for festive nuptials, as he harboured sleazy thoughts related to food, charming conversation duly followed by sporting heroism of the horizontal variety.

He couldn't get rid us quick enough while he was frantically polishing the place and practically hovering his housemates out of the front door. However, there was a slight problem with the gas supply but a man was due over on Christmas eve to fix it up in time for Mike's' sexmus feast. We could see that at least he was going to have a really festive time this year as opposed to the usual bollocks. The gasman fixer duly showed up on Christmas eve early afternoon, tinkered about a bit, turned the supply off for safety reasons and told Mike that he had to 'pop out' to get a spare part to complete the repairs. Mike patiently waited all afternoon for the engineer to return but as the minutes and hours passed it became dreadfully obvious that gas repair guy had decided to start his Christmas holidays early, and left Mike minus any cooking facilities over the season of good-willy.

This was when we lived in the 'silent years' a time long before most the general population owned mobile phones, which rendered us unable to 'chase up people' from the comfort of one's living room, toilet or squat kitchen. As Mike waited on the lookout by the front window like a curtain shifting old lady for the repairman to return, it eventually dawned on him that the guy was probably in the pub downing festive pints and that he was definitely fucked.

Thereafter it was cold food, no heating and little in the way of Nordic pleasures for Mike that Christmas. He was naturally well pissed off and earned our sympathy when we all returned from our respective holidays expecting a graphic account of his hot Scandinavian nights, which sadly for him had turned as cold as Sweden in January.

17 – Happy Hours and Whore Alleys

In the spring of '87 Des, Mike, Brendan (Des's brother) and I decided to ride the ferry over to Amsterdam for the weekend. Though none of us had previous experience of the Dutch delights we did have a vague idea what to expect.

After the somewhat cold, sickly, overnight crossing of the treacherous North Sea, followed by a short train ride to Amsterdam Central, we booked ourselves on one of the then popular (but sadly no more) 'Floating Hotels'. These 'Floatels' were dotted all around the centre of downtown Amsterdam, they were a cheap, fly-by-night accommodation for all types of travellers, squatters, bums, students and smoke-heads from everywhere on the planet you could possibly imagine.

Basically, these contraptions were medium sized boats on a secure mooring offering small bunk rooms and 'En suite' shower, which basically consisted of a sloping floor with a plughole in the middle of it. The 'Reception' was commonly manned by a Brit hating Australian bitch with a high pitched whining voice who we could tell would bully us at every opportunity during our brief stay. The cheap bar onboard was utilized day and night for drinking and spliff testing by the motley bunch of low rent tourists.

If you were travelling 'really low budget' style you could always hire a bench to bed down upon in the bar area on these vessels, that's if you liked trying to sleep perched on a hard pew around twenty inches wide whilst trying to sleep among the sounds of stoned laughing a few feet away. There were loads of these boat hotels to choose from, and we ended up on one run by an amenable expat, though we only used his vessel for sleeping purposes. Besides that, the Floatels all operated a happy hour policy, so one could move from one boat to another and consume Amstel lager far into the small hours.

But we didn't want that, we wanted the full on in-yer-face hardcore that was downtown Am'dam. Soon after booking into the scuzzy floating hotel and taking turns to wash above a hole in the floor, off we went in search of the local Dutch culture. The other guys were not really hash smokers though I was, but we did visit various popular coffee and stoner shops such as Future, Mellow Yellow and of course Fancy Free where I took my order from the spliff menu and proceeded to get wrecked, Dutch style.

Later, we found a good restaurant and ate heartily in preparation for the pleasant after dinner stroll along 'Whore Alley' as situated down some much footed back streets of this rather odd city.

Up to this point in my life I felt that I could not be taken aback by much anymore, having seen 'some shit' in my life I considered myself a liberated, open minded guy. Accompanied by the other Battersea squatters we wandered along the red lit canals of Amsterdam, being continually confronted by the window selection of various brothels that this small city is much renowned for. It was a sight we'd barely expected but a revelation too, should prostitution be legalised everywhere? We discussed this possibility being appropriate in Britain, especially as ours is a country globally known for sexual repression. Therefore, if we had legalised brothels in the UK then maybe this could lead to a sharp drop in the numbers of sexual assaults in our country?

A major stumbling block to such liberal ideology would of course be the upper middle class, curtain shifting, Mary Whitehouse following stiffs of middle England who would pursue every legal avenue in their considerable right wing power to veto any such legislation. Besides that, who wants a brothel in their street anyway? Lowering the house prices and bringing sleazy low rent crime into your area especially as it seemed the UK was already riddled with criminality by the latter part of the 20th century anyway.

As we wandered the pretty Dutch streets of Amsterdam agape at the sight before our eyes, I was now making a mental note that many of the women on offer, they were really good looking and some were knocking politely on their windows and calling after yours truly. This must've been the fact that I was currently wearing the spiky bleached blond 'Billy Idol' look which appeared to be generating interest among certain ladies of the Dutch night.

What also struck me was the general good atmosphere up and down these busy streets, with a lack of threatening rowdiness you'd expect in the dark alleys of Kings Cross. In the coolly lit streets of the red light district Amsterdam all was well organised, unpoliced and very civilized. The Dutch seemingly have a sense of taste in their uncomplicated view of mankind's need for sleaze.

But within moments, our pleasant observations of Dutch culture were suddenly smashed as we became aware of the sound of a familiar tune floating from one of the bars we were approaching…The sickening rendition of the tune known as 'Land of Hope and Glory' was being cranked up ever louder as we arrived at the location and collectively craned a confused look through the open doors of this bar. What met us next was that deeply embarrassing sight of a bunch of really pissed English blokes, a couple of whom were wearing union jack T shirts, while standing on tables and goading on a real idiot who was drunkenly swinging from the light fitting above, much to the amusement and bemusement of other punters looking on.

After a glance through that door, the four us immediately decided that we wouldn't be English for the remainder of the evening, as we hurried off to a calmer bar far away from our shame inducing compatriots. What only minutes ago seemed like a good case for the legalisation of prostitution in modern Britain, now became laughingly obvious that this cultural step forward was a pretty unlikely prospect in our country anytime soon.

Speaking of English, we did find The Bulldog Bar that had a selection of live bands on the bill, though they were usually local musos and a pale copy of some lame prog rock dinosaur type affair from the mid seventies. But at least this venue was far enough away from the drunken (and stoned) English dickheads we'd left back along brothel canal.

Apart from the drinking, marijuana and whorehouses of Amsterdam, there was the Rembrandt Museum (if etchings are your thing) the Sex Museum, pretty bridges adorning canals, lovely buildings and a cool flea market on we stumbled upon during our strolls. There are a few things that strike you about Amsterdam (apart from the relaxed attitude to cannabis and prostitution) – one being a world famous stamp collector market downtown on Sunday afternoons, especially for the anoraks. Another Dutch curiosity are the 'open plan' exterior urinals for men, which involves pissing in the street behind a screen while you can crane a look at everyone passing by, very strange. There once used to be a big squat community outside the city and much of the floating hotel business were connected with as regards income generating. The strange coin operated food dispensers in the streets are another quirky thing about the city, I did eat something from one of these greasy cubicles but to this day I don't know what the fuck it was. Then of course there are chips with mayonnaise, Belgian style apparently, to which I've indulged in ever since.

Finally, and never forgotten, are the minefields of dog shit on the streets, though I didn't recall seeing any dogs when we were out. There was crap everywhere, including a lot of shit that looks suspiciously like the human variety too. You literally have to watch every step you take in Amsterdam. I think the Dutch eventually invented the pooper scooper motorcycle to clear the problem up, but it was really bad in those days.

With all considerations taken into account, Amsterdam is a great place for a long weekend, to party on in true liberal style and let your hair down. This is the city of cheap smoke, hash cake; chilled bars, cool clubs and low priced brothels, or at least it was in the mid eighties.

But to partake in a two week holiday in the place is plain madness, unless you're on the guest list or a judge at the famous annual Amsterdam Cannabis Festival, smuggling diamonds or on a 'fuck every whore in town' type vacation.

18 – Sink Plunging from Above

Despite our collective, stoical efforts to live in Emu Road, some of us decided to make the break and find somewhere else to reside. We'd also had news that the previous landlord was now initiating a private eviction order; therefore in view of what Stan and I had already been through regarding bailiffs, it was time to get the hell out.

Leaving Emu Road was especially important as this property was owned by a privately as opposed to being council run. We had nervous visions of a gang of privately hired neck-less thugs kicking the already flimsy door in and turfing us all out into the cold street in the middle of the night wearing only our boxer shorts for comfort.

One Saturday afternoon Ian, Stan and I once again collected the aforementioned 'Squatters Toolkit' and made tracks for pastures new, namely Brixton. We three liked the idea of residing in SW9, and knew it to be a magnet for squatters at that particular time. Added temptations were many local drinking venues most of which we already knew, these being The Prince Albert, The Atlantic, The White Horse, The George Canning and The Railway. There was also the Ritzy cinema, the Fridge Club as well as the famous Academy venue which held big gigs in their large Victorian built auditorium.

Brixton's famous market is always a colourful attraction too as well as an assortment of various back street dub clubs and late bars to frequent on any given night.

Therefore, this part of south west London was our first choice for obvious reasons.

We furtively stomped the streets around Barrington Road one mild Saturday afternoon, constantly on the lookout for our next potential home. We spent much of our day riding the piss smelling lifts to start on the top floors of council blocks and work our way down checking out seemingly empty places as we descended. This took hours of patient and nervous work, all the time waiting for a resident to come out onto the narrow landings to ask questions and generally make things uncomfortable for us.

We broke open a few non starters which one always expects in these situations, there were a large selection of complete shitholes closed up and just left to fester. A couple of flats were filled to the front door with two inches of swampy, stagnant water that a saltwater crocodile could feel at home in and often the heating had been wastefully left on for weeks or months whilst the property laid unoccupied. Nearly every flat we broke that day offered the usual bag of offensive, stinking horrors awaiting you beyond their mouldy front doors.

Eventually, we found what we'd come for, a corner flat, five floors up, with balcony view, the electricity on and hot running water too. However, it was only a two bedroom flat on two floors with an upstairs toilet and bathroom, though the kitchen sink was seriously blocked up with a lurking life form from the deep.

After a brief discussion it was agreed that we could live with these minor setbacks and be able to unblock the kitchen sink, eventually. It was agreed to keep the front room vacant which included the balcony view, and that we would draw straws in a democratic manner to see who'd be sharing one bedroom, and who'd have the other to themselves. Ian held out three matches, I drew the longest twig and therefore my own bedroom at least for the time being.

The following Monday evening a van was hired, I drove, the familiar nasty squat furniture was stuffed into it and soon delivered into flat number 71, Kettleby House, Brixton. We took turns to chisel out the door frame to fit the mortise lock firmly into the half wreaked front door frame. This was always the first job on the list for any self respecting squatter; home security for our pitiful belongings. We already owned a quality Chubb lock (the only ones to buy) which had served us well at the previous two squat addresses in Bermondsey.

The living room was relatively clear of clutter and had a glass fronted door opening onto the high balcony Brixton view overlooking Barrington Road. Jazz the cat liked the place straight away and leapt onto the small ledge to get a good view of his new domain. However, the brown patterned wallpaper (unchanged since the mid seventies) throughout the ground floor certainly wasn't from the William Morris collection, and on close inspection we observed faded blood splashes rising on the walls next to the sofa areas. We soon realised that this was formerly a junkie flat, where the occupants would squirt the residue blood from syringes after jacking up while slipping into a near coma on the sad, brown sofa as left behind.

This was an unpleasant situation for the three of us to contemplate, especially as the current Aids crisis was all over the news regarding junkies, needles, unprotected sex and the usual red top tabloid paranoia around during that time. We decided to get the rubber gloves on and bleach the fuck out of the whole flat, squatters we were but definitely not junkies who could live with that level of degradation on a daily basis.

We went hard at it on a Saturday afternoon and soon enough in the back of the kitchen and bathroom cupboards, used syringes were discovered floating about inside water filled plastic coke bottles.

Exclamations of 'Yuk!' and 'For fuck's sake!' were heard that day as we disinfected the place from top to bottom. The kitchen sink was a real heave-ho, retching, barking up type job, we took shifts with the plunger, a bent wire coat hanger and other improvised jiggery pokery tools to eventually free up the thick brown sludge lapping up to the overflow limits. The 'Rice Soup from Hell' was eventually defeated and all was washed away with gallons of clean water and bottle or two of industrial bleach.

Later, we sat back in our new, cleansed apartment, arranged the furniture around the living room (which of course included my portable telly) and rolled a number of spliffs to erase away the gory memory of that afternoon's grime evictions.

We were happy having sourced and cleaned up a pretty good flat, with an elevated view over the trees, a tube station close by, and all the other Brixton benefits as previously mentioned.

'Sorted' as we used say.

Ian decided to cook a celebratory meal in our new, bleached, germ free kitchen on the cooker so kindly left by the previous occupants. However, this simple task did provide us with yet another slight problem; the damn electric cooker had a fault and a dangerous one too. This ancient oven had an earth problem which meant that you'd get a shock if you used a metal utensil anywhere near the pots and pans.

Receiving a small whack up your arm was quite uncomfortable when one stirred the contents of a pan, though we got wise to it soon enough and only used wooden utensils when cooking. I tried to fix it one afternoon but it was all spaghetti under the bonnet so I gave up. We did buy a second hand cooker within a few weeks and then manhandled the dangerous one into the pissy lift and down to the crowded bin area. We neglected to leave a warning note for a soon pleased, unsuspecting fellow semi homeless person to drag it to their miserable squat only to be killed instantly via culinary electrocution.

We managed to persuade the gas board to hook us up as we needed a supply for our new, 'safety tested before sale' stove. Our utility supply was eventually procured for an exorbitant deposit of cash having filled in the boring paperwork, as being squatters and therefore viewed as totally untrustworthy; they required all manner of personal assurances before they'd send a man with a wrench and leak detecting meter and a bad attitude towards squatters.

We settled in and began to enjoy the night time delights of south west nine without having to contemplate the long (and usually drunken) trek home to either Bermondsey or Battersea. We were locals now and living among the thriving squatter scene going on in a lively part of London during that period.

Brixton was indeed a cool place to live, loaded with musicians and arty types mixing it with the Jamaican community and the young Europeans who were squatting in south London too. Once again, the usual friends came over to check out our new address and admire our balcony view as well. One of which was a former heroin addict who used to score smack in that very flat, which confirmed the blood stained wallpaper and the unpleasant bathroom discoveries. He also happily informed us that a dealer had been murdered in the place a year or so previously, which may have been the reason it was unoccupied when we turned up to thump the door in.

By the summer of that year (1987) we were all working in full time jobs and full on social lives too. We were out watching bands locally or up in the west end venues. Stan was the only one actually in a band at that time, the lively outfit called Lightning Strike who were becoming well known on the London gig circuit.

Things were ticking over nicely as we got on with our lives, while Jazz regularly scared us with his high jinks acrobatics on the narrow balcony ledge. Cats just don't seem to have any fear of heights, or at least our one didn't.

19 – Brixton Brew and Jam Jars

One day, a collection of equipment arrived from somewhere enabling us to procure our very own home brew. Included in the kit was a large plastic fermentation bin, plastic pipes, a funnel and simple instructions on how to produce strong lager or cider in a matter of weeks. I chose the cider option, bought the mix from Boots one Saturday afternoon, briefly scanned the instructions, poured the stuff in the bin along with water, yeast and sugar, pressed the lid down and lugged the heavy bucket of home brew out on the Brixton viewing platform to ferment for a couple of weeks.

Three weeks later, the warm bubbling froth was then sifted into twenty washed out Merrydown bottles through said funnel, sealed shut and lined up along the balcony for soon consumption. One evening, about a week after the bottling process, whilst we were sitting in the living room, there came a sudden popping-of-glass type explosion from the balcony outside. On investigation we found that a bottle of my 'home boy' cider had blown up due to the serious pressure that had obviously been building up inside.

This must be good stuff then? We concluded, so in that case we'd better get stuck in before the whole lot blows up like a cheap explosion, we further deduced.

Tentatively, I opened a bottle at arm's length and carefully poured the brownish coloured liquid into three glasses. Although this monk mead tasted slightly bitter and was therefore not quite ready, we knew instantly that the alcohol level was surprisingly close to that of tin slurping street wino proportions.

In other words, half a bottle was about all one needed to blast your fuckin' head off.

Over the next couple of weeks, three more bottles self destructed while in 'production' out on the balcony. Maybe the temperature changes overnight had affected the process? Or perhaps I'd failed to measure the ingredients correctly? Who knows? Who cares? But this countryside hobby became my one and only foray into the anorak world of home brewing.

My infamous 'Home Boy Cider' often procured a serious frontal lobotomy type headache after about half a bottle and thereafter completely erased your short term memory far better than the whirly device in the film The Ipcress File. The damn stuff got me into plenty of trouble which culminated when I put my hand through the frosted balcony door window and spending a Saturday afternoon in casualty waiting to get my little finger stitched back together. Not only did I have to repair the damn glass door with a fucked finger for my troubles, but I still have the scar on my pinkie to this day. No wonder this home brewing lark has a reputation for sending people either blind or mad, or invariably both.

It was around about this time when some friends came over to chill out in our cool squat (with balcony) on a Saturday afternoon in the heat of that summer. We hooked up Ian's guitar amp to the ghetto blaster in the living room and rolled spliffs as the dub reggae thundered out from the serious sound system as rapidly organised. We neglected to remember that there were neighbours all around us in this tower block, as we selfishly carried on with the excessive volumes before going clubbing later that evening.

On returning home many hours later, we stumbled upon a scribbled note stuffed in an old jam jar left for us by the front door. It simply read; 'Come up and see me sometime u cunt' and was signed Eward DeBono. Although realising that we'd obviously pissed off a neighbour or two with our admittedly very loud reggae that afternoon, Stan was having none of it being extra brave and full of Guinness he decided at that moment (4am) to 'go up and see him'. We reluctantly followed him upstairs to the next landing as he marched along the passageway holding the jam jar note aloft and drunkenly calling out for its author.

Nobody came out to reclaim their jar, nor thankfully to throw him and the rest of us over the ledge, this being six floors up.

We never received another note from the creator of the jam jar message, but we did cool the music levels down as after all it is only manners. Stan then scrawled the message 'Eward DeBono for President' on the living room wall in marker pen to remind us of the secret jam eater in our block.

20 – Vote R.A.B.I.E.S. Party (The UK General Election 1987)

Speaking of Presidents, the 1987 General Election campaign was now getting underway as Thatcher and her cronies were bidding for a nightmare third term in power, which was indeed scary. This could not be allowed to happen; there had been the Miners' Strike in which the workers of Britain had witnessed the crushing of that industry in '84. Other northern based heavy industries such as engineering and steel production were slowly being destroyed too. The increase in personal greed, wealth and selfishness brought on by the yuppie culture had lead to an 'I'm alright Jack' attitude among many of the general population of the UK.

Britain was now a divided country; the prosperous south versus the grim north.

Across the Atlantic that buffoon Reagan was running (and ruining) America too, with his shaky old finger on the Armageddon button and ever keen to climb into bed politically with Thatcher during this era. But the drawback was that Britain currently had a booming economy, a strong pound, and high levels of employment, at least in the south of the country. The working classes were now being persuaded into taking out mortgages their run down council homes, as part of a 'Home Owner Britain' con thought up by someone in Mrs T's cabinet.

All this amounted to a major challenge for the political opposition and probably an impossible task to overcome too.

The people of Britain had been duped into the 'me me me' way of life and had temporarily forgotten about the industries and people who'd been totally shafted by the Tory Government since 1979. Thatcher and company shrewdly chose the right moment to hold a General Election.

But many of the population of Britain were still compassionate souls with a conscience, and the 1987 General Election was fought on hard and real human issues by Kinnock's Labour Party, and from the right in that irritating relaxed 'You've never had it so good' attitude by the smarmy 'already in power' Conservatives.

The swords and sabres were drawn and honed by all the fringe parties in the UK during that particular General Election and thereafter a vitriolic, scathing, bloodthirsty and backstabbing battle for power commenced throughout Britain's hustings.

Through our squat front door during this vicious political campaign came a tatty leaflet with the answer to our voting dilemma. In big green words the message was printed loud and clear; 'Vote R.A.B.I.E.S. Party'. Members of this non mainstream 'Political Party' invited the squatting Brixtonians to attend a 'Mass Public Demonstration' in which their 'policies' would be publicly (and briefly) aired and the show would culminate with the brutal hanging of a life sized effigy of the Iron Bitch from the large tree outside the Ritzy Cinema the following Saturday afternoon.

We were of course sold on the humorous distraction of these politicos as frankly, politics in most people's lives had become bloody a joke by this stage. Besides that, we all secretly knew that Thatcher and her Tory sidekicks would probably walk the election once again anyway.

The three of us residing in Kettleby House may well have been squatters but we'd all registered to vote, were legally allowed to do so, and we were damn well going to use them too. After our usual Saturday shopping in the market we strolled over to the alternative and colourful election rally outside the Ritzy which was being fronted by three of the crazy party leaders who were representing 'The Rabies Party'.

One candidate, standing on a beer barrel, reeled off a load of total nonsense policies, such as free larger on Sunday's, ten pence tube fares, a countrywide ban on leg warmers and the compulsory wearing of shades from May to September while interjecting the party phrase 'Burrahhhhh' as he hoisted a can of cheap lager into the air. Members of the voting public were invited as 'guest speakers' to soapbox their own opinions on the state of anything they liked, loved, despised and hated in 1980s Britain. This political event was climaxed (as promised) with the hanging of a rather good effigy of Thatcher many, many times more noisy exclamations of 'Burrahhhhh' from the cheering, jeering crowd.

The whole desperate charade (also amusingly observed and policed by the Brixton Constabulary) was over in about thirty minutes, then we returned to our squats and prepared for government.

The Rabies Party polled 171 votes in our constituency on the 11th June 1987, with one of those 'wasted' votes being cast by myself. Of course, Thatcher and her junta were duly returned to absolute power during the course of the night with a slightly decreased majority of a mere 101.

It was noted and discussed in the media after the 1987 election that many voters secretly decided on polling day that they really couldn't bring themselves to vote for a ginger Welsh geezer who kept whining on and on about the poor bloody nurses. The Labour leader had been filmed on a long lens falling over on a windy beach during the election campaign which was much aired on TV, this setback probably made the case for his leadership of Britain a less likely prospect the more it was shown.

So that in effect was that for yet another five long years, as the nation awoke the next morning to watch the power mad and beaming Iron Lady in blue waving to her throng of equally wide eyed, crazy followers on GMTV from an upper window of Tory Party Office in the west end.

21 – The Great Escape (Glastonbury Festival 1987)

Very soon (as in the next day) after this political tragedy of national proportions in the summer of '87, Ian decided that it was time for travel. Besides the fact that there were three of us sharing a two bedroom flat, he felt like a change of scenery and packed himself of to foreign shores for an undisclosed period of time.

Meanwhile, back in Blighty, Stan and I also needed a distraction from the grim reality of yet more Thatcher; and what better way to absorb the blow than a trip to the Glastonbury Festival?

As far as festival going went in 1980s Britain, nothing was ever subject to foresight or pre-preparation beforehand (at least not in our squat) we would just decide to go a day or two before it kicked off.

Stan and I made the supreme effort to get down to Wiltshire and bunk into Glastonbury over the third weekend in June. This trip would be 'planned' with hardly any money to finance the travel requirements, let alone budget for luxuries such as food, alcohol or our recreational drug requirements for the full three days of joy in the West Country sunshine.

Some of our friends would already be down there to greet us, and encouragingly, Stan owned a two man tent for our accommodation purposes. We left the flat with the minimum of weight to carry on our backs as possible on that mid June Friday morning, and set out (in the rain) to hitch a ride in a general westerly direction from the slip road under the Hammersmith flyover.

We waited for what seemed like hours in the drizzle, taking turns to hold up our specially designed and colourful hitchhiker's plaque as the traffic splashed by. Eventually we were picked up by an American woman driving a hatchback who was on her way to the festival herself, so no turning back now.

After a relatively uneventful couple of hours drive to the outskirts of Glastonbury, we were duly flagged down by the cops and directed into a small car park fitted out in temporary style with a few random grey mobile cabins. Stan and I were mildly searched and found to be clean, but our American friend however was invited into one of the plastic sheds for about twenty minutes. She eventually came marching back to the car, looking furious, and we soon learned that she'd been strip searched and given the full marigold glove inspection. But this was on account of her previous form which was drug related. It was bad luck, but she was in this instance clean and we could now drive to the festival ten minutes away.

Stan and I, however, had other plans as we drove round the grassy edges of the site eyeing up the fences for weaknesses to undertake the old 'Dash and climb like fuck!' routine.

Our stateside driver dropped us off at a quiet spot wished us luck and drove away.

Stan and I scanned for an area less occupied by cops, traffic, and crusty stewards holding back their mangy dogs on lengths of dirty rope.

Within a few minutes we stuck upon other squat types dotted about as they too sussed the fences surrounding the site. In reality the best way into Glastonbury is undercover of the night, as the site security was pretty slack and they'd usually be drunk in the evenings anyway. However, if you did get caught, you'd be arrested and deported to the train station in a van, or worse still kept in a local jail all weekend and miss the fun, which was crap luck indeed.

Suddenly, we observed a number of scruffy types make a break for it as they hurled their bags over the fence before them, and started the twelve foot climb up the wire. Within seconds the two us were also running at top speed with our light rucksacks swinging from our grasp as they cleared the 'obstruction' before us and thumped onto the grass on 'the other side' We hit the fence climbing and laughing as we clambered upwards towards three days of festival joy. For a few seconds as I scrambled up the wobbly fence I half expected to hear a shout from somewhere behind us

'Achtung! Holt! Non ticket holders or I will fire!'

This would inevitably be followed moments later by that familiar sound of a Bren-gun being locked and loaded, then commencing with that sickening rat-at-tat-at-rat-at-tat-a-tat-tat, as bullet riddled hippies and punks released their grip on the chicken wire and fell stone dead in clumps of bad hair and dress sense on the wrong side of the 'freedom fence'.

But no, this is what should've happened when the wee Jock made a break for it in the famous WW2 film The Great Escape, as the fence was duly cleared by this shabby group of cheap festival goers. We jumped the last ten feet on the other side hitting the grass beyond, grabbed our rucksacks and sprinted the last fifteen metres until we made it into the 'inner sanctum' of Glastonbury '87.

We were in, and the wonderful world of festival awaited our pleasures.

The drizzle had finally cleared and the sun was now out, it was looking like proper festival weather as we gazed out upon the twisted chaos that lay before us from our raised vantage point. We had an idea of where to find our friends on the site, and made our way mostly in a slow manner to the back fields and over the stoner bridge somewhere in the distance.

Eventually we found selection of the familiar Brixton faces and were welcomed with a couple of cans of beer and a spliff or three.

Soon enough was decision time for Stan and I, do we erect the tent now or go and watch Robert Cray on The Pyramid Stage and leave that little chore until later? We chose the easy option and made our way to the gig only stopping to buy some acid on the Bridge... Besides, surely it'll be a piece of piss to put a two man tent up later even when tripping out of our minds?

By the time Cray had finished his blues routine we were well and truly trashed, seemingly along with the rest of the crowd that is the multi headed festival audience. But next up was Troublefunk who introduced a mix of fat funk sounds and rap to an expectant throng. Their line up also consisted of an amazing and fearless teenage drummer who impressed the crowd with his stick skills.

It was all looking so good, and then it got a bit cloudy, followed by light spots of rain and soon after it kind of poured for about hour.

This being Glastonbury, and in the open countryside, it didn't take too long before areas of the site descended into a brown slopped, slippery mud fest. As soon as a decent, man made mudslide had been created by the movement of wet people, it was then game on for the soil surfers and their expectant, soaked, earth covered audience.

Entertainment of one sort or another is always present when thousands of people mob together in a few fields, collectively we seem to create new angles on life and develop a sense fun; though I'd expect that the alcohol and the acid had something to do with it. I remember seeing a bloke having a great time in the sunshine wearing his brand new bright orange rucksack during the Cray gig, which he'd probably bought especially for the festival the week before. About an hour later I saw him again, still wearing his rucksack, only this time he was lying on his back in a sloppy, deep puddle, laughing his head off as his nice, new, soon-not-to-be bright orange rucksack sunk under him into the oozy slime beneath.

You'll see a lot of sights like that at Glastonbury, sane people turning up all smiles and then reduced to drooling, babbling wrecks within a couple hours of arriving, let alone the twisted madness of it all after a couple of nights under the stars. Over the course of the evening, one loses the people you came with within the massive and constantly moving crowd, until you eventually stagger back to your camping area. I went off to see other bands and the weird sights of that crazy festival until I found my way back 'home' to find Stan in a comical mess, covered in mud, pissed on local cider and no doubt as ready to 'put the tent up' as I was.

We managed to make a drunken, stoned effort to erect his disgusting tent, complete with green mildew patches and furry rot stains from being taken down (years ago) and packed away while still damp. We needed a few bongs to smoke out the musty smell before we'd contemplate three cheesy nights under that grim canvas.

We woke in the morning to find the tent had sagged so much during the night that it was now 'touching cloth' and both of us were soaked through from the West Country morning dew. It was probably a better idea to sleep by the fire under the stars, though I hoped for lots of sunshine to bake the canvas dry over the next two days…

After that first day and night the rest of the festival was filled with getting smashed and watching bands you'd never see nor hear of again, but they were usually up for a good laugh and were probably just as stoned as the happy, hedonistic throng swaying in the breeze in front of them.

By the end of the second day we were out of cash, food and spliff and had to resort to blagging the occasional meal from friendly festival goers who'd brought along enough grub to supply a marooned platoon under fire and happy to share anyway. We'd seek shelter in the comedy tent when it occasionally drizzled, stumble around stalls selling all manner of shit we didn't want, and eventually found the serenity and calmness in the 'Green Field' with like minded chill out people late into the night.

It was a good three days (and nights) at Glastonbury '87, the only time I have sampled that festival, and better still the weather was good after the first day's downpour. One hears stories of how it has changed over time, it was a good festival period in Britain; everybody had their complaints regarding Thatcher's crimes knowing that there was more to come. But the humour of it all was regularly aired in marquees, fields, on stages and by the Stoner Bridge by respected musicians, orators, comedians, crazy hippies, not so crazy hippies and various other alternative thinking people.

But now it was over, as we woke on the Monday morning to contemplate the journey home. Our friends packed up and had to leave us to it as they didn't have any spare room in their vehicles. They wished us good luck as they closed their car doors, trying not to show their obvious pity for our dilemma.

So, we were going to hitch back to London, along with about 10,000 other punks and hippies were we?

As we left the site, unshaven, stinking and filthy dirty I asked Stan a simple question: 'How much money have you got left?'

'Nothing, I spent it all two days ago,' he replied, bluntly

I kind of expected that answer as I reached into my pocket and counted out eighteen pence.

'We'd better get on the road and see if someone will stop and give us a ride' I enthused.

We joined the throng of other mucky hitchers, and started to walk in an easterly direction. Thankfully the weather was bright enough so at least we weren't going to get soaking wet for what looked like all day.

We plodded along with the other festival hitchhikers and gradually began to spread out as we collectively strode at our own paces. There were still many vehicles passing us for the first couple of hours as we attempted in vain to thumb a lift even if just a few miles up the road.

After about an hour we came to a petrol station, which was crammed full of other festival types stocking up on supplies for the long trek ahead. It was then that I choose to buy one Twix bar with my remaining eighteen pence and to pocket another while surrounded by other spiky tops, who were also helping themselves in various acts of random thievery whilst the staff were distracted and overwhelmed by the sheer number of invading townies descending upon their isolated countryside garage.

On exit, I laughed as I handed Stan his stolen Twix bar

'Enjoy it mate, it might be the last thing you'll eat in a while!'

We chomped our energy giving sustenance in seconds and once again proceeded on our way east.

As we walked and walked for hours, the slowly diminishing procession of overloaded cars and hippy vans droned past us, as the afternoon drifted on. The orange sun slipped ever westwards and after a good deal of mileage behind us our legs were beginning to feel the pace, we now had to periodically stop and rest.

Yet more hippies and punks whizzed by, shaking their heads or making 'We're full up' gestures to our disappointed faces.

At last a salesman driving a typical salesman type car complete with jacket hanging on a hook in the rear door pulled over.

Stan climbed in the front, I flopped in the back, and he drove off immediately.

'Been to the festival guys?' he enquired.

'Yeah' we wearily replied in unison.

'Where are you heading?' he asked

London, or anywhere near,' Stan replied in hope

'I'm going some miles in that direction guys, but I'm turning off on a back road to Bath, I'll take you a few junctions along so you can pick up another ride on this road' he offered.

'Thanks a lot,' we replied

We listened to a regional radio station as we slipped by other souls at the roadside pleading for a lift.

Within no time at all we reached his turn off, but even those ten miles had given our sore legs a break from the march east.

We thanked the guy as we stepped out onto a near empty B road and watched him speed off into the distance. In front of us now was a road sign, offering us an alternative, do we carry on and try to get a lift on the A303 or we try to make it to Bath and jump a train or two back to London?

We discussed the possibilities, but decided to keep going along the A303, as it was more likely that festival goers would still be passing late into the evening.

We walked, and walked, now getting pretty shagged out as the miles very slowly ticked over as more tatty and full up vehicles slipped by as we flashed our 'London please' makeshift cardboard sign in vain.

The afternoon wore on; by now we were alone, it seemed that every other festival goer apart from us had scored a ride today.

On we dragged ourselves on now mostly in silence as the afternoon sun started to dip further over the western horizon. I was feeling a bit demoralized and was beginning to think about various criminal alternatives to get us home. I looked around for a car to steal in the loneliness of each tiny village that came and went, even though I didn't know how to hotwire, I'd cross that bridge when we came upon it. Stan kept his spirits up and assured me that eventually we would get a lift, I however wasn't totally convinced.

As the dusk approached, we were exhausted, hungry and in a word, fucked. We plodded on yet further until the light faded and we stood on a slip road of a roundabout leading down to a faster part of the London road.

We knew instinctively that the traffic below would be moving too quickly to stop anyway, and besides that who in their right mind would possibly pull over at night for two dirty and dodgy looking hitchers in any instance.

We looked over the fence into a field and decided to pitch 'the tent' and spend a restless and hungry night by the noisy roadside and try again 'fresh' in the morning.

Just at that moment a VW Camper came hurtling over the roundabout indicating towards the slip road we were waiting at. We both ran out to the edge and frantically flagged at the hippy wagon, which immediately slowed down and stopped on the slip road.

We ran to the passenger door with new life in our legs.

'Hi there,' we announced ourselves in unison.

'Are you going to London?' was the direct question asked by the female passenger.

'Yeah, anywhere near town is great for us.'

'Get in guys,' came the reply from the male driver.

'Thanks,' we replied as we practically fell in through the side door as opened for us by their rear passenger.

'Have you been on the road all day from the festival?' the driver asked as he slipped through the gears and slid onto the fast road towards London.

'Yeah,' replied Stan as a pouch of tobacco was offered our way.

'We've been walking since Glastonbury this morning,' I added.

'Long way,' interjected the front passenger. 'We're nearly thirty miles from there now,' she added.

So we'd walked about twenty of those, allowing for the salesman lift earlier I mused to myself.

We smoked our first cigarette of the day and felt happily dizzy as we explained that we were just about to set up camp in a field when they pulled over and how grateful we were that they did.

Very soon after that we were peacefully fast asleep as the miles slipped by under the reassuring purr of those ever reliable Volkswagen engines.

We stirred back to life some hours later as the lights on the outskirts of London neared, and it was time to find out where we'd be dropped in the middle of the night.

'Where do you live?' Stan enquired.

'Camberwell,' came the reply 'and you?' asked the driver.

'Brixton' came ours in unison.

What a result I thought, a walk from there was a breeze compared to the miles we'd already covered that day.

'Anywhere in the area is great thanks,' replied Stan.

We passed the south western districts of town and then into the familiar areas of south London, and soon enough the driver asked us where we'd like to be dropped off. They took us all the way to Loughborough Road and let us out under the shadow of Kettleby House.

We thanked them for saving us from a sleepless night in the countryside, stumbled up to our humble abode, threw our grubby bags on the floor and crashed out within minutes, not stirring until the evening.

22 – The Hurricane Season
(London, 16th October 1987 – Night)

So that was Glastonbury Festival 1987; Great fun, good vibes and even the hitching there and back were on reflection, a good experience too. That West Country weekend was soon consigned to our collective memories as we quickly returned to our inner city lives. I resumed my search for yet another indecent, obnoxious, self indulgent, darkly noisy band, having been invigorated musically by the recent 'Festival Experience'.

Stan and I were doing a lot of weekday clubbing and going to gigs in the west end as well as managing to hold down full time jobs. Mine was a particularly unpleasant occupation at that time; I took a job driving a blood splattered butchers van, dressed in an equally bright claret soaked white coat delivering dripping carcasses of all descriptions for a meat distribution company and spending each weekday morning among the gore and guts at the famous Smithfield Market. This job gave me a woozy feeling each day while carrying all those bloody livers, slippery cold meats and the other assortments of animal parts into high class restaurants in Chelsea and Mayfair. The feelings of nausea were usually a result of the taste still lurking in my stomach from the previous evening's' excesses down in the dark bars of Brixton town.

One evening that now infamous 'Weather Forecast' by Michael Fish was aired on the BBC news in October 1987. The night when the BBC's number one meteorologist informed us all reassuringly that contrary to reports and despite it being particularly windy around the country, there certainly *wasn't* a hurricane on its way to the shores of Britain.

I didn't catch that particular bulletin, so was therefore like many others, completely unaware of the impending 'end of the world show' due later that night as I eased into bed after another hard day carrying bits of dead animals into posh west end kitchens.

I remember waking up a number of times during the night thinking to myself how windy it was outside, then slipping back into lucid dreams involving the tower block we lived in leaning far over under the strain of 1000mph gales.

Car alarms were going off with every mighty gust and the whole breezy effect felt somewhat amplified from five floors up. I slept on and off through the night, waking periodically as the noise outside pulled me back into semi consciousness.

I had to get up for work at around 5.30am for the meat packers, so my first view from our elevated balcony the following morning was an eerie and strange sight. I panned my eyes across the London landscape as the chaotic wind blew about at the sight of the entire city bathed in total darkness. The only lights I could see across London were the three triangular red spots emanating from The Nat West Tower in Canary Wharf. All else around at every compass point was unnervingly dark.

Even after hours of gusts the hurricane was still blowing at severe gale force, as I watched cardboard boxes, paper cups and city rubbish hurtling past my window at dangerous speeds. I even saw a piece of 4' by 6' chipboard chaotically glide past my block at a height of about sixty feet.

The whole spectacle was an alien and foreboding demonstration of nature's power, making it even more of an unusual sight than anything I'd witnessed before. We certainly weren't in the tropics and the fact is that we don't get hurricanes in temperate climate Britain, do we?

I watched a lone man in the street below battling against the gale, with his coat flapping madly in the breeze as he struggled to even open his car door. There were a few trees blown down in the surrounding streets and it all looked kind of apocalyptic from my lofty standpoint. I made my way to work by pushing my craning body against the forces of nature along the deserted, unlit streets. In the chaos around I soon realised that this might not be a good day to be driving a high-sided vehicle full of butchered animals.

When the gales finally died down by mid morning, John (the other carcass delivery driver) and I were then sent out to negotiate the traffic chaos of central London. Everywhere you looked were fallen trees, smashed dustbins, floating rubbish and debris spread across the streets all over town. Cops and traffic wardens were hopelessly trying to re-direct the increasing tailbacks as the city was without traffic lights or any power to most of central London. There were cordoned off streets in the west end as some of those period buildings were leaning dangerously close to collapse. Drivers grinned to themselves as they slipped slowly past a very large tree lying over the bonnet of a very nice metallic blue Porsche 911 parked outside The Ritz. Oh well, one less yuppie in a fancy motor in the west end no great loss I mused to myself as I eased my white van around the debris.

Despite all of nature's wanton destruction, Kettleby House remained standing, so we still had a home, at least for now.

This totally unexpected and unforeseen event was extensively covered across the newspaper headlines the next day, as news crews were busying themselves in competition with each other to gather the best footage and stills of nature's carnage all around southern Britain. People flocked to the pubs after work that evening to exchange excited stories of their views and impressions on an event that really shouldn't have happened in this district of the northern hemisphere.

The town of Sevenoaks in Kent was briefly renamed 'One Oak' as the tropical freak of nature gradually passed into the annuals of bad weather forecasting history, and a number of people died during the storm.

But once more and yet again, we were faced with another eviction when I returned from a trip with my girlfriend later that month. The notice from Lambeth Council was left sitting on the living room table by Stan for me to find instantly on my return. He knew that I'd prefer to hear the bad news immediately.

Annoyingly, we'd almost sorted the flat out, having dragged some half decent furniture in and generally made the place comfy enough to live in. Stan had creatively tacked some posters up on the walls to cheer the place up a bit while I was away too. What a bloody disappointment, again. Who else was going to live there in any near future? The place would need to be totally renovated and fitted with new appliances before any legal tenants could be offered a tenancy there. We knew that the flat would be closed up to fester once again, possibly for years. What a fuckin' waste.

But this time however, we decided to try and take on the council and ask them to let us keep that flat. Stan and I made an appointment with a local housing officer to plead our case. Although the young man listened intently and was totally sympathetic to our dilemma he told us in no nonsense talk that it's was the policy of all London councils (which included Lambeth) not to house squatters under any circumstances. This was despite the fact that I'd been on Lambeth Council's huge housing waiting list since 1984.

He added, 'If it was up to me lads, I'd hand over a tenancy agreement now, I totally understand your situation.'

He knew that we were the sort of squatters who'd be very grateful of somewhere permanent to live, and he also knew that we'd maintain and look after the place better than many. But he was governed by rules and could do nothing but offer us moral support.

So that was that then? The colossal and un-shifting weight of bureaucracy plods on unabated, without reasoning, where rules are thought up by unimaginative, autocratic people who live in a world so very far detached from the rest of us, well at least far away from squatters in south London.

Fuck them, we concluded over a cup of tea back at our soon-to-be-evicted-from-squat. Let them close down and board up 'our flat' and allow it to gradually rot away while the details of it were quietly filed away in a back draw under the section; 'New Accommodation to Let'. Bullshit as usual.

We knew the score so well by now as once again our flat opening skills were called into action. We'd be out in the dead of night and opening up other places by our well honed hook or (more likely) crook methods sooner or later.

It was just a question of where in the streets, estates or even the tree lined avenues of sunny Brixton we'd strike lucky next...

23 – Villas and Mansions

A few days after Guy Fawkes Night in 1987 Stan and I attired in the obligatory dark clothes, moved quietly through the deserted back streets of Brixton. Once again, our squatter's toolkit had been collected together in preparation for another night time sortie involving breaking into locked up council properties in the SW9 area.

We wandered furtively among the dimly lit and dirty corridors of run down tower blocks in the Loughborough Estate. Being old hands at this game by now, we instinctively knew how to score free accommodation in south London in those dark nights of the mid nineteen eighties. It was always a question of luck and astute intuition as we went about the business of busting open empty flats on any given moonlit night.

As we 're-opened' one flat after another we'd invariably stumble upon the usual horrors; those stinking scuzzy shitholes harbouring festering life forms lurking within closed and long unplugged fridges. All the while you'd be slipping about in the darkness upon slimy, rotting bin liners filled with months' worth of rotten food and god knows what else.

Most of these places wouldn't get a second look beyond the door as the rough aroma of old rotting vegetables hit us in the hallways and we'd turn around and leave within seconds. A lot of these empty flats hadn't been cleared out when the previous occupants had left; they were just sealed up by council workers regardless of the filth that may have been left behind. They probably considered it not to be their job and the current news about AIDS was probably another factor, bearing in mind the discoveries we'd made in our own place. Therefore, these flats couldn't be occupied by anyone apart from the seriously brave, street tramps or inexperienced and desperate squatters.

We didn't fall into those categories, and knew that perhaps the next place might not have been formerly occupied by Neanderthal Man. As difficult as it often was to find somewhere marginally above the level of a cave dwelling, we had our standards and would keep searching until something turned up that we could make habitable in a short period of time.

We had a certain threshold in our living standards and wondered how some people could possibly live like that. We were also aware that a small percentage of squatters were giving the rest of us a bad name, but then again some people who are legally housed really do live like cave dwellers, so those types would be classed as your typical nightmare neighbours from hell.

This pointless and appalling 'Housing System' as adopted by many inner city councils was the result of bad management, corruption and a total waste of housing stock, especially in view of the housing shortage in London during that period. This dreadful situation is what encouraged so many people to squat in the city during this 'Golden Era' of free housing as part of our own accommodation policy. There was an abundance of poorly secured empties all over the inner city estates to which the local authorities had little or no information on, which meant in some cases people could sometimes squat a property for years before being 'discovered'.

A couple of hours into the hunt we came across an unlit flat in a local tower block that appeared empty from the outside. Having already forced our way into a number of sealed properties that evening we were getting irritated and losing patience with our evening's failures. After booting the flimsy door in we soon found that once again there was no electricity, which was always the first thing we'd check when we entered anywhere. We nosed our way through the flat while stepping over the usual shite and rubbish until we came across one room at the back of the flat which had a nicely made bed, a case of clothes, a few candles and a clock sitting on a crappy bedside table. This place (or rather the room) was obviously somebody's home and therefore belonged to another squatter.

We left quickly closing what remained of the front door behind us.

Now almost at the point of giving up for the night having opened about ten, rancid, pissy, sleazy, death smelling apartments that evening. We finally ended up strolling along Villa Road in Brixton. This whole street looked pretty good and better still, it kind of looked squatted as well, and judging by the colourful variety of front doors, it had that arty look about it too. We both liked what we were eyeing up as we strolled along the street.

Villa Road consisted of about twenty large mid Victorian terraced houses, with a couple missing from each end of the road, and tatty as they were, each one seemed to possess its own distinctive character. We stopped outside a really dark and unoccupied looking house in the middle, number 29. There wasn't even a front door just an 8'x4' piece of chipboard nailed onto the frame with '29' daubed large on it in bright drippy red paint. Looking up at this sad building we noticed a few broken windows, and in the darkness of winter the place looked like real shithole to be sure. We ventured down the side steps to the basement below and pushed on an old wooden door, which just like in a horror movie, simply creaked open before us.

This was at least an encouraging start; as no loud metallic tools would be required to break this place open.

What awaited us inside this small mansion was a total mess; autumn leaves filled the dark purple painted hallway as we made our precarious way forward. Dozens of empty half bottles of White Bacardi Rum and crushed cans of Red Stripe cluttered every inch of floor space. Nasty, tan coloured 'fire trap' type plastic covered, foam filled furniture from the 1970s adorned the various rooms we stepped into, one after another. There were astonishing piles of junk and rubbish everywhere we looked, and plaster rubble over the floors on every level. We crunched our precarious way from one horror room to another holding our candle and flashlight up to the dank misery that adorned our eyes with every turn into each room.

This was a big Victorian place consisting of five floors from basement to attic, with open fireplaces, sash windows and those high architrave decorated ceilings of a bygone period. The house had plenty of character but the truth was the whole place was in a serious state of disrepair as we climbed the banister-less rickety stairs ever upwards. We then realised that it was fallen ceiling plaster that was adorning the floors and especially covering the stairwell landings. By the time we reached the top of the house we discovered to our dismay that around half the slate tiles were missing from the roof, and had been for a long time by the look of it. Therefore the rain, sleet and snow had been free falling into the building for some time, loosening the thick, aged wattle and daub plaster from one floor to another in an ever increasing manner the more the weather got into the property. This inner decay must've been ongoing for years judging by the condition of the upper floors. One could just about see the night sky and stars from the 2nd floor landing while standing outside what could loosely be described as a bathroom and toilet. We took a moment to check the clear night sky and laugh before resuming our stumbly tour of this former Victorian Villa

On top of all that, there was nothing coming out of the tap in the horrible sink downstairs, though we found that the mains supply tap in the basement hallway which had been turned off. I gingerly opened the valve while Stan stood in the kitchen to observe, we soon heard the rush of water through pipes which was quickly followed by

'Turn it off! Quick! Turn it off!' shouted Stan

He'd been hit by a six foot jet of water that came jetting from a roughly cut pipe sticking out of the wall below the sink.

'Looks like the place needs some serious plumbing too then?' I said

Unbelievably, the gas and electricity supplies were on, of sorts; Stan lit the ancient oven in the trashed and now wet downstairs kitchen area and eventually we traced a botched electricity junction box by the basement door. There hadn't been a meter reader calling at this address for a very, very long time, and it seemed the gas meter had also been 'fixed' to deliver that ultimate squatter's dream; an endless, free supply.

The electricity meter had been completely by-passed, there was a wooden board nailed up on the wall with a regular four pin extension board attached to feed the whole damn house. We'd tested the supply as we moved from room to room with our squatter's switch tester and although none of the ancient sockets elsewhere in the house were active, there was juice coming via the dodgy plug board and butchered junction box in the basement. This set up looked highly dangerous as it buzzed away in front of us in the dim candlelight, but we at least had limited power coming in and some of the overhead light sockets were still live too.

After a long evening of stumbling about in dank empty properties, Stan and I sat down opposite one other in the grimy basement around a circular table with green baize mysteriously tacked over it to discuss our emergency housing dilemma. Stan could somehow see the potential of 'owning' such a large house; I, however, could only see the mess, a roof missing, a dangerous electricity supply and the general fucked state of the entire place.

We sat in the silence momentarily of what was now deemed the downstairs kitchen, he rolled a spliff as our eyes adjusted in the dim candle light at the chaos surrounding us. We cracked open a couple of Red Stripes and rolled a spliff in the semi darkness then proceeded to discuss the pros and cons of residing in a rubble ridden, semi roofless house. By now I'd grown pretty pissed off with living in total dumps which we'd have to completely clean up and bleach out before even daring to make a cup of tea in. The Kettleby flat, despite formerly being a smack dealers house, complete with an electric shock stove and heaving scum filled sink had been cleaned thoroughly and made secure, by us. But this mansion was a different sort of challenge. How much more bad luck would we have to endure when it came to housing? But then again the reality was that we weren't going to be paying actual rent for anywhere to live anyway, so therefore these were the limited choices squatters like us had to work with.

We also had to consider the timeframe before we'd be evicted from Kettleby House which was now only days away, let alone the lack of funds either of us had to pay an extortionate rent to a greedy private landlord, to reside in a cupboard. Neither of us relished the prospect of being housed in a place like Emu Road ever again, or stuffed into a grubby wardrobe sized bedsit right next door to a creepy, greasy haired serial killer.

But this place was in need of some serious building work, skills that neither of us possessed, we could fit a mortise lock, wire a plug and put a shelf up, but we knew nothing about roofing or plumbing.

No water supply? Just how the fuck were we going to manage without even that basic necessity? This was a rare occasion when Stan and I ever argued about anything, I wasn't keen at all but he was committed, he liked the idea of having a house and said he was prepared to move in alone if he had to. As there wasn't an alternative address anywhere to be found that night among the numerous horrors already visited, we both knew that we'd be out again tomorrow night for an evening for much of the same, with the added bonus of getting busted by the cops at any moment.

Therefore, with the looming prospect of squatting alone I was reluctantly sold on number 29 Villa Road, knowing we had little choice and even less time. We downed our tins of Red Stripe, pulled the basement door semi closed after us and decided to knock on the house next door to get some info on the street in general. Our potential new neighbour came to his door and helpfully proceeded to give us a brief synopsis on the street and some history of the house adjoining his.

Thankfully, the good news was that the entire street was indeed squatted, the bad news was that number 29 was what's commonly known as a 'blues house' run by a local gangster currently serving time at Her Majesty's pleasure. The place had been used for some serious all weekend type parties going back about ten years; hence the reason for the empty beer cans and Bacardi bottles everywhere.

Our soon-to-be new neighbour, Mark, seemed keen on having a couple of willing blokes move in as the house desperately needed living in providing we were prepared for the clean-up and brave enough to confront the gangster if and when he showed up again in the future. A number of other people had tried to live there but had been turned out violently by this guy on the spot; the place had an established reputation as a local party venue and brothel so we'd have to take our chances.

Apparently the street was full of Mercs and BMWs during the party season, so only the bravest of squatters would have any chance of staying in number 29 before being threatened to fuck by the Brixton underworld. However, as long as this guy was locked up, it seemed that we'd be okay. Mark gave us a moment to collect our thoughts on his doorstep, and then raised a sly smile as he kindly offered to loan us a broom to clear the mess up. But he basically knew full well that what we really needed were industrial masks, boiler suits, a job lot of strong rubble bags, some large shovels and a couple of deep skips parked in the street outside for a few weeks.

The next evening we moved our stuff into our new/old Victorian mansion, about three trips in all as we pushed our meagre belongings in a busted wheelbarrow the quarter mile round trip from Kettleby House. We were already coved in dirt and shite after spending just a few hours in this house, and without a water supply just how were we to get clean, have a shave, or make a cup of tea sometime? This was just one of many problems for a couple of now hardy squatters had to deal with, one piece at a time.

That first evening as we stumbled about in the darkness we discovered a pub sized pool table buried under cardboard and curtains in the front room on the ground floor and soon after the slate for it turned up behind a piece of chipboard leaning against a wall. This discovery was at least a positive aspect of the general misery around us as I do like a game of pool, but shooting a few frames in the dim candle light wasn't exactly a top priority right at this moment. Besides that even though there was a full selection of red and yellow balls there wasn't a cue anywhere to be seen, let alone the prospect of having to climb over piles of rubbish and crap each time you wanted to line up a shot. But this was a cool find and a ray of sunshine peeking through the darkness of our mansion sized problem.

All around us and in every direction one looked were tons of dusty broom and shovel work to be getting on with, and this was just to clear an area in the only room that could be occupied and slept in at that point. This being the adjoining living room next to what was now termed 'The Pool Room'.

We stacked plenty of dry wood and rubbish next to the big open fireplace on the ground floor as we gradually cleared the shit up around us. Lighting a nice fire is a warm comfort at the end of a dirty and tiring day, as we sank back on the scummy brown sofas from the disco era to skin up, eat chips, crack open a few cans of beer and settle into our new mansion in front of a roaring blaze. Those first nights were spent in our sleeping bags on those grubby settees in the ground floor living room.

One quiet night, about three days after we'd moved in, as we slept soundly on our cheap sofas, I was abruptly eased back into consciousness in the middle of the night by a strange ripping sound followed seconds later by a crash and a heavy load of weight upon my legs. I jumped out of my slumber, half trapped by the weight on my lower legs as I reached for my torch in the dust cloud to find most of my legs buried under a mound of broken ceiling plaster. We were both literally covered in plaster dust and rubble which was also liberally spread about on the floor as well.

It seemed that some more ceiling had once again become dislodged with all this new activity and disruption in the house and had let go at that very minute. Stan (who'd sleep through a prison riot) hardly stirred on his miserable sofa and simply turned in his restless sleep slightly and went back to his open mouthed snoring. I struggled in my bag to kick off the debris, and looked wearily up at the hole above us, laughing sarcastically to myself within the now settling dust cloud as Stan mumbled a couple of 'What the fuck happened?' statements in his sleep. I reached for a half finished joint smoked it with a grin on my face and eventually slipped back into dream world; which consisted of cream painted mansions, with sunken baths, marble floors, walls adorned with awesome pop art, double fridges full of cold beer and bronze skinned babes oiling me down in the hot sunshine next to the clear blue, kidney shaped swimming pool dug in the delightful, expansive back garden as viewed beyond the living room French windows… And then I woke up again.

When we viewed the new hole above us the next morning we realised that we'd been quite lucky. It's quite a long drop from a Victorian ceiling and had our heads been at the other ends of our mucky sofas, one or both of us could've been seriously injured or even killed just by the sheer weight of what had dislodged and dropped from above the night before. There would be a number of other near misses involving falling plaster and the subsequent dusty mess to clear up afterwards in our house. This was considered to be just another dangerous squat hazard to be aware of when you least expected it.

Within a few days our various friends started arriving to gaze around the nooks and crannies that was our 'new mansion' and then in sympathy would often lend a hand to help with the massive clear up. As every room was still in a shitty state we'd be sleeping in the front room for a while yet. Gradually, the electrical extension leads began making their way upstairs, floor by floor.

Fortunately, we still owned the 'Brixton Brew' fermentation bin which was used bi-daily to ferry our precious water supply as gained from the 24 hour garage which was thankfully only at the end of the road. This 3rd world water system was performed for a number of weeks until one of our good neighbours came over on a Sunday morning and plumbed in our first tap in the basement 'kitchen'. This was a major step forward to actually be able to boil water, wash and make tea in London in the late 20th century and not having to live like pikeys most of the time.

It wasn't long before the word got out among the street that number 29 was now occupied and that the two guys living there were prepared to stick it out. The other residents of Villa Road knew only too well the sheer state our place was in and some came by to offer hot baths and showers on seeing this pair of squatters going about our filthy daily business. We soon found out from the various neighbours that the street was occupied by around ninety people of all ages and backgrounds, and had been squatted since the mid 1970s. This was indeed music to our ears; could this mean at last that we may have a place to live for a bit longer than the usual four to six months?

This encouraging news seemed to make all the shit and mess stacked up around us somewhat diminish in volume before our very eyes, and perhaps we could make some longer term plans in our lives now?

24 – Sieges and Sirens with Eggs

During a proposed redevelopment of numerous 'run down areas and estates' in England (namely areas in Sunderland, the north east of the UK and Brixton) in 1978, Lambeth Council duly decided to demolish both sides of Villa Road and also one side of St John's Road in order to create a 'Park Area' next to the Brixton Road as part of this 'redevelopment'

This would involve evicting the now well established squatter community of hundreds who'd been occupying those houses for years. Although there is now a park (Max Roach Park) where at least half of the street used to stand, this fairly large green area was formerly the back gardens of the even numbers of Villa Road and likewise the odd numbers of St John's Road opposite and across the park.

When we moved into the street there were only the odd numbered houses left in Villa Road on one side with the small park situated across the road which was where the even numbered houses had once stood. Back then, this was a pretty big community who immediately lodged dozens of complaints about these 'proposals' at the council which were as usual ignored as after all, these people were dirty squatters, so what rights did they have?

Despite the fact that this community were maintaining these neglected houses simply by living in them and that many of these residents ran workshops and businesses from their homes made not a scrap of difference by the 'March of Progress'. If

Lambeth Council would give permission to have the infamous Barrier Block designed and built on Coldharbour Lane, then one can assume that they were capable of sanctioning any awful architectural venture if it meant a good deal financially. Besides that, would any Lambeth councillor actually volunteer to live in the Barrier Block after its completion?

This new 'residential block' was due to sit next to (or even under) a massive link-road flyover, which would then cut through Villa Road further into Brixton This was a nightmare piece of colossal and expensive designing, in an era when sizeable areas of London were still ugly, corrugated walled off enclosures of bomb sites left over from WW2.

This bureaucratic stupidity within the isles of Lambeth Council was guaranteed to lead to some level of confrontation, which in due course, it did.

The residents of both sides of Villa Road and one side of St John's Road were then served with the inevitable eviction notices. This must've amounted to a couple of hundred people at least; all were to be turned out of homes they'd occupied for a long time. People were naturally angered by this forthcoming action, they got themselves organised and decided on mass to raise a little mayhem and make things very difficult and (expensive) for Lambeth Council.

What happened next is now a part of squat history in Britain.

Although the siege of Villa Road happened long before we'd arrived there, I've since been given details and often hilarious accounts of what went on during that period by some of older the residents in the street. I've also conducted some research of my own into this particular episode of squatter history. It's that old story of bad town planning, a waste of resources and more so, the determination of a lot of people to keep their homes, squatted or otherwise.

Demos were organised, which were supported by various industrial unions, as they'd been given the support of the squatters' collaborations during the 'The Winter of Discontent' at the end of the Callahan's Labour Government in the late seventies.

These Villa Road squatters of 1978 prepared themselves well for the inevitable day when council bailiffs and police arrived by the truckload to forcibly remove them, house by house on both sides of the street.
    I was informed by these hardcore squatters that for three long months the authorities would arrive at 9am in the morning, seal off the whole road and arrest anybody leaving any house for the hours that they tried to get into any of the buildings. I've heard stories of a wartime siren being erected on the roof of one of the even numbered houses to warn all when the evictors showed up. One guy who lived in number 13 actually made a drawbridge which could be pulled up over his door making this man's squat truly his castle. Every house on both sides of Villa Road sealed up their ground floor windows, with bars and corrugated steel; doors were treble locked, thus making the bailiff's job twice as difficult. All this went on and on week after week as Lambeth's 'eviction process' bill grew heavier by the day.
    There are tales of ageing hippies and young punks moving furtively from one rooftop to another to pelt the bailiffs and cops with rotten eggs and potatoes as they shuffled along the street below seeking out a weak spot in any of the houses.

It must've looked like a scene from a medieval uprising, a full on siege, the same shit every morning for weeks on end. By all accounts this uncomfortable situation was gradually stretching the council resources, and wearing thin the patience of all those officials standing in the street in their high viz tops while they were stink bombed from above each day. Kevin, (who lived in number 11) said that the council's adopted policy was to maroon the residents in their houses during this siege, instructing that they were to be literally starved into submission by not being able to leave their houses during the day.

Services were cut off as houses were plunged into darkness, but those still with (free) electricity fed extension leads to those without. What made us all laugh around our felt covered kitchen table was when Kev said that the bailiffs had forgotten to seal off or even man the back entrances to the houses; this simply meant that people could slip out via their back gardens to get the shopping in and return to the anarchy and mayhem 'after lunch' to relieve the rotten vegetable throwers.

Now that's what I call organisation...

On a number of occasions the residents' of Villa and St Johns Road noisily invaded public meetings relating to the Villa Road development, thus creating a lot of disruption and disturbance to help make life ever more difficult (and expensive) for the planners. At one particular meeting, loads of the unwashed of said streets stormed into a session and even managed to climb desks and throw masses of the paperwork into the air. Democracy at work, in a democratic state? These ongoing events soon made the front pages of the local rags and began to attract news reporters and hacks from the national press to this 'squat city siege' in Brixton. All the while the residents battled on day after day to keep hold of their homes.

Eventually, the residents of the siege decided to seek some legal advice, and gained the trust of a reputable local solicitor to champion their collective cause. He soon discovered that the Villa Road houses could be graded as listed, historical buildings as they were late Victorian, circa 1880s in design and build. This therefore meant, in the eyes of the National Trust that the fronts of the buildings at least had to remain intact. Now it seemed, a legal loophole was found and would soon be acted upon, legally.

Sadly however, during this time the bailiffs had managed to get into one of the even numbered houses and quickly started to evict its occupants. One big problem here was that the residents in many of the houses on both sides of the street had knocked some of their internal walls through into next door's house and so on all along the street. These internal doors would link the neighbouring homes on various floors in different houses, thus leading to a serious domino effect. Once the bailiffs had gained entry into one house they were able to move onto the next one on both sides and so forth, as obviously these internal doors were not as secure as the fortress style gates holding up the exteriors against the siege outside. The occupants on the odd numbered side of the street had to sit tight and endure the sight of a mass eviction across the road while they stood firm and courageously held out.

While the evictions were underway; the head of Brixton Police stepped into the fray and really threw a spanner in the works to add another headache at Lambeth Council. On seeing the proposals he raised objections to the fact that the whole of Villa Road would not just be demolished, but the actual street would become part of the proposed park. This in effect meant that the police would now lose their quick access through Villa Road onto Brixton Road from the back streets behind the police station in Canterbury Crescent.

This wasn't good news at all for Brixton Police as they'd now have to use a longer alternative route around the local one way system, adding precious minutes to answer their calls. These are the very planning proposals that any emergency service will object to the most in these situations, road closures, and lack of access leading to reduced response times. This was excellent news for the squatters and seriously bad press for Lambeth Council.

By now the diggers and demolition crews were bulldozing the whole street on the even numbered side of Villa Road as well as the houses backing onto them via St John's Road, and were currently too busy to be ready for the odd side of Villa Road.

The architects were called in again to redesign the whole mess and it was soon decided to go ahead and create Max Roach Park after demolishing the even numbered houses on Villa Road, as well as the other houses in St John's Road and have done with it. This way Villa Road and St John's Road would remain accessible for all including the police, and Lambeth Council would get their park.

So, having spent a shitload of the tax payer's money on police services and no-neck bailiffs it was decided to give the still standing squatters of Villa Road a stay of execution until an unconfirmed date in the future. The word on the street was that after the lunacy of the expensive and abandoned plans to evict hundreds of people, Lambeth Council secretly decided to wash their hands of Villa Road and its thorny residents, and the remaining side of Villa Road was now in effect theirs to occupy and do what they will with, until the whole lot fell down around them.

Lambeth Council decided that from then on they would offer no help, structural or otherwise, to Villa Road ever again. Which in layman's terms meant that the hundred squatters had won a fierce battle and could continue to live there and look after their houses as they'd been doing so for years anyway.

There were other political and design flaw reasons as to why all those crazy plans were eventually axed by Lambeth. The link-road flyover was dropped too, though the now dreaded Barrier Block was already under construction by then.

As we gradually got to know our fellow squatters over the time we lived in the street, we in number 29 were given occasional snippets of those amazing stories about the siege of Villa Road often with a beer and a spliff around our battered old pool table. These tales were amusingly reeled off by the very people that were there at the time and were still sitting pretty. I was warmed by the fact that this community had mobilized themselves against the full power of an inner city council, and with joint determination had beaten the long odds against them.

These people were a genuine bunch, and had developed their own community. They looked after each other and offered various technical skills such as plumbing, carpentry, roofing and rewiring to other occupants, as and when required for the good of all. People had to dig up the street outside their houses to repair broken Victorian sewer outlets, at their own expense as only too aware that Lambeth Council would only offer eviction as a form of help should they ask for any, therefore nobody ever did.

Now that there would be zero assistance from the council after the expensive siege, our new neighbours were willing to help out because our place was now by far the most run down in the street. Number 29 desperately needed occupying if it wasn't to collapse sooner or later, probably bringing down the rest of the houses like skittles around it as it was centrally situated. As most of the Villa Road squatters had at some point in their past been in exactly the same position as we were now, it was in their own interests to assist the new blood on the block.

There were still a fair number of the old school squatters in the street when we moved in at the end of 1987. Though some of the previous hippies who'd resided there in the late 60s and 70s were middle class and university educated, who often came from moneyed backgrounds and could've walked out and bought a home at a moment's notice anyway. But in those days they were often living the squat life for altogether different reasons than we were. Whereas they were highly politicised and involved in all manner of world changing movements so popular during that heady era, we on the other hand just needed somewhere to live during the worst political era of modern times – Thatcher's Britain.

A recent TV documentary called 'Lefties' told tales about the squat life in Villa Road outlining the relation between the squatter movement of the late 70s and radical groups such as IMG (International Marxist Group) whose offices were actually stationed in Villa Road. One would usually find these serious left-wingers waving the banner of Trotskyism on demos and marches leading up to the demise of the old

Labour movement at the end of that decade. If feminism was your thing then you could always join the Primal Screamers of Villa Road too; though neighbours and passers by in the street must've wondered what hideous murders were being committed in hippy town on those balmy summer afternoons and evenings.

I guess in a way theirs was a similar lifestyle to ours (minus the Primal Screamers) by the time the 1980s were upon my generation. Only we were often without the higher education, better job opportunities and probable family money that many of our predecessors had to look forward to. There was almost full employment (if you wanted it) in swinging Britain of the 'You've never had it so good' sixties. It wasn't until the mid seventies when the OPEC oil crisis, the three day week, and the mess that the then lame Labour Government got themselves into that eventually led the UK into eighteen years of greedy, self serving Conservatism.

Granted, they were squatters of another era, but of better times (or so people say) and could've walked away from poverty, sieges, evictions, and blocked drains if they'd wanted to. We however couldn't, and were stuck in a roofless shithole complete with pigeon rooms, rats, buzzing electricity and bollock bowls. If we'd had the choice (and of course the money) I doubt if we would've have chosen to live in those conditions.

25 – The Spirit of Community

Meanwhile, back in the present, Stan and I struggled on, he was out a lot rehearsing and gigging with his band, I was the one with more time on my hands to get on with the multitude of house repairs and D.I.Y/botch jobs.

It was hard work just living in conditions like that, but thankfully within a month two Australians Jim and Marlene (who were connected with Stan's band at the Intrepid Fox Pub in the west end) moved into the 'available flat' aka 'dungeon dwelling' in the basement.

Although it was a dry room, the exterior facing windows were sealed on the inside and bricked up on the outside, so without any natural light down there, they had to live encased in cabin fever conditions under constant artificial light. It took Jim about a week to hang a heavy door on the room via the half wreaked frame but they also had access to the 'kitchen' next door. They lived in that cellar for about five months before another room became available upstairs, with the added bonus of real, proper daylight.

Ian then arrived back from his travels in the Middle East, and after finding that Kettleby House had been sealed up by the council he was directed to his 'new home' by one of our other mates in Brixton. Being full of life and enthusiasm as one generally is when you return from a few months abroad, he was ready to write more songs and form a new band. He loved the place the minute he put his rucksack down and accepted a spliff before his arse even hit the rubbish chair behind him.

Some weeks later, Dean arrived too. We came home one evening and found him sitting quietly in the candlelit front room drinking Stella and staring at the pool table with a big smile on his face. Now somewhat recovered from the accident though he effectively only had one arm and his leg was still very weak having been screwed and pinned back together again. All those rickety stairs were a rough prospect for the guy, but he was welcome to endure the hardships along with the rest of us.

So now we were six, our Victorian mansion was adequately occupied so anything was possible…

We'd heard from a neighbour who called around one afternoon (probably for a nose about) that there was once a cooperative run by the residents of Villa Road to help each other out and occasionally raise funds for vital building work when the need arose. With our place being nearly derelict, we were definitely in that particular 'desperate squatters' league. Ian and I sat down one evening and constructed a note, made copies and posted them to every house in the street; we were calling a meeting at number 29 to introduce ourselves to everyone and to discuss our serious roofing problem.

Quite a few of our squat neighbours showed up on an evening a couple of days later and filed into our makeshift living room, some with an obvious morbid curiosity to see inside 'the blues house', besides the fact that a number of them had been regular attendees at the wild parties at number 29 in the past. All were in agreement, willing to help, and wanted us to make a go of it, as should this place collapse it would seriously undermine the whole street.

There was a real eclectic mix of people in Villa Road, artists, eccentrics, students, musos, Marxists, writers, acid casualties, low rent recreational drug dealers, media types and mixed bag of differing nationalities too. But at this time the people who'd prove more useful to us right now were those with plumbing, sparking and general building skills, and they were dotted about in the street too. It had been discovered that a couple of hundred quid was still sitting in 'The Villa Road Fund'. After a quick show of hands it was democratically decided that it would be offered to buy the materials needed to fix our leaking roof. By now we were into the winter and the rain was regularly pissing down the inner walls in the upper floors.

The pitfall here in the (non existent) small print was that although the slates and new batons would be purchased out of this street fund, it would ultimately be us who'd be climbing up onto the roof and repairing the damage ourselves. This represented another problem; despite the height involved, none of us knew how to fix roof tiles and we were rather hoping that would be done for us by a kindly neighbour for some cash, food and as much spliff as he (or she) could smoke.

But no, the deal was the same for us as everyone else, we were loaned a roof ladder and a slate ripper but it was our baby to sort out. The slates, nails and batons arrived by flatbed truck a couple of weeks later and our mate Donkey Paul turned up to show us how easy it is to fit roof tiles from the bottom upwards. The ladder was then manhandled down the street from someone else's roof and out through our attic room and gingerly perched over the rickety eaves. Nervously with deep breaths some of us climbed out of Stan's attic window and onto the ladder to check out the windy, elevated and pant browning view of a nice section of south London around us.

Initially, Ian and I decided to throw a large tarpaulin over most of the (large) hole and tie it securely to the window supports for a week or so until enough of us in the house became available to get on with the frightening job at hand. After an hour on that lofty death trap getting half blown off while clinging on for dear life, Ian and I secured the feeble botch job down and retired to the kitchen for warm tea and a spliff to calm our fears and hope that the whole business in hand would simply just go away.

26 – The Pigeon Room

Before we could contemplate the treacherous climb to our untimely deaths up the north face of 29 Villa Road, there was a serious problem involving squatters of the winged variety. A couple of hundred pigeons and their families had made their homes in the eaves of the house, and were now well bedded into their own forms of bird comforts having been a long time freely able to fly in and out of the busted roof without restriction.

After spending many happy and reproductive years occupying the top two floors and the rafters of the house, it was now time for them to squat elsewhere.

This of course turned out to be an extremely frustrating job, we chased them out of the broken windows in the two rooms below the roof, waving brooms and sticks at them, but the fuckers would fly straight back as soon as you left. I even sent the cat up there, a brave boy was Jazz, but he came back two minutes later complaining of being seriously outnumbered.

Marlene volunteered to go up there and shovel knee high levels of pigeon shit into bin liners, and came back asking what to be done with all the eggs and chicks everywhere. Sadly, there was only one option by this time; do we live side by side with dirty, disease-ridden birds, which were carriers of some rather nasty ailments including tendonitis, this being an unpleasant affliction especially for people (like musicians) who need finger dexterity.

Or do we evict these flying rats out of our own desperation regarding our own housing needs? By now along with everything else that we had to contend with in this rubble filled house, I was well past caring about fucking pigeons, so I clambered up into the low rafters armed with the slate ripper and within half an hour of 'orrible flapping and chirping, a serious number of bird murders were committed. If those chicks couldn't fly when I arrived then they had three seconds to learn on the way down via the gaping hole in the roof. It was a mêlée of blood, straw and feathers in all directions, accompanied by bits and pieces of street rubbish that had been airlifted in down the many years for nesting purposes. It stank like hell up there, like a chicken coop on a midsummer's afternoon.

On top of that, this was also a microscopic insect universe of the multi legged variety, there were hundred-footed creatures making good their escape as the slate ripper in my hand just seemed to have a will of its own, as it clubbed and crushed various life forms in an orgy of sickening violence as I reclaimed our loft.

The street below was very soon littered with the splattered remains of pigeon chicks and eggs in various forms of development. It was a brutal and bloody ritual I know, but it was either us or them, anyone would probably make the same decision if confronted with that choice too?

Ian, Stan, Marlene and I clung onto that roof ladder for four days as we wobbled and balanced our every step eighty feet above a straight drop to certain death on the street below. Meanwhile, Dean kept the supplies coming, mixed the concrete to seal the edges and periodically passed up the tea. In hindsight and looking back we really took our lives in our hands, just one slip and you'd be flailing off the edge without a chance, flapping in the air and soon enough brown bread on the cold street below.

Slates would slip from our grasp and hurtle towards the pavement followed by our shouts to anyone happening to be passing the house below. No ropes or harnesses were available to bind us either to one another or onto something solid like a chimney stack. Health and Safety in the workplace was not an option here, we took our chances and were as careful as we could possibly be. We did become slightly more at ease about our lofty predicament after a couple of days up there elevated in the breeze, overlooking the local landmarks.

This, as opposed to the those nervy, scary moments we all felt as one by one we eased our way up through Stan's attic window in that first hour.

We soon adopted a disciplined teamwork type system and watched each other's backs, we handed tools to one another often at arm's length. There were usually three of us working at any one time; someone would take a break from the main work to prepare the next step or level, while the other two got on with it. There were even the odd joke moments when something (usually a pigeon) a long time dead was discovered buried between batons and slates, or fell past you on its way down to the street below. Their skulls grinned out at you, and the musty smell of pigeon shit filled your lungs as their feathers periodically tickled your face as they slipped away in the wind.

We wobbled on that ladder (our only safety net) and swung about in the breeze, but we just gripped on hard in our determination to finish the task.

Fixing that roof must be among the most dangerous things any of us have ever taken on, most people don't really like open air heights with very limited supports, but hanging onto the last rung of the ladder with one hand and cementing a crack right at the end of the roof with the other is something I'd prefer not to have to do more than once in a lifetime. It was a fiddly, awkward, cold and dirty job, but we kept up a sense of humour and a 'never say pigeon' attitude.

We didn't quite manage to cure all the leaks, but around 95% watertight was definitely good enough for the likes of us. The house now seemed to have a new lease of life, though the real test of our workmanship would come during or after the first heavy downpour. But it was at least a relief that one ghastly and pretty dangerous squat job didn't cost any of us more than a small cut or a scary heart-stopping moment.

However, it did cost the once resident pigeons considerably more.

27 – Bollock Bowls and Old Boilers

Now that we had a roof, a couple of miles of extension leads, a gas cooker and one (cold) tap for the entire house, we were pretty much in business. Jim and Marlene moved upstairs to a room I had cleared out, I went up a flight and took a room at the back of the house, Dean temporarily moved into the front room and slept on the pool table, Ian got a back room upstairs and Stan took the attic. That left the windowless basement, which was now being eyed up as a possible rehearsal room. Everyone chipped in with the painting, repairs and clearing up the slowly diminishing piles of rubble, as we created more space by the week.

We'd learned how to fix a roof and somewhat conquer our fear of heights, and a good neighbour by the name of Colin had taught us the basics in order to 'design' a network of dodgy plumbing as and when the need arose. We also acquired the largest water boiler for the makeshift bathroom I'd ever seen. Jim manhandled it through the basement door one afternoon and plonked it down in the pool room for us all to admire. This huge aluminium kettle type contraption was a real life saver and when plugged into the already overloaded house supply it certainly added yet more strain on the national grid.

Despite the fact that we didn't as yet have a water supply to the bathroom or taps on our antique bath, we fed a garden hose up from the tap in the basement to fill up this boiler for our bathing facilities, which then in turn took a good three hours to boil. But a hot bath, despite the wait, was next to heaven considering what we'd been used to, even if you did have to book it on rota it a day in advance. The days of boiling kettles and using an old saucepan; better known as 'The Bollock Bowl' for us were now almost over. It took a while before we learned how to plumb the toilet in so we were still bailing used bath water (via the bollock bowl) to flush it in the meantime.

Of course this giant industrial kettle used shit loads of electricity and the lights throughout the house would dim considerably the moment one plugged it in, but we did after all still have a free supply entering the house. It wasn't until a flat blew up somewhere in Brixton that the gas board actually wandered over and started checking all the dodgy houses in our squatted street soon followed by the Electricity Board who wanted to sniff about in Villa Road too.

Ian was caught short one day when someone from the L.E.B. called. The man in the street below was looking over the house as Ian stuck his head out of an upstairs window and was immediately asked if we had electricity.

'No we don't,' quipped Ian with positive authority.

'Well, what's that then mate?' asked the meter man, duly pointing his pen at the light bulb switched on above and behind Ian.

Ian simply turned a looked back at the guy and in a split second answered, 'Ohh, we've got some lights mate, but that's all' adding with measured degree of bullshit.

'We've just moved in and getting it all sorted out soon,' he lied further.

The electricity rep took another quick look at the state of our place followed by a wandering gaze up and down the street, and then with a shake of his head, he ticked something off on his clipboard and walked off grinning to himself.

That was the last time we worried about the criminal theft of essential utilities until the next time it came up, legally or otherwise.

28 – Party Season

With a multitude of urgent repairs now completed, we were ready to open up the place and party down. We'd also acquired a very sturdy exterior steel door and fixed it in the place where the previous wooden one had hung in the basement.

This secure door was the only entrance into our house, but we now had a new member to the family, a Rottweiler called Slippery who was temporarily accompanied by both of her parents on loan in case the aforementioned local gangster came calling once again. A word about Rottweilers at this point, although I'd never run into that breed of dog before and was naturally wary of them, as they look quite scary and have a bite around 50% harder than that of an Alsatian. However, these animals are simply the best guard dogs on earth, highly faithful, obedient and comfortably quiet animals, unless roused.

Slippery was a nice bitch, she loved Jazz the cat, but he obviously wasn't too keen on her, or the parents Roadster and Sophie for that matter too, although they returned to their owners after a couple of months, leaving just Slippery with us. A funny thing happened next, I'm convinced that a now adult Jazz grew some more when he saw the size of these black monsters that had moved in with us. He suddenly became a really big cat, who could take care of himself and gradually got used to Slippery. Jazz was once seen curled up and sleeping nice and snug on the same sofa with all three of these beasts on one very below freezing January morning.

We all chipped a few quid into the pot, bought a pool cue and a box of chalk from a local sports shop and were soon on the way to becoming pool hustlers. Even Dean with his one arm became pretty good in no time using his newly developed technique to skilfully slam the balls noisily into the pockets. Whenever guests came over, the pool table was generally the central attraction, many fun evenings of 'winner stays on' or 'killer' were enjoyed with a few beers and spliffs. Finally, we were beginning to enjoy our new abode as the winter began to slip away and along came the spring.

Ian would often hastily organise a pool competition when a party was in full swing, offering his own never played records and other assorted tat as 'prizes' to the winner. However, the irony was that being the best pool player in the house, he usually won these competitions, and therefore had to accept his own crap back after a mini ceremony was performed in front of a drunken, jeering crowd.

We then stuffed some old mattresses (of the non scabies variety) into a hole in the wall downstairs that partitioned off the windowless room; which now served us as a band rehearsal room. My drums, various amps, and a selection of guitars were set up and we could now all practice away at any time of the day to our hearts' content. Ian and I took a drive to Newcastle in my van and picked up his 300 watt vocal PA from a friend who'd been storing and occasionally using it up there for years. It worked a treat; it had just enough output to serve for vocals over the rest of the instruments.

We were all going to be rock stars yet, with three musicians in the house, all in different bands, playing different styles of music. It was just great to climb out of bed, have some breakfast and then sit behind my kit for a few hours of practice on a weekday. The thick walls absorbed a lot of the noise and there was at least one floor between the music room and people's living quarters, but it could get pretty loud down there when full bands were hard at it rehearsing for gigs.

This was great, our very own rehearsal room! What more could a squat muso possibly ask for?

All of our separate bands were now practising regularly during the week, and gigging in the usual venues around town. Other bands we knew on the circuit, or connected to us via roadies and crew techs were soon booking time in our music room too. They'd gladly pay the £5 an hour to rehearse; especially when they could knock the balls about on our pool table upstairs too during their tea breaks.

Number 29 began to be the place to live, people from all over would stay over at our house, and these people arrived mostly through our west end club connections. Some of them were great company, generous contributors and very welcome, a few were dodgy drifters, and one or two were just plain trouble.

During the summer of '88 we threw parties, lots of parties. They were usually busy and full of the Brixton set; these being musos, artists, oddballs, local squatters as well as the hedonistic west end crowd. We had some trouble occasionally, but the steel door and Slippery's growling kept the idiots out. Our parties went on throughout this large house, up the stairs into people's rooms, and often out in the back garden too. The pool table would become mobbed so we had to organise a names-on-the-board system so that all could play. Sometimes the PA would get switched on and improvised gigs would kick off downstairs.

It was a riot of squatter party fun during that summer of 1988.

One morning, I woke on hearing a lot of commotion going on downstairs, thinking it was perhaps a minor a domestic argument or a band practice I turned over and returned to sleep mode. Later on that morning I was to find out that the said gangster had returned and stationed himself in the street and was periodically throwing bricks at our rickety and newly hung front door. Also, he had a few mates waiting in the wings to charge in and give us all hell if and when the door was either opened or simply fell in.

Stan had heard the commotion too, and after climbing out of bed in his boxers, he armed himself with a huge cartoon type meat cleaver from the kitchen in one hand and a leashed Slippery in the other. He then answered the door to our unwelcome visitor, to which the mobster upon seeing our dog, nervously mouthed the words

'So, you've got one of them have you?' pointing at an equally nervous young Slippery.

Then as Stan opened the door a bit wider to reveal the comedy meat cleaver, he replied, 'Yeah, and I've got one of these too' as the gleaming blade flashed in the sunlight.

At that, the man groaned some more about 'his house' to an uninterested Stan, but knowing the risk wasn't worth the effort; he fucked off, collecting his hoods along the street on the way.

He was never to return. Times had now changed and he was a part of Villa Road history, not its brighter future.

The house was beginning to come together, and soon enough there were eight of us living there. Paint was thrown on the old walls, and loads of ancient newspapers and magazines that had been discovered tucked away in cupboards were soon creatively pasted over the decrepit, crumbling basement walls by Jim. They had a good effect, and there was always something interesting to read on our kitchen walls. There were lots of those hand-drawn advertising slogans from the thirties and forties. Creative pictorials of the era displaying banners such as 'Smoke Black Cat Cigarettes, For a Stronger Taste'

These magazine pages were a record of good, honest advertising (apart from the cigarette promotions and the wonders of the mass use of DDT) from an innocent and even quaint period in the history of the 20th century as plastered up in every available corner to cheer up an otherwise dower basement kitchen. These vintage ads would often include the archetypical happy, piny wearing housewife from the post war years, holding a box of Omo while standing next to one of those now antique top loading washing machines. How times have changed…

The rehearsal room was being now used a lot, and in the heat of that summer we 'fixed up the back garden' and held regular barbeques out in the balmy evenings. I'd improvised a repair job on the back steps by burying an upturned motorcycle frame and creating some steps out of it. A touch precarious, but they worked considerably better than the large gaping ravine from a previous collapse which you'd have to leap over to make it to the garden below.

The rain still crept through in various places when it fell heavily, especially down the back wall as it wasn't covered by a sloping roof. We eventually sorted that problem out by designing a makeshift corrugated interlocking roof that held out the worst of the downpours. Of course the whole place complete with high ceilings, broken windows and gaps under ill-fitting doors, was naturally as cold as Greenland in the bleak winter. But the cool visitors we had calling, along with the general goodwill and socializing that went on in number 29 always raised our spirits while we lived and coped with our numerous and difficult living conditions.

Dean's leg was gradually getting stronger, although he was still full of pins and sometimes found it a struggle to climb all those stairs, especially when full of beer. He did manage to fall off a skateboard one evening thus snapping his leg again. But it needed re-setting anyway, so he went back to Essex and had it all screwed back together once again. He came back after a week on crutches as he was missing our faithful guard dog Slippery to which he'd built up a close relationship with, and she was now definitely recognised as part of the family at number 29.

Slippery was a funny, soppy dog, with friendly eyes and a quiet disposition, probably due to the fact that she was surrounded by drunken people crashing in from club land most nights, all full of love and joy. Dean had also got to know another Rottweiler owner locally, and had once offered to look after his dog for a few days while the said owner was away, although he neglected to tell all of us in the house of this neighbourly arrangement. When Ian came home one night half pissed and conducted the usual maul-the-soppy-Slippery-in-the-dim-light routine, he soon discovered (to his drunken horror) on this occasion that this particular rottie *wasn't* our Slippery, and quickly made his panic ridden exit locking his bedroom door behind him completed with a rickety chair jammed under the wobbly door handle. I made the same mistake too on another occasion once in the dim basement darkness; easy done when all Rottweilers look pretty much alike through hazy, pissed-up eyeballs.

As for my life during this time, I was condemned to support myself with various menial jobs in order to fund my musical aspirations. These 'jobs' included building work and something relating to self employment performing 'light removals' in my Dodge Comer van. This vocation usually involved moving large items of furniture for people living in high rise flats with broken lifts. The words 'Only a few bags and boxes, mate' soon became a two-journey-type-deal while the overloaded rear suspension rubbed upon the wheel hubs. Soon enough, I became pretty pissed off with that particular profession, as well as occasionally filling my van up with a dodgy load of builder's rubble to illegally dispose of 'somewhere quiet'.

I handed out Camden Palace flyers outside The Brixton Academy, did the cloakroom and side door at The Marquee Club, in which I usually ended up getting very pissed as Ian worked behind the bar there too and alcohol would be periodically supplied throughout the evening. I got into some film extra work too, appearing in such gems as *Soldier, Soldier* and *The Unknown Soldier* and a few band videos, one of with was a mass hysteria scene at the Brixton Academy featuring Scritti Politti...Oh the things one does for fifteen quid.

I then found a job as a cashier at William Hill the bookies, I'd always liked a flutter, and here was a chance of ear wigging some advance betting tips from the various managers in the shops. Sadly nothing substantial in the way of winnings ever really materialized during my brief employment in the world of betting. The fact remains that betting is a mugs game unless you can afford to lose or have the ready cash to take the bigger risk. I did have my share of winners though, but working in the bookies is not much fun when you see desperate men putting next month's mortgage or rent on a horse, and subsequently watching it disappear in the already full till in three minutes flat.

All these so called 'jobs' were just extra cash to keep that musical dream alive, and living it was our dream. My playing was reaching a higher standard, although I basically knew I'd never be a really technical player, as I'd not been trained from a young age. In view of this, I went with the fast, tribal and busy drumming style that suited my realm of noise creation. I also wanted to be in a dub reggae or ska type band, as it was the music that attracted me a lot in the eighties, but I settled for more realistic aspirations in a south east London Crustafarian type band instead, and grew a set of dreadlocks on top the of my head in the popular 'pineapple style' of the period.

29 – The Rat Trap

Along with the lousy living conditions and hygiene considerations we had to put up with in Villa Road, it was discovered that there was an even dirtier squatter in our midst. Some of us were slumbering in front of the telly one evening in the basement kitchen when the sound of scuffling could be heard among the plates balanced in the rack next to the sink.

Dean lent back silently in his rickety chair and whispered the word 'Rat' back at us with a big smile on his face. We all stood up and charged towards the sink as the big brown scavenger made his rapid exit through one of the many holes in our grubby basement.

We announced our new resident to the rest of the household and it was jointly decided that a suitable trap would be purchased, which in due course should hopefully take care of the dirty rat. The mass produced deadly wooden device was bought from the local hardware store, carefully set with a tempting piece of bacon and cheese and left under a loose floorboard beneath the kitchen table.

We then waited expectantly for that sickening sound of a whack! Unfortunately, the instantaneous execution of said rodent wasn't as immediate as we'd hoped, so we'd periodically re-set the trap and move it to other dark locations in the kitchen. We experimented with a number of different delightful dishes (including chocolate) which were skewered upon the vicious spike, usually by Dean, who was good at that sort of stuff; but still our sewer dwelling guest evaded the goodies on offer.

One morning, Ian came down for breakfast before going to work to find our rat leaning halfway into a large pan of his homemade winter vegetable soup and thoroughly enjoying a free spicy meal. Once again Mr Rat made good his escape and Ian, then pushed for time, made his way to work. When he came home for lunch four hours later he walked into the kitchen to find me (who'd just got up) watching the one o'clock news and getting stuck into his delicious culinary delight...

It was a number of years before he told me that I'd shared his veggie soup with mister ratty that morning as well, to which of course in hindsight was taken in good humour as I'd not turned purple, come out in unsightly boils and then died horribly of the Black Death two days later.

However, Mr Rat was still among us, though time would eventually turn against our dirty basement tenant. One morning soon after the soup incident, the trap was found to have mysteriously sprung. There was a blood deposit left behind and the tasty snack was absent. This meant that ratty had suffered an injury but had made off with the free meal all the same. We duly set the trap once more with another enticing treat and awaited rat's return.

The very next morning when I came down to the kitchen, Paul had left us all a present hanging up and in easy view upon entering the room. Mr Rat was no more, this time his luck had run out as he was now pinned across the neck by the steely spring, stone-cold-brown-bread.

It was obvious that it was the same rodent as the previous day as the now stiff corpses' nose was bloodied and obviously crushed by the very recent near miss. The trap was immediately thrown away, with attachment still hanging on by its now broken neck. Rodents never return to a trap that has been previously and successfully used as rats and mice seem know something that we don't, and therefore you cannot catch two separate rodents in the same trap.

We had another incident with a big grey rat a month later, when Dean, Paul and I cornered an unfortunate stray in the upstairs kitchen one Sunday morning. He managed to dodge Dean's wild swings with the pool cue, and also the determined swipes from Paul armed with a hard broom as it bounced on the floor missing ratty by inches with each swipe.

But I had a firm grip on a handy piece of two by four about three feet long, which proved his downfall. Ratty was duly clubbed to death and without a great deal of mercy.

Apparently, even though you're never more than twenty feet from a rodent anywhere in London, the word must've got around in 'Rat World' after the brutal slaying of that particular snack seeker, as it appeared that no more vermin ventured into our house again.

30 – Medical Curiosities

During this era of non stop partying at our London Town House, we all needed an income of some sort or another to pay for our regular needs and general luxuries such as food, cigarettes, alcohol and spliff.

None of us were actually earning anything from our musical careers (as is usually the way of the artist in the 'early years') we had to fund our lifestyles through various meaningless, menial and mostly temporary employment. This strategy included one of our number who worked as a cashier at a well known high street bank in Brixton. He'd often come home at lunchtime for a few games of pool, a sandwich all topped off with a couple of bongs, before he returned to his cubicle and somehow managed to serve the monetary needs of the many and varied Brixton public while smashed out of his afternoon head.

We all worked at The Marquee Club on Charing Cross Road in one guise or another during these times, either behind the bar, the back door security, the cloakroom or with the heavy mob on the front door, this usually being Donkey Paul's particular gig, as he was tattooed, from the north and tough.

The worst possible work scenario at the venue was 'side door supervisor, Sunday evening' which involved manning the emergency exit inside the venue on that night, as was often my part time job. Live performances were often a schedule of soft rock, tedious metal or yawn inducing prog rock type bands from the dinosaur period.

At least for myself, this was a long shift which involved standing by this emergency exit and forced to endure the scream of twiddly chord progressions while observing complete wankers watching total dickheads, dressed in the standard 'rock gear' uniforms. Many of these bands it seemed had travelled down from some non descript town in the industrial midlands to gig at one of London's premier venues. They busied themselves in front of a brain-dead audience as hammer cords were the order of the evening, accompanied by 'comical' ad-libbing between songs in false American accents. More often it was a long night's work standing through three or four of those performances.

Despite being grateful for employment at a world famous club, I'd arrive hoping for a half decent band on the bill to ease the whining, painful drivel of hammer chords, or saving that, at least an evening rubbernecking decent looking women, who'd often be impressed by the mere fact that you actually worked in a famous London live rock venue.

Sunday evenings aside, there were some really good nights after hours up in the green room, always a good mix of exciting and creative people to chill out with. Eventually, The Marquee Club woke up from their prog rock coma as the Acid House/Rave scene ushered in a new breed of clubber at the start of the 1990's. Hence The Marquee soon became a hot venue on Saturday nights and started to pull in the crazy ecstasy generation through the doors for long nights of wide eyed dance madness.

This was the 'happy time' for punters and staff as those wild nights continued on until the really small hours; as everyone got immersed into the rave generation as it happened before our eyes. There were plenty of new people turning up at the club and often ending up in Villa Road too, either sleeping on the ever-available pool table, or somewhere else in the house.

Jim and Marlene were quite well established at The Marquee and Camden Palace by now, we were always getting freebies and guest lists for Gossips and The Limelight too. It was a time when we really didn't stay in that often which was a welcome break needed from the chaos that was 'our home'. Besides that, it was still hard work just living in a place like that, one wanted to go to the pub to get away from dust, bad plumbing, bollock bowls and the risk of being killed via the aerial threat of falling Victorian masonry at any given moment.

There came a time when Ian and I were completely skint, and after hearing about these 'Drug Research Clinical Trials' we decided that it'll be a good idea to put our healthy bodies forward in the advancement of medical science, as advertised in *The Evening Standard*. We made an appointment for a general medical at a clinic in Farringdon, to which of course we both passed with honours, and were booked in for the following week to start 'the trial' with duration of six weeks in total.

This particular 'Research Study' involved orally taking both an anti depressant and a blood-thinning agent simultaneously. This was a new treatment aimed at those suffering from various forms of mental illness and/or Schizophrenia. Therefore an ideally suited drug cocktail to be administered to anxious, heavy drinking, unemployed, hash smoking, twenty-something, musician squatters then? It really did sound like a barrel of fun for the 450 quid promised in appreciation of 'our cooperation'. This programme required us to make our way to the clinic every couple of days or so to give a blood sample and to collect more blue or white pills. We were also to attend an overnight stay at the clinic as part the 'Advancement of Medical Science' while our young bodies were given away in lieu of monies as contractually agreed.

The worst news for us to digest was that we were forbidden alcohol and recreational drug use for an incredibly long period of six weeks. This was a tall order to ask of us we thought, but Ian wanted to give drinking a rest, and I could always handle life without alcohol anyway, but being denied a spliff for weeks on end would indeed be a serious 'drug test' in itself for us both.

Ian and I kept up the sterling work and jointly avoided such temptations for what seemed like forever. We were managing without the booze okay, but it was painful watching all that excellent spliff floating about under our noses day after day. This nice little earner was going to be a much harder discipline than we'd anticipated.

The drugs we were given to take on a twice daily basis did induce some rather weird side effects, at least for me they seemed to. Whereas Ian's constitution appeared to be up to the challenge; I was soon having some quite trippy, frightening nightmares accompanied by uncomfortable sleeping patterns. Various side effects were mentioned and described by a number of other pitiful 'subjects' who'd also signed up for the research trail on grounds of poverty verses scientific advancement.

We were booked in on the third week to spend one night in the clinic with the other desperados as part of the process. The administrator handed over a membership card for the local video rental shop, to which we were expressively told not to rent The Texas Chainsaw Massacre on account of the continuous screaming and the fact that the staff had seen it a hundred times already.

This overnight stay involved having a tap (also known as a cannula) 'fitted' on your arm for easy blood sampling on the hour or 'as required'. Scarily, this attachment also meant that one could be periodically drained while sleeping if the doctor on duty managed to extract your life force without the need to wake the 'subjects' up.

We, the guinea pigs, ordered a take away from the menu provided, played some board games among ourselves and looked forward to watching gore movies (bar the one already mentioned) one after the other for the rest of the evening.

All the above included the added bonus of knowing we'd have to angle a shit into a small plastic pot the next morning, and then hand it through a cupboard door to a gloved scientist person to poke about with for 'examination' purposes.

'Ahhh, the things we do for money,' I mused to myself in the white tiled clinical toilet as a pushed a thankfully dry one out into said beaker after breakfast the next morning.

On the last week of the trial we went along to Camden Palace to see a friend's band play… surely, just one beer can't hurt can it? I let more than a few slip down, followed by lashings of vodka and white wine backstage afterwards, and then I knew I was really in trouble. I was completely legless by the time we got the night bus home having consumed a greedy amount to make up for the puritan living over the past few weeks. Ian and I were of course taking these pills everyday as instructed and I'd also been getting some funny sensations in my legs and felt somewhat uncomfortable and buzzy all the time, much like the sensations one feels when you're on the tail end of an amphetamine come down. Not a pleasant feeling and I wanted this to be over soon.

But that next morning after all the excesses in Camden, I really felt like hell, and was completely all over the shop, I was semi conscious and unsurprisingly extremely hung over as we readied ourselves to give up yet another blood sample in the city. By now our arms were full of holes from the regular extractions and we both looked like a couple of junkies when we rolled our sleeves up.

I certainly wasn't feeling up for more painful and badly administered bloodletting from the doctor on duty, with the usual phase…

'Just a little prick, coming your way, now'

The doctors did often say that I had very good veins for drawing 'samples' out of, but it didn't make the process any less painful first thing in the morning, after a night definitely not on the wagon.

I had a truly terrible day that day, well fucked up and travelling to the city in rush hour with the mother of hangovers. The doctors had warned us not to drink as these drugs currently in final 'human trials' were going to be prescribed for those suffering from schizophrenia. Obviously these pills didn't agree with lager, wine, vodka or my particular personality. I lied about the heavy drinking the previous night and decided it was best that they didn't know that we'd been smoking hash through a homemade bong bucket during the 'week off' either.

Hopefully, by the time our alcohol and hash soaked blood samples came back from the lab our money would already be banked. Never again would either of us be prepared to put ourselves through that much misery just for four hundred and fifty quid.

A short time later Ian and I received our cheques and appreciation note for our part in the 'Advancement of Mental Illness Science', to which we immediately spent on bills, clothes, food, lager, vodka and a massive lump of spliff…

Still, one hopes that the desperate financial situation which drove us to briefly become 'O Lucky Men' has much helped to keep the corridors of institutions such as Broadmoor nice and quiet ever since.

31 – Wot's That Smell?

One afternoon, during the hot summer of '88, Ian, Billy and I were happily rehearsing in our cool basement studio at the house when we were suddenly overwhelmed by a wafting smell of shit; that rough aroma immediately introduced the suspicion in us that a sewerage drain must be blocked somewhere nearby.

Upon investigation, it turned out of course to be our very own outlet drain. After I gingerly lifted the steel cover at arm's length with a lever what met us (apart from the awful stink) was a four feet deep main outlet in the back yard overflowing with pink toilet paper, rice, shit, sanitary towels, yet more soupy, runny shit and all topped off with the occasional floating condom.

Ian gasped momentarily for air and duly ran to the nearest telephone kiosk and immediately alerted Dyno Rod of our dilemma, who's even more rapid response was, 'We don't unblock drains mate, we only jet them through after 'it' was 'removed" or words to that effect.

This meant that collectively, we were now thigh deep in our own mess and seeking 'options' on how to 'remove it'.

It looked as though we were up shit creek without a hose and may even have to move, again, as none of the house members knew the first thing about sewerage bar the fact that once the toilet was flushed it had nothing to do with us anymore. After a brief house discussion, it was unanimously decided we had no alternative but to dig a big pit in the back garden and bury bucket loads of our own shit in said hole.

Twenty minutes later, as our shit-pit deepened we realised just how much of it needed shifting from one place to another. While Jim and I were busy digging the hole the rest of the poo gang were changing into clothes that needed burning anyway, and procuring various bucket like utensils to get on with the filthy task in hand.

Then it was hankies over the face and really down to it, Dean, Ian and Marlene took turns with the bailing, initially employing an old aluminium saucepan (formerly known as 'The Bollock Bowl') into a plastic dustbin, which in turn was dragged across the lawn to the now Jurassic sized pit and sloppily teemed in whilst Jim and I temporarily leant upon our digging implements, laughing and gagging.

An old silver tea urn that had been hanging about and unused was then excellently employed to the business of shit collecting. This meant that one could get a really big, sloshing 'full load' with each bail, therefore making the job quicker, which in turn would make it go away as soon as possible. Dean really got into to the filthy task, he soon became director of shit bailing down on his hands and knees with his one arm reaching ever further into the stinking hell as the level gradually dropped.

In due course our neighbours were probably getting an idea of what was going on in number 29's back garden. Maybe it was the smell? Or perhaps the laughing and scooping sounds had drawn them to observe us from safe distances over their garden walls and pass the occasional comment such as: 'Ohh shiiiiitttt'or 'My, that's a shitload to shift huh?' Or 'Do you guys need to borrow a shiny shovel?'

The Poo Crew took it all in the right spirit and returned with a couple of our own such as:

'You can laugh now, but it'll be your turn to bail shit next week when your sewer blocks up!'

The friendly banter aside they were offering plenty of moral support, but obviously not going as far as to volunteer themselves for a turn on the saucepan or better still, the tea urn. Most of our neighbours were forced to make sometimes costly repairs on various structural problems at some point on their own houses too so they knew the score. As we didn't own our houses and no landlord was going to come over and sort it all out for us, this was our problem and we had to deal with it.

This was another one of those everyday events proving that 'life is full of shit'. By the time we'd prodded it through, buried a ton of (our own) human effluent and eventually had clean water running freely along the drain the unpleasant task was over, but it had taken all afternoon. Thankfully and gratefully we were all offered bathing facilities in one neighbour's house or another after 'the shitty job' had finally reached completion.

At this point we all yearned for a long, hot wash to conclude a smelly afternoon of shit filled madness. As our giant kettle type water boiler was the single facility available for washing and took hours to boil, which meant that only one person could bathe at number 29 that day, while the rest of us went elsewhere in the street, courtesy of that communal spirit.

A small earth hillock slightly higher than the rest of the garden remained for years to remind us of that particular afternoon. To this day buried deep in the middle of that pit are a black plastic handled aluminium saucepan and a medium sized tea urn, minus the lid.

In hundreds of years from now, what might future archaeologists dressed in their combat shorts armed with small trowels and brushes make of those two metal artefacts as they slowly retrieve 'A slice of 20th Century Civilization' from the earth? Then enthusiastically discuss just how they ended up being buried together under a canopy over lunchtime sandwiches and tea…

Or maybe one of them will take the bollock bowl home and impress their dinner guests by reusing a historic cooking utensil to serve up a delightful meal made 'the old way'.

32 – The Ghosts of Brixton

Speaking of pasts unknown, there should be a mention of our various 'resident ghosts', as no Victorian townhouse should be without one, or two. During our residency at number 29 some very peculiar and odd things occurred, usually (and traditionally) in the dead of night.

On a number of occasions people's personal possessions randomly disappeared only to turn up later in someone else's room. This usually happened to the women for some reason, and we were sure that it was due to at least one spirit perhaps being a bit on the mischievous side as opposed to the downright macabre.
    Stan and his girlfriend lay in bed one dark night listening to a full blown party going on throughout the house for what seemed like hours. On finally getting the bottle up to open their door all the sound dissipated and they were left listening to an echoing 'post party' silence. Ian woke up one night to see a middle aged woman standing at the end of his bed, which must've been a wee bit scary.

It was Dean who by luck appeared to be the 'sensitive' one and seemed to regularly attract our resident spirits. Maybe they could enter into his sixth sense though he was the late sleeper and usually patrolled the place late at night on his own. He told us of one particular night when he was in the basement re-assembling a motorbike gearbox, when he suddenly felt the urge to look through the open door that leads into the rehearsal room and watched 'The Victorian Butler' flit past in one swift motion and silently enter that room, through the closed door for added spookiness.

That incident must've made the hair stand up on the back of his neck; I know mine did when he relayed the creepy tale to me later the next evening as we tinkered with the gearbox in the very same room. He mentioned that 'The Butler' was attired in the height of 'Victorian Service' fashion and he was seemingly the most frequent spectre at number 29.

Although I am a believer in such things, I rarely had any opportunity to take in a sighting, and consequently never did. I know I felt a 'presence' every now and then, but whoever these spirits were, they usually left me alone. Only on one occasion when the building work was going on in the house via the housing association did I seriously get the fear. This was when we had all moved out for a couple of months during the refit work and I needed somewhere to stay for a night, so I choose number 29 that night for convenience.

It was a dark and very quiet house as nobody else was home; it creaked and groaned like old houses do when they're readjusting themselves after the exit of people. But because the building was currently a work site with piles of rubble everywhere, the only place for me to sleep that night was in that windowless rehearsal room in the basement, the room our 'Butler' regularly haunted...

It was pitch black and dead silent when I switched the light off and ran the three paces to my cold sleeping bag. As I lay there in the extreme quiet and darkness I started to get a little nervous, I had the feeling that someone else was in the room with me, standing there and watching, along with a sense of anger towards my being there. I felt that any minute now I'd hear something move, or worse still, something muttered in 'Olde Englishe' from a corner of that silent, pitch black basement room.

After a mere ten minutes of sheer, paranoid terror, I jumped up and ran for the light switch, even afraid that once I flooded the room with artificial light I'd have to turn around and face 'The Butler' angry at the presence of a squatter from a forward century. Thank god or whomever that nobody was standing right behind me, wearing a stiff collar and a sterner glare to mess my head up for a lifetime.

I was out of that house in seconds flat and proceeded to wake up our next door neighbours briefly explaining my ghoulish dilemma on their doorstep, which was viewed with immediate sympathy, as they also had their 'very own ghost too'. I slept peacefully and without interruption on their comfy couch for the remainder of that night.

When Dean moved up to the attic after Stan had moved out, he woke up one night to watch a white spectre buzzing around the room. On another occasion he noticed weird handprints all over the ceiling, after a frosty night. Maybe it was the ten cans of Stella and seven spliffs before bed? Or perhaps not?

We never did find out who (or what) placed someone's jewellery in another room, we counted out human interference as we all knew that none of us were the sorts to rifle through each other's belongings the moment everyone left the house.

We hear stories of houses that seem to hang on to the past a bit; Villa Road was a mid Victorian terraced street built in the 1880s, and similar in design to many of the period.

These houses were mostly occupied by the well-heeled middle classes of the day; those who could afford to employ a few servants who'd work in the basement below and sometimes reside in attic quarters up top.

These were the areas of our house where the majority of these haunting incidents took place. 'The Butler' it seemed, was a somewhat angry spectre and perhaps rather put out or inconvenienced by all the disruption, therefore probably not keen on the presence of a bunch of 20th century squatters busily redecorating his once proud home.

33 – White Lightning Weekend

One very hot weekend in June '88, Ian, Al (our friend from Essex who'd provided the scabies riddled mattress) and I decided to take a trip in my faithful Dodge Comer van to the Milton Keynes Bowl to a festival organised by Amnesty International. With a decent schedule of bands and good weather predicted, it all sounded ideal for sitting in a field in the sunshine and getting smashed.

We drove all morning, the three of us side by side in my faithful truck eventually entering the bland interior roads of Milton Keynes before being confronted by an endless series of roundabouts, total directional confusion and bad signposting. We kept passing the same hippy and punk mobiles over and over again at these almost identical crossings surrounded by fields occupied by the local bovine population, as we roasted in the cab atop of the centrally positioned engine.

    Eventually, we found what was termed a 'campsite', paid our fee in and parked. As usual the pre-festival preparations were poorly thought out; we'd just thrown a few blankets and sleeping bags in the carpeted rear cab before we left and therefore no need for a tent. Besides that it was going to be a very warm weekend and who wants to erect a simple tent after consuming a keg of beer, ten spliffs and a dose of mind altering hallucinogens only hours before? In view of the previous Glastonbury experience, the back of my van was a good alternative and there was plenty of space for the three of us.

We took the short, crowded bus ride to the MK bowl, along with other and various assorted music lovers, this to initially recce our ability to bunk in. Despite the fact that this festival was organised for a good cause, we were seasoned blaggers and it was second nature for us to climb fences and make the dash to the safety of the throng before being accosted by random (and usually drunk) stewards. That was part of the fun, to test one's wits against the odds of being caught or embarrassingly rejected from an event by a person holding 'the guest list' on which your name wasn't present. I'll make a donation to the wonderful Amnesty International one day to pay off my Karmic debt.

Having successfully charged laughing through the dense undergrowth (along with an assortment of other non payers) we stood at the top of the bowl looking down on thousands of revellers sitting out in the afternoon sunshine.

We found a spot to sit down and proceeded to do what we always do at an open air gig; skin up, drink warm lager, and get gradually hammered from then on in.

Within no time, various hippies and cold box sales people were offering us the usual selection bags of grass, beer, mushrooms and the old favourite, acid. We took the unanimous decision to buy three White Lightning blotters from one of these hawkers, this was in the days when acid came in either microdot or blotter form. The blotters would be named during production, and likewise be illustrated with a tiny picture of that particular batch; for instance there were the Superman trips with our leotard wearing hero standing erect with cloak flowing behind and right arm raised afore. Then there were the ever popular 'smiley' trips, which were still doing the rounds in the wake of the acid house generation. Our purchases had a lightning streak zigzagging design across the tiny card. We'd take half each for now, and see how we got on…

Meanwhile, the bands entered the stage, played their bit and exited to generous applauses. Joe Strummer got up to do a set and asked if anyone else had driven there too? Stating that he'd got completely lost in the ludicrous 'new town' roundabout system as well. He then launched into a lively set which of course included some popular Clash numbers.

There were a few side show bands playing around the site, the usual hippy stalls selling hippy stuff, and a large red and white striped marquee situated on the other side of the site.

We waited patiently for our microdots to come up; nothing had happened for a good half an hour, we were beginning to think that perhaps we'd been ripped off?

We spent several more anxious minutes and discussed the possibility of hunting the man down (in a field of thousands) to get our money back, despite the fact that we'd never recognise him again anyway. It was around about then that Ian decided to take his other half as the first 'wasn't working'.

About eight to ten minutes after that when we began to feel the effects of the half trip coming up…

Shortly after, we started to feel that this acid was pretty damn strong as all around began to echo, warp, blur and shimmer in the sunshine.

Al and I thought it best not to have the other half, while Ian had already done his and would soon be suffering from the horrible consequences of his premature actions.

Within an hour we were out there with the fairies, pissing ourselves laughing, in between the gagging and drinking, as the bands played on in the backgrounds of our now twisted, trippy and addled minds.

Al went off for a walk as Ian awaited the 'second half' to kick-in, I was just about coping with the dose I'd taken, and there was no way I'll be swallowing the rest today. I was already seeing butterflies in the sky and the rhythmic crack of a distant, amplified snare drum was ec–ec–echoing past my inner ear anvils.

Eventually, our curiosity got the better of us, so Ian and I decided to visit that large stripy marquee just to see what was going on in there, like a couple of curious kids on a fucking cake walk.

As we entered the coolness of this colourful and sparsely populated marquee, we were immediately struck by the music emanating from the stage which appeared to be about half a mile away in 'real distance' through our tripped out tunnel-vision eyeballs. We stumbled along the walkway and decided to take a couple of seats near the back of mister large, circus like marquee to take in the show before our wondering eyeballs.

We sat down hard on the flimsy deckchairs, Ian handed me an appallingly rolled spliff as we turned in unison to watch the band on a stage far, far away.

We leant back in our cheap seating to absorb the sounds of said band up on the stage, Ian and I (being musical types) were always interested in listening to different bands and musical genres.

I soon observed that the stage was occupied by around twenty assorted musicians, all busily playing their various instruments at the same time, in what looked (and sounded) like a crescendo of fucked up, mixed tunes in the worst form of music torture ever created; Jazz improvisation. I gazed partly in awe and the rest horror, from one manic muso to another as this mess of tuneless drivel began to ratchet into my brain and seriously affect my already tripped out mind.

At that moment I turned to the left to gauge Ian's opinions on this particular musical nightmare before us, but couldn't immediately see him; but as a checked again I found him leaning far back on the last rung of his stripy deckchair laughing his equally minced out brain off!

That started me off too, as we rocked in our wobbly seats at every jazzy twing and twang going on all around us.

The horrifying, tripped out cacophony of sound was resonating from every corner of the cheap marquee and ringing uncontrollably in our rattled brains. As the assorted musos played on, and fucking on we curled up in hysterics until we had an overwhelming urge to leave this hell immediately and return to sanity if we were not to suffer permanent and irreparable musical damage.

We stumbled towards the exit of the large tent holding our aching chests now painful through laughter, as we at last made it through the floppy-flappy door and back into 'the real world'.

Should 'The Happy in the Head Orchestra' or whatever the fuck they call themselves happen to be playing a gig in your area, be sure to take a really strong dose of hallucinogens and reserve a seat near the door for a quick exit.

Meanwhile, as the two of us staggered clear of the musical abyss now receding behind us in another time, the bright afternoon sunlight hit us (as did the full effect of the second half of Ian's trip) and we suddenly had an overwhelming desire to treat ourselves to an ice cream. This was considered a just reward from the near fatal overdose of jazz head fuck only moments before. Ian stepped up to the Mr Toni ice cream van and managed to order two 99 cones from the grinning proprietor; who'd probably seen us falling out of the large tent nearby crying in hysterics just moments before.

The large (still smiling) curly-haired-ice-cream-vendor-man then moved inside his wobbly truck to process our order, whilst the two of us tried to maintain some sort of dignity during the endless twelve second wait. He then turned abruptly and passed two 99 cones about the size of upturned traffic cones down the nine foot drop from serving window to Ian who was by now quivering with laughter. I however, was trying to look the other way as the tears streamed along my cheeks as the now receding sound of The Trippy in the Fuckhead Orchestra still rang on in my ears. The only comfort I could find at this moment was the knowledge that I'd only taken half of the strongest trip I'd ever bought, and was at this point seriously worried if we'd ever fully recover from that particular musical trauma.

We then tried in vain to consume these massive cones as they melted in the heat and dripped down our fingers. After what seemed like twenty minutes or more, we'd managed to finish what we could eat and were consequently covered in sticky white ice cream.

This period in time was back in the days before mobile phones, meaning we had to traverse the site to find Al, rather than simply ringing or texting him to arrange suitable a meeting point; but preferably not in *that* marquee.

We found each other quite quickly and settled down in the sun to try and bring some sense back into the day, with warm larger expensively bought from a bloke carrying a cold box on a speedy mission. Even Howard Jones's set sounded like the best gig we'd ever seen compared to what Ian and I had recently been put through, as we rolled a few spliffs and watched the big orange ball in the sky slip slowly in the west. It was the hottest day of 1988, and we had been suitably British, having left the sun block at home and were therefore roasted like oven ready chickens in an open field that boiling afternoon.

Then the announcements for the end of the day's festivities came over the PA as people started to move towards the exits and line up for the free bus ride back to the campsite.

After the short, swaying journey over many roundabouts in a stuffy, sweaty bus, we were delivered (along with an assortment of also sunburnt campers) to our weekend commune in the middle of middle England.

As the late afternoon slipped into a warm evening, small fires were lit by the better prepared and organised campers around us. In due course we sidled over to our festival compatriots next door to share their warm flickering fire, as the day's trip thankfully mellowed with each passing hour.

We bartered spliff in return for some of their food, which was duly accepted by our fireside campers, followed by the usual chit chat on the day's events, favourite bands and where we were all from.

After an hour or so some parka wearing individuals arrived at our laid back site to introduce themselves. We offered a spliff straight away and likewise our neighbours offered whatever wares they could spare, but all was rejected by these strange invaders, as they keenly moved around and among us.

We were just at the point of becoming slightly wary of these people, when Ian checked the back of one of their parka coats, and immediately arrived at the answer as to the intentions of these odd people. He beckoned to Al and I to check for ourselves as he grinned broadly. On passing inspection of the backs of these new visitors we saw large homemade stitched emblems stating that they were members of the 'Jesus Army' in that Californian 'over and under' Hell's Angel design.

This revelation brought on more sniggering laughter; especially from Al who had a deep suspicion of everything related to organised religion. All the previous confusion ebbed away by those among us with any common sense at all, as the 'God Squad' penny dropped. These oddities were then suitably ridiculed in a subtle way over a brief period until eventually they gave up on converting us to whatever they had in mind and duly slipped off to God bother some other campers.

The image we formed in our spit roasted heads as we drove back to the sanity of London the following day, was that the acid is well strong, there are way too many roundabouts, head fucking jazz bands, not enough firewood to hand and some really weird religious cults based in Milton Keynes.

34 – Squatting, Dutch Style

In December 1989 a few friends and I decided to 'do Amsterdam' for the New Year. We'd heard that it was a gas over the seasonal period of joy, so four of us which included two women (one of which was heavily pregnant) and I made plans to set the city of sin alight with our raunchy presence during the drinking festival.

The ladies and Paul all took the sickly ferry to the Hook of Holland, whilst I planned to arrive in style by air, as to date I'd still not flown high up there in the little fluffy clouds. Flights to Europe were priced at an all time low at that time, so I booked myself on a jet plane to Schiphol Airport on New Year's Eve, and on being asked at the check in counter I requested a scary window seat view behind the engine, overlooking the wobbly wings. If I was going to fly I may as well be able to look out of a porthole at toy town far below as we rose frighteningly ever higher.

The strange thing about flying for the first time is when you are taxiing on the runway. You sit strapped into an aluminium tube weighing 300 tons and are almost convinced that even though you've seen aeroplanes take off a million times before, there's no way on earth something this big and heavy can possibly get off the ground. That is until the damn thing hits about 200 mph and the pointy bit at the front lifts up, as does your stomach. But being an adventurous type who was first time flying, on New Year's Eve, I knew the time was right to enter the world of 20th century travel. Even if this meant being crammed into a pressurized cabin, breathing everyone else's air, with the possibility of being involved in an un-survivable catastrophe should anything mechanical go wrong while travelling at 500 mph, a mile up, over water.

In fact, the morning I came down with my bags packed ready to leave, Jim and Stan had been watching a news montage on my crappy telly of the unusually high number of tragic air accidents around the world during 1989.

Jim was just reaching for the channel button as I walked into the front room, so I only got to watch one Boeing 747 exploding on impact in a giant fireball, a couple of miles from its final destination. All references to air safety in the modern era were suppressed immediately as Stan passed me a spliff, and Jim handed over a fresh coffee.

I couldn't give a shit anyway; I was going to get on that plane even if it was painted black, flight numbered 13 and was leaving on a Friday night, in a blizzard.

Of course the plane was up and down in fifty minutes, hardly enough time to 'enjoy it'. I then jumped on a train and enjoyed the short ride to Amsterdam Central Station.

We'd arranged to meet in 'Future' a well known coffee shop cartel sporting a bright pink florescent marijuana logo and just a click away from the station. We'd all been to the city before and knew where that particular smokin' establishment was located.

First thing to do was grab a coffee and 'the spliff menu' and get the weekend underway. But within no time I was informed that all the hotels; grotty or otherwise, were fully booked up for the forthcoming mayhem yet to come, and that sadly the Floatels were no more around the Port of Amsterdam. My travelling companions had been wise enough to organise their digs in advance, I however hadn't bothered; it simply didn't cross my mind that a good deal of the population of Europe like to celebrate the New Year in that fair city as well…

The looming possibility of living like a hotel-less hobo for the weekend was soon forgotten as I stored my bag in the station lock-up, thus leaving both arms free to hold both beer and a spliff at the same time.

The four of us hooked up with a few other revellers from London at The Bulldog Bar, and then did the rounds along the sleazy bars adjoining Amsterdam's canals, as we geared up for the midnight hour.

When the last few minutes of the soon ending decade approached the midnight hour, the streets were jammed with people; all were seemingly waiting for something spectacular to happen. Suddenly as if on cue, we could hear in the distance a sound that at first resembled the rat-a-tat-tat of machine gun fire. We stood motionless for a second before we were pulled along with the crowd as everybody started to run towards the loud crack-cracking.

As we neared the increasing noise, we realised that it was in fact the sound of firecrackers which were loud and of course Chinese made. The big Chinese community in Amsterdam were out pining large Catherine wheels onto their restaurant doors and duly entertaining the baying throng of pissed-up stone heads with the delights of their ancient, noisy invention.

Just as the firecracker exploded off its last loud bang, another one would start up somewhere around the corner, thus the chase was on again to find its source. This went on for about half an hour, as we chased through the streets and canals following the sound of New Year, in a Chinese-Amsterdam style.

We ended the night gate-crashing a party somewhere south of the city until the early hours, when thoughts of sleeping arrangements (at least for me) began to slip into our minds. It was deemed that I wouldn't be able to 'ease past' reception at the small hotel my friends were already booked into, therefore the search for my 'evening accommodation' began in earnest as we started to walk back into the centre of the city.

As the four of us staggered towards Leidseplein we came across a large domed shaped building sitting alone and in darkness. All around the immediate area of this odd looking building were the tell tale signs of dereliction, this being piles of bin liners, rubbish and the usual look of an unoccupied venue. We stumbled around the place and found an entrance which led into a cool looking large open plan hall, with stairs leading upwards in a few directions. It seemed that we were alone, so we climbed one of the rickety staircases up to the next level. After a good look around I announced that I was perfectly satisfied with bedding down in a vacant corner for the night, and they were free to go back to their warm hotel.

But my companions would have none of it, and being streetwise they all decided to stay with me for the night. This decision was partly out of a sense of camaraderie, and also because Amsterdam (at least in those days) was a decidedly dodgy place, continually occupied by passing rogue travellers and criminality. They obviously didn't want me to come to any harm, so we all roughed down on cardboard boxes (including pregnant Jane) and fell asleep within no time. We were disturbed briefly during the night when a couple of party people came upon us while also scouting for shelter. They apologised jointly as we stirred and soon found another corner in that odd building to fall down in.

The next day was spent recovering in The Bulldog and an assortment of other bars in the centre of the city, culminating in a visit to the flea market (which was closed) in the 'dog shit borough' and the Rembrandt Museum, situated in his house. But sadly, unless etchings are your thing, the whole tour was over in minutes and altogether rather boring. We should've visited the infamous Sex Museum, as that feast for the eye was probably more up our street, artistically speaking.

I slept alone at the hippy squat in Leidseplein the next night, as there still weren't any hotel rooms available in central Amsterdam. The others had a good night's kip before getting the boat back to England. We met up for a coffee before they left; and as I'd booked a charter flight returning after a week this meant that I'd be staying 'somewhere else' for another five days.

But I did have the phone number of a Dutch friend, Gus, who'd squatted in Brixton and was a regular at Villa Road; he was now living in Utrecht which is only twenty kilometres from Amsterdam.

I rang him and he offered to put me up at his squat and show me around Utrecht for a few days, which in view of my other accommodation alternatives, I accepted straight away.

Holland, like its neighbour Germany, is also a great country for the hitch hiker; I made my way to the road heading in that direction and was picked up very quickly and given a ride all the way to the Utrecht station. I rang Gus and within five minutes he turned up on a typical old black and well used Dutch bicycle. I climbed on the back with my pack over my shoulder and we wobbled our way to a quite respectable street nearby.

I was then introduced to the squat life, Dutch style. Gus lived with four other people, two guys and two girls in a relatively spacious town house. This dwelling was in excellent condition throughout, well maintained and decorated with all the utilities working properly and a big kitchen used by all. Their place was of a much higher standard than the trashed house I'd been living in for a couple of years now. There was also a good deal of organisation to this house and its occupants, everyone took turns to cook, do the recycling (unheard of in Britain at that time) general house maintenance and cleaning.

It was a relaxed and friendly atmosphere, almost middle class and very homely. Each person had their own room; Gus's place was comfortable and like everyone else's decorated with style to suit each individual's character. It was a bit of a revelation as I was shown around from room to room, duly impressed with the way these Dutch squatters lived, although they did have a better house to start with than the pigeon filled, roofless shit hole we'd moved into in Brixton, to which Gus had visited and was well aware of.

There were different laws regarding 'squatters rights' in the Netherlands at that time; Legal Notices were not pasted up near the front door, and it was in effect quite difficult to evict squatters from occupied houses. Gus told me that the only way to evict people from properties would be if the authorities could acquire your name in relation to the address you were living at. The simple solution to this problem was to never have any letters delivered to your squat. Therefore, all self respecting squatters used Poste Restante to collect their mail, problem solved, and they paid their utility bills directly to the suppliers. Gus pointed out that if I were to write to him at any time I was to use this method. This, by all accounts was quite a liberal, civilized system really, and so typically Dutch.

I spent four days with Gus and his friends, visiting local bars and hanging around the small town. We borrowed a couple of bikes and went out for a ride one day to look at the windmill filled local countryside too. Though it did take a while to get used to their cycles, as one has to pedal backwards to brake. This odd mechanical stopping system led to a few close scrapes and a couple of 'nearly over the handlebars' moments, but one eventually gets used to it.

I took my turn to cook for everyone, and enjoyed their hospitality in Utrecht as well as this insight into the squat life in Holland. I bid my farewells to Gus and his friends after a few days and hitched back into Amsterdam in order to catch my flight back the next morning. I had, however, now nearly run out of money and was enduring a diet of chips and those awful 'What the fuck am I about to eat?' Gilder-a-time slot machines in the streets for my food. At the end of my last day in Amsterdam I made my way back to the odd squat in Leidseplein for one last uncomfortable night in the local public doss house.

This time I decided to aim higher and book into the 'Penthouse Suite' for added comfort and security. This trek involved climbing ever higher and leaping across ravines that had been formed by the collapse of old wooden stairwells in the dilapidated building. On arrival at the top floor, I found that most of the floor space was taken up with rubbish of all description as I stumbled around in the dark, tripping over old clothes and even older (used) porn magazines. The upper floors were in worse condition than the lower, as I crashed into a small annexe situated off a large room. My heart stopped momentarily as I heard a stirring from a dark corner of this room, as my eyes adjusted to the dim light I could make out a couple of blokes laying down next to each other in a tiny space they'd cleared out for sleeping purposes.

'Who's there?' I heard an English voice in the darkness

'It's alright guys, I'm just looking for a place to sleep' I answered honestly.

'You English, mate?' came a midlands accent in reply.

'Yeah, I'm from London, going back tomorrow,' I replied.

'Help yourself, mate, if you can find a spot that ain't covered in shit and spunk, and watch were you put your head' he advised.

'Thanks,' I said as I inspected the floor space with a lighter held up for guidance.

I kicked the assorted porn magazines and old jeans aside and got my head down for the night. Despite the zero star accommodation, I did get a good night's sleep and awoke next morning to find two bearded, greasy bikers fast asleep in 'their corner'.

As I walked back through Damrak towards the train station I jiggled the last three Gilders in my pocket and contemplated how best to spend them until my flight later that evening. There was no way I'd be actually paying for the short train ride to Schiphol Airport, I'd eat and smoke the remainder of my spliff supply during the long wait until check in.

I spent the bright, cold winter's day sitting and watching the Dutch world go by, until it was time to catch the train. When the ticket man appeared at the other end of the carriage, I slipped into the toilet cubicle and waited until his heavy footsteps receded, a bit like a scene in a spy movie I thought as I puffed away on a fat spliff in the miniature loo. I obviously needed to get rid of all my remaining pot before I got to the airport, and I still had a fair bit left. I left the remainder in an easy-to-find place by the toilet for an unsuspecting punter to enjoy on arrival.

I then spent hours waiting for my flight as I wandered the brightly lit halls of duty free heaven, looking at goods that I couldn't afford and didn't want anyway.

By the time I got on the plane in the early evening I was worn out, in need of a bath and very hungry.

The 'air meal' was consumed in seconds when it arrived, as we endured a bumpy and scary flight back to Heathrow. I managed to get through customs without incident; even though I was 'clean'. But one still feels guilty every time you walk briskly through the 'Nothing to Declare' channel and out the other side to the platform for the long trek back into town on the Piccadilly Line.

There were a few people still up when I arrived watching of all things live news coverage of a plane crash earlier that evening in over the M1 shortly after takeoff. The uncomfortable fact here was that I'd just flown back with that particular airline only hours before, and remembered how shaky and bumpy the flight was in the bad weather as I'd nervously viewed from my nearside window.

We were now in the 1990s, and the new, final decade of the tumultuous 20th century was about to get underway. Would it get better for us or just the same old rulers exerting the same old power?

One possible answer lay in a demonstration being planned by the British public who would duly deliver a stunning message of the real meaning of 'People Power' to our despised and apparently unshiftable Iron Lady...

35 – Maggie! Maggie! Maggie! Out! Out! Out!

At the start of the new decade political tension was running high in the UK. The government was now in the final planning stages and about to re-introduce a formerly medieval money collecting practice known as 'Poll Tax'.

This punitive tax was last levied on the British public in the year 1381, which soon culminated in two weeks of raging riots in central London bringing the capital to near siege status. The Arch Bishop of Canterbury was dragged from his supposed fortress in the Tower of London and executed in the street by the angry, unwashed mob. The army was called in, a truce was made and the fifteen year old King Richard agreed to meet the rabble on Blackheath Common. Apparently, after a quick discussion between the boy King and the pissed off peasantry the demonstrators were brutally horse crushed into the mud and their leader Watt Tyler subsequently lost his head for treason in the traditional and very public manner upon a raised platform, which ironically for him was erected just outside the Tower of London.

However, back in the 20th century, demonstrators were now getting organised and in some instances managed to invade live council meetings in numbers during the setting of Poll Tax rates by often reluctant councillors many of which were also against the concept of Poll Tax. This direct action was regularly being aired daily on the news channels, feelings were running high and it was causing massive disruption in council chambers up and down the towns, shires and cities of

England, Wales and Scotland.

The heat was being turned up by the week and a big demonstration was planned in Trafalgar Square on the last Saturday in March. Around half a million angry people who'd travelled from all areas of society and every corner of the country joined together in a common cause to march to Parliament on that fateful day. It appeared that the people of Britain were finally united on masse after eleven long years of Thatcher.

The cops were lining the route, dressed in the latest of riot gear fashion and seemingly ready to wield their bright new, ergonomically styled truncheons. But even they were surprised by the turnout and knew that our sheer numbers were going to make an awful lot of noise that sunny afternoon.

The march commenced at high noon from Kennington Park and made its slow way over Westminster Bridge and on towards Britain's best known town square, where various speakers from the political to the absurd were airing their views on this levy about to be forced upon the people. A large group of demonstrators staged a sit down in front of the newly fitted, high security glossy black gates that were recently erected on the entrance into Downing Street. This impromptu mini demo made the police nervous and ever more anxious to use their space age clubs. It seemed only a matter of time before the authorities lost control of the situation, and soon enough they made a big error of judgement by stampeding the crowd on horseback in an effort to drive people away and to supposedly keep the procession moving along towards its final destination.

But due to the fact that there were now so many people packed into Whitehall, most of us could not move in any direction apart from skywards as we scrambled up railings, lampposts and the historic monuments to the safety of higher ground and to avoid being horse crushed, medieval style. This action really got things going in a bad way as the disorganised mounted police were now crushing sections of demonstrators with our backs against unmoving stone walls.

Young children on a fun day out at the revolution were being trampled in their buggies as the cops surged and anxious mothers screamed at them to back off. Many in the crowd were middle aged people who were angered enough to make the trip to demonstrate against the Poll Tax. They had travelled to London in organised coach pensioner parties to air their grievances' peacefully against Thatcher's poorly thought out, dark ages style tax levy.

The behaviour of the mounted police seriously got the crowd buzzing, as the friendly, democratic, drum banging party atmosphere soon began to turn ugly. Objects started to fly through the air in the direction of the police and the always present hardcore element of demonstrators who wanted a fight anyway suddenly organised themselves in moments. Before long the shit hit the fan, as the missiles rained down heavier, the police who'd already shown that they couldn't cope with the numbers made the stupid decision to literally try to push the whole crowd out of Trafalgar Square and onto the various connecting routes that fed into this major west end hub.

This was indeed a poor error of judgement as they tried desperately to separate a huge crowd into lots of smaller, 'manageable' units. Thousands were pushed up Lower Regent Street, Northampton Street and Charing Cross Road, and as everyone knows that as soon as 'the running crowd' starts then that's it, the free-for-all riotous mob mentality commences unabated.

Within seconds total chaos reigned in the west end as the crashing sounds of large, plate glass windows could be heard going in all around. Cars were overturned pushed into the roads to act as barriers and set alight.

Having already been crushed against the railings and cold stone walls of Whitehall, then denied our democratic right to demonstrate, the mob now fought back, and fought back hard. Within half an hour it was a full scale running battle, the like of which had not seen in Britain for about six centuries. Many people were simply trying to get away at this stage but couldn't as the police wouldn't permit anyone to actually exit the chaos which in turn angered the crowd even further as elderly folks and kids were now mixed up in running battles and periodic police horse charges.

Soon enough, the usually genial demonstrators and your everyday law abiding man and woman in the street were fighting their own brutal afternoon battle just to actually get out of the area. Thereafter, we the mob, fought the police tooth and nail all day. It was a horrifying sight to witness, but majestic too; as each time the cops came forward wielding their batons and shields they met a considerable force and were repelled again and again, to the unified chanting of a hundreds of thousands of disaffected British voters: 'Maggie! Maggie! Maggie! Out! Out! Out! Maggie! Maggie! Maggie! Out! Out! Out!'

The revolution resonated noisily on under the lofty monument of Britain's' favourite nautical hero. Our Lord Horatio Nelson, Admiral of the Fleet (when Britain once ruled the waves) looked impassively down Whitehall as he has since his stunning victory at Trafalgar, while a modern day chaos of rioting continued on beneath his large, metallic grey, pigeon shit covered feet.

The Iron Bitch must've heard us all the way back at Chequers as she and the commissioner of the Metropolitan Police cowered in front of the live TV pictures now being broadcast around the planet. South Africa House, a symbol of the hated Apartheid soon went up in flames, and I saw with my own eyes police reinforcements streaming out of that building and hitting the demonstrators hard on the flank. Just how the fuck did they get in there we all asked? Are there secret underground tunnels connecting it directly from the corridors of Whitehall? This quick theory was momentarily put forward to the crowd by an observant bloke in the middle of the anarchy as he then turned and ran off in a different direction.

Extensive road works and building refits were under construction throughout the west end at that time, and consequently the whole of central London was one big building site. Construction creates a lot of waste and there were skips of it everywhere, these being full of bricks, rubble and weapon-sized wooden clubs in which to arm the revolutionaries on hand to even out the odds. One could hear the continuous sound of shouting, windows being smashed and thousands of feet running in one direction or another. The outnumbered police force were taking a bit of a beating but the truth is they had it coming, how could they send vehicles hurtling through crowds of people unable to see from which direction they were coming through the dense crowds and simply couldn't get out of the way in time?

The national television stations had set up shop from the usual vantage points as their cameras were turning and gathering endless footage of the carnage going on all around. I witnessed a lot of people having their cameras seized and smashed on the ground and this also included the assembled press photographers, who were being sort out for special attention by radicals or persons who'd rather not be photographed throwing an empty can of lager at a policeman balanced on a horse.

The whole lunatic charade dragged on all day and into the night, rumours that the army were close to being called into action were filtered around as law and order seemed to be breaking down everywhere. Despite the anger and violence being played out in the running battles and cavalry charges all day, it was a miracle that nobody had lost their life during the whole ugly and violent mess.

That fateful afternoon of the 31st March 1990 was the day the death bell finally tolled on Thatcherism. As the chaos commenced all around it was obvious that the worm had turned and the symbolic nails were at last being hammered down into her political coffin. The British people once again showed that they will stand together and fight with a bulldog spirit when the collective need arises. Our history is full of such demonstrations going back to the invasions of Romans, Vikings, French, Dutch, Spanish, occasionally the Scottish and our footballing best friends, the Germans.

Thatcher, supported by various members of her (soon-to-be de-selected) cabinet and accompanied by a few high ranking police officials appeared on the evening news channels, expressing outrage and disgust at the 'appalling antics' of the mob and the wanton destruction of the West End. Ministers offered stern promises to capture and prosecute the 'Anarchist and hooligan' protagonists of the riot having ordered the television stations to hand over their news footage of the mayhem directly to the law. However, the police were by all accounts rather humbled by the club wielding public kicking they'd just received care of 'we, the pissed off people'. However, our revenge would come in the weeks and months to follow.

The summer of 1990 was the summer of riots, another big one kicked off in Hyde Park after a demonstration over yet another putative new law that was rapidly white papered through Parliament regarding the 'disturbing sounds of repetitive beats' and those now infamous warehouse parties. The Public Order Act was a repressive one indeed as our panic stricken government (who still held a decent majority) pushed it through Parliament in a couple of months. This new law now allowed the police to arrest a small group of people who were gathered around a beatbox and listening to the dangerous new form 'rave music', and if anyone gave any them trouble, they could be read the riot act and then legally beaten to a pulp. Warehouse parties were now against the law and our fun was yet again diminished further in what was now becoming a worryingly oppressive 'New World Order' state.

But what was rather comical during this time is the fact that the police were often reduced to little more than car park attendants at most of these raves when thousands of revellers showed up at isolated locations where there were only a few cops on duty to police these regional towns and villages. They either had to stand by and await the arrival of heavy back up or wait for the ecstasy fuelled excess to end, this being usually sometime past dawn.

Yet throughout all that turmoil and anger felt by the people of Britain during the spring and summer of 1990, the England football team actually managed to make it to the semifinals of the World Cup being hosted in Italy that year. For a few weeks (at least in England) the beautiful game took centre stage until Germany reduced at least one Englishman to tears and then went onto take the golden trophy back to their newly reformed country.

However, back in the real world The Poll Tax Act was hurriedly renamed with a slightly less imposing tag; 'Council Tax' and duly passed into law.

Therefore, the revolution had failed, again.

36 – Secret Four

As the dust finally settled on the people's failed uprising and our once again missed footballing glory, I found a job as a cashier at William Hill the bookmakers. I'd always liked a flutter now and then and had learned a few useful tips about betting systems. But I also saw a lot of disappointed punters losing heavily on a regular basis, and got sick of it pretty quickly, as I do with most jobbie jobs.

I decided to quit this employment after a couple of months as it was just plain depressing, and collected my final wages from a branch in Vauxhall on a sunny Saturday afternoon in the autumn. I looked at what was inside the brown pay packet, and immediately knew that the meagre funds available weren't quite enough to take me on a trip somewhere warm in southern Europe. So I decided to spend that afternoon trying to win enough money for a vacation from within various betting establishments of William Hill, Coral and Ladbrokes in south London.

This I deduced might be possible from the skills, luck, knowledge and the tips I'd picked up during my employment with Hill's bookmakers. I walked to the nearest Ladbrokes and bravely placed my first bet of £5 on a horse, which then romped home at a cool 9/1. A winner, and now already £45 up, this could be my day I thought to myself as I next gazed down the complicated dog statistics on the card at Romford track that morning.

I had another £5 on a dog whose name (and recent form) I fancied and within seconds that young pup also came in for me as well. I decided to stick to my original plan which was to change bookies and try my luck elsewhere. I strolled ever southwards until I came to the next gambling house, a William Hill branch maybe I could earn some cash back for all the hard work I'd put into that organisation in the last few months? Again another winner, I was now definitely in the pink but wasn't making any risking high stakes; £5 bets were my limit at this stage. I had a couple of low priced losers to accompany my earlier good fortune, but ahead I was, though still not enough funds had yet been accumulated for the soon hoped for summer holiday far away from fucking Poll Tax and Mrs T.

I then moved onto a branch of Coral's on Brixton Road; I'd used this little betting shop occasionally before, and it had actually been quite a lucky venue for me during some really hard times. This was a place where in the past I'd entered out of desperation with about a fiver that I couldn't afford to lose, and often left with double my money. I'd always known when to quit and count my losses (or winnings) if it meant the difference between eating at least something that evening, or being able to buy a few 'extras' through my good luck and some astute betting.

I examined the form on a couple of flat races due off in the next fifteen minutes along with other betting shop desperados. All this day I had been using the (often considered unlucky) number four in my betting where possible, which had been a relatively successful ploy as I moved from shop to shop.

My reasoning behind the selection of this numerological digit is that I'd had a lucid dream some weeks before in which I observed the letters '4EC' scraped into fresh snow at night in a car park location somewhere. The symbolism of this dream had been etched in my mind since then, and I'd remembered it again that day, so I thought it a good idea to use the number four as part of my equations while scanning the form sheets.

I made my choices by either using the racing position number of a horse or dog, or perhaps a combination of that number; such as the number 13 (as in 1+3= 4) or by using some other numerological and mysterious methodology that I'd decided to rely upon with esoteric hope that afternoon.

I scored yet another winner, once again chosen using the above formula, which now put me around £90 ahead. Next up, the 4.30 at Kempton was approaching the stalls, this one was a real cavalry charge; a five furlong sprint with twenty-four runners, we'd all be sure to lose our money in the twenty seconds it takes for big race horses to cover such a short distance. This race was basically a real no hoper for most of us, supported by pot luck decisions. Just select the stud in form and hope that he doesn't get blocked in yards from the finish line.

I cleared my mind, fixed a blank stare on my face and slowly scanned down the long list of aptly named horses, standing alongside various other also soon-to-be-losing punters crowded around the newspaper cutting pinned up on the bookies wall.

As I hopelessly inspected recent form, jockey weights, jacket colours, and searched deeper for 'horse inspiration', I soon and without doubt, found the horse for me. There he was standing out (at least for me) above all the other brown, four legged friends of man on the long card. Horse number 22 (that's 2+2=4 (I deduced) and he was named 'Secret Four'. How could I possibly not bet on this nag? He was sitting out there quietly with odds at a most reasonable 10/1. I looked at his current form, not bad I thought and a big strong horse with a good jockey on his back. The next bit of processing was deciding how much of today's luck would be gambled on this last ditch venture. I decided that a tenner on 'Secret Four' to win at 10/1 would be a fair risk at the end of a pretty good day at the bookies. I made my bet, keeping the odds at the start of the race, and then settled back with nervous excitement to watch the race in expectation alongside the other Saturday punters.

Being late afternoon and nearing the end of the day's racing schedule, most of the 'customers' in the shop were having a last bet on this wild race too. The odds on so many 'no hopers' were long and tempting enough even for a stake of a few quid. At least this race was a quick sprint and therefore none of us would have to wait long to make for the exit, losers yet again. A five furlong race is over in a flash, I tried to ignore what was happening in the first few furlongs as I'd seen the leader overtaken in the last few strides on many occasions before. But with about seven seconds of this charge remaining I heard the immortal words bellowing from the overhead speakers

'And here comes Secret Four with a furlong left to go!'

My heart began to flutter as the last few metres to the line grew ever closer as my horse came home at a streak on the final knockings, charging in from an 'also ran' position to wiping the floor with the field from the rear.

I was a ton up and gathering from the silence around me it seemed I was the only one in the shop who'd backed 'Secret Four'.

I kick myself for not sticking a cool £50 on the nose of my secretly dreamed about horse, I really had nothing to lose, as without a decent winner there would certainly be no holiday fun for me anyway. I knew it was the one I'd waited for since that weird dream, it was out there in the universe, etched into my subconscious. I ask myself why o why didn't I put my money where my mouth was and brave a proper stupid bet and walk out of there with a monkey or more in my pocket.

However, I was more than a couple of hundred ahead for my day's work, so definitely not a completely wasted Saturday.

37 – Revolutionaries in Flight

After a brief search the following Monday, I found a special offer in *The Evening Standard*...Athens £19 one way'. Even with a £10 airport surcharge, I'd be hard pushed to find a better travel bargain with the resources I had. I called the agent in Victoria and booked the ticket to be collected at Gatwick Airport where I'd depart from in a few days. I didn't have much of an idea about Greece, only that it had an interesting history, good weather and known as a cut price popular holiday destination for Europeans.

There was the added encouragement of perhaps being able to find work there and to be able to stay longer than my meagre funds would cover. This was after all a one way trip, so I gathered what money I could and also invested in a couple of 'homemade' twenty pound notes that were doing the rounds in south London at that time. Perhaps they'd be convincing enough to slip under the counter in a place like Greece as opposed to getting immediately nicked trying it on in a high street bank in Britain.

It was now the time for a foreign adventure and some new scenery, far away from politics, baton charging coppers, angry brick throwing mobs and punitive taxation.

I queued for my ticket at Gatwick, along with various other squatters who were probably on the run from Thatcher's post crushed revolution witch hunt too. As the plane taxied and soon rose into the sky, I slipped out of the country feeling somewhat like Ronnie Biggs as I hid grinning to myself behind a daily newspaper. The flight was uneventful, as chartered, cheap class economy travel usually is. I spent just one night in the smog filled city of Athens, dossing down in a shared mankey hotel dorm with an Australian bloke who was on the same flight earlier. I spent just one day wandering around in the warm sunshine in the home of democracy, visiting the old stones at the famous and now crumbling Acropolis.

In the late afternoon I went to the port of Athens and made enquiries to various travel agents as where the best locations to find work were in Greece. The unanimous reply from them all was Crete, this being the biggest and wealthiest island in the country, and bang in the middle of the Mediterranean. I was assured that this particular island was full of opportunities in such grand professions as orange or olive picking and building work to accommodate the rising tide of tourism.

It took about two seconds to decide that Crete is where I should be the following day.

An overnight ferry took me to the port of Chania in West Crete where I met an English couple from Kent who were seasonal workers in the orange groves. They could instantly see that I was a first timer on the island and offered to take me to a village about eight miles along the coast to introduce me to some of the other working travellers. These people were nearer to your true traveller than the usual pretenders, and most came back every year to work for a few months on Crete, then move onto other locations in Europe as they followed the continental fruit picking seasons.

Some of these characters were pretty rough and couldn't go back to the UK due to one minor criminal misdemeanour or another. But in all, they were a good bunch of people. They showed me the ropes and told me how the local employment system worked. Then there were the language lessons too; they taught me how to get by in pigeon Greek and which words to use and understand when it came to finding 'Dolia' (the Greek for 'work') on the beautiful island of Crete.

The British have a reputation for laziness regarding our efforts to learn a foreign language when abroad, but here in Greece being one the originators of European civilization, there was a common respect for a culture that gave us democracy (also a Greek word), political voting systems, the Olympics, Socrates, Aristotle, Archimedes, Hippocrates, Pythagoras, the Trojan Horse and every young boys favourite; Jason and the Argonauts.

Therefore, the least one could do was to learn enough of their language to get by and give yourself a chance of getting work. I then patiently waited outside the café each morning hoping for 'Dolia Semera?' also known as 'Work today?'

I booked into a cheap, functional hotel in the town, paid a couple of weeks rent in advance and spent my first days enjoying the beach and watching the sun shimmering over the Mediterranean for the first time in my life. I learned how to play a few card games with my new traveller friends and soon made some interesting foreign acquaintances too. However, even though I got out of bed at 7am each morning and waited outside the Café Neon next door to the hotel for work, no 'bosses' showed up to offer 'Dolia' and after three weeks of this I had very little money left.

The proprietors who ran the hotel could see me getting up early in the mornings to wait at the café, so they knew I wasn't just on the piss all the time and neglecting the rent. They eventually did the same deal for me that they usually do for all the poverty stricken foreign workers; they duly took my passport from me with the assurance I'd get it back after the rent I owed was paid up when the fruit picking season got underway. Apparently, many unemployed backpackers before me had painted that hotel at the end of the season in order to get their passports back and leave Crete, and I wasn't about to add my own painting skills to that statistic.

Living on the beach and swimming in the sea sounds idyllic to many, but I was now getting quite near starvation levels and was soon living on tomatoes in bread rolls and tap water. I could only afford to buy the most basic food (as above) from funds raised by returning empty Amstel beer bottles I collected every day down on the beach. Things were getting pretty desperate for many; the season was late that particular year as the weather hadn't turned yet. When the skies finally opened and the torrential rain fell in buckets from above, there was a lot of excitement in the town, much like a harvest festival atmosphere as the locals knew that the time to earn their years' wages was about to commence.

Crete, being situated geographically on the cusp of a tropical food producing country, is dependent on the right conditions before harvesting its main export crops of olives and oranges. The island is also quite unique in that it is also the most northerly sited banana producing region in the world.

In the weeks that preceded the coming of the rain, I'd managed to get bits of work here and there. This was usually manual type labour which mostly involved shovelling heavy pebble ballast into a cement mixer in the boiling sun on a groaning, empty stomach. This toil would generally be performed under the watchful eye of a stunted Greek wanker who'd be 'tac tac tacing' me all fuckin' day. I soon learned what 'Tac Tac' meant in Greek, it roughly translates as 'Quick quick!' or 'Chop chop!' Which is all one needs to hear when you're suffering from sunstroke and close to buckling over from the lack of stomach sustenance. It wasn't much fun working for a couple of meals and a cold beer, but the alternatives were equally unpleasant, as I'd heard that the prison in Iraklion in the middle of the island always had plenty of 'rooms available' for foreign thieves.

It was during this lean time that I also learned to play backgammon, the Greek way, which is fast, tried some of the local food which I liked. Retsina, the local tipple could be palatable if distilled longer than my Brixton home boy cider venture. Metaxa, a cheap brandy was often a good addition to spice up the morning coffee before a day of Greek employment of one sort or another.

As regards the beer, I soon swapped to Heineken in an effort to avoid some of the local brews to help cut out serious hangovers possibly induced via chemically imbalanced brewing systems in Greece. At one desperate point during the wait for the rain, I had to make the decision to trade in one of my dodgy twenty pound notes in order to eat for a couple of days. I showed the bent note to a fellow Englishman outside the café, who after a brief inspection, passed it as very convincing and added the opinion that 'They'll never be able to tell the difference round here anyway'. He reassured me as I could hear the sound of his stomach rumbling from across the café table too.

I drew up the courage from within; this much helped along by my also empty belly, as I crossed the road to the temporary money exchange wagon, stood in line and quickly slipped the counterfeit note furtively under the window when I stepped up at my turn. The cashier didn't even give the note a second glance and promptly counted out an exchange rate of 5,500 Drachmas'.

I sidled back across the road to the café with the money in my fist and a raised eyebrow as my two grinning accomplices nodded in my direction.

I ordered us all some food and a beer as we settled back to play a few rounds of backgammon on that mildly sunny afternoon. I kept watch over my shoulder hoping that the counterfeit cops wouldn't suddenly turn up and take me off to the cells at Iraklion, thus completely ruining my somewhat dodgy 'working holiday'.

38 – Mountain Men

My willpower (and hunger) was always on call to get me up early each and every morning to spend a few hours waiting (usually fruitlessly) outside the Café Neon along with a couple of other guys in the same boat as I. Eventually, my determination (and relative hunger) to work finally paid off, the long waits in the morning breeze had obviously been noted by some of the locals. I was offered work picking olives for a couple of months in a small village called Kolumbari, which was about five miles inland. This little olive producing community was pretty isolated in the interior of Crete; but I immediately took advantage of a change in fortunes and became a 'Mountain Man' as we were popularly known back in town.

    I moved into a derelict shed with a guy called Rod who originated from somewhere in the north east of England. We would share a 'kitchen and shower' (if one could call them that) with the couple in the 'flat' next door which more resembled hobo's a tin shack from the dustbowl era.

Our work or 'Dolia Team' consisted of a German girl and her English boyfriend called Mark who was okay but saw himself as a seasoned traveller and reckoned he could tie any knot ever invented as he was born in Southampton, this being a big ship building port city full of nautical history. He and Rod had 'Done the Olives' before, they knew each other from previous seasons, and soon enough fell out, and then proceeded to stop talking to each other for the next two months in that typically English, unforgiving, sulky manner.

This meant of course, that I would have to adopt the position of the fucking mediator as usual. Rod was probably a closet gay, though he wouldn't admit to it, being a tough, no nonsense former army type, but a down to earth bloke who had some hardcore stories to tell about war and his tour of duty in Northern Ireland. But all the same he was a good bloke and a hard worker, as those from the northeast generally are. Though all he ever consumed for lunch were about twelve cheap Greek cigarettes, smoked one after the other as he sat on his own far away from Mark enjoying his peaceful, smoky 'lunch hour' in the groves.

The other three and I on this 'Olive Team' were due to work for a guy called Stellio, he being a well known and respected giant of an olive farmer on Crete, who I'd meet soon enough. But in the meantime I had a few days' work with a local family, picking olives for three thousand a day (about fifteen quid). I'd be up early in the morning chill waiting in the tiny village square for the 'Bosse' to show up in his wrecked pickup truck. It was hard work as I expected, especially as I'd not been eating well during the poverty weeks on the beach. But I soon livened up when I was given huge lunches during those days, to the effect that one could hardly move to work again for the afternoon shift. I fell on my ghastly bunk in our horrible shed on an evening, happy in the fact that I had a few Drachmas in my pocket, and that one day, I may be able to go back home.

But right now, I rarely thought of Brixton, England, long faces in the middle of the grey winter that was no doubt taking hold of that island until sometime around March the following year.

After my short education on the ancient art of olive picking, I finally met my 'Bosse' for the next couple of months; Stellio, 'The Olive King of Kolumbari'. He was an unassuming man in his late fifties living with his withered mother (dressed always and only in black) in a large self built white house that centre pieced a huge TV which occupied a large share of the kitchen table. I didn't see the rest of his house, but by all accounts it was probably in the Greek Villa style.

He usually employed a western work gang to pick his olives, and although many others were directly in his employ, he would be out with us every day. Greeks like to employ European workers, this partly being seen a sign of prestige and to be able to afford 'European rates'. He was one of the wealthiest men in the area (in Greek terms that is) and boy did he have a lot of olive groves all over the place, they went on and on, grove after grove, bloody millions of them.

Our gang soon got into the swing of it by early November, now that the weather had noticeably changed and it was generally cooler. The working hours were 8am till 4pm with an hour for lunch, when it was nice to just lie down in the groves and chill out in the wooded silence. Rod and Mark operated 'The Machines' while I and said German girl collected the falling berries on the mats that we'd laid out around the trees before Rod and Mark moved in with 'The 'Machines'.

'The Machines', for want of a better name, were small, petrol driven generators that converted into air compressors, which in turn were attached to aluminium poles that drove floppy tubes of rubber spinning at speed and simply knocked the olives from the branches. Rod and Mark worked 'The Machines' around us, one (usually Rod, being tall) using the longer pole to reach the higher branches, whilst the two of us below commonly known as 'Mat Scum' simply rounded up the berries and filled large sacks up as we followed their lead.

'The Machines' were a labour saving modern invention to empty trees of olives in no time at all, and must've been a godsend for the likes of Stellio when someone sat down and came up with such a modern solution to an ancient farming method. Olive groves were abuzz with the sound of small genies, whirring away hour after hour, day after day up and down the valleys of Kolumbari during the season. Rod and Mark were paid 5,000 Drachmas a day, as they were 'Machinists' and therefore higher up the pay scale than the likes of us 'Mat Scum' who earned a mere 4,500. I didn't really care too much about the difference in pay; I was now eating regularly again and actually saving a bit of money.

Speaking of savings, Stellio had a system in place to 'help us' save money and more importantly to encourage us turn up for work each day. He wrote down the pay figure for each of his four workers in his book every day, as did we. Therefore, when we needed money for groceries and such like, we'd ask him for some cash to which he'd reluctantly hand it over asking if you were going out on the piss for the night.

I seldom did this, I got up and went to work 95% of the time as the recent memory of half starving on the beach drove me to those eternal olive groves each morning. I decided that I'd rather work while it was going. However, we all occasionally had the need to get away from our dreadful living quarters and 'village life' to hitch a ride back into town to have a meal and get completely shit faced. As they say 'All work and no play…' and besides that, I was supposed to be on a 'working holiday'. Sometimes I needed a night out and away from the two sulking English blokes I worked with every day.

On one occasion I visited the hotel in town buy my passport back at the princely sum of 17,000 Draks, this in the knowledge that I was definitely going to be leaving Crete one day…

I gradually began to learn a few words and phrases in Greek and to increase my respect for their heritage and ancient history. This is a culture with plenty of both, these people were creating an empire, an alphabet, electing governments and advancing scientific and mathematical knowledge around about the time when the ancient Britons were clubbing each other to death over an evening meal of a rotting carcass. This island had a recent history as well, thousands of German paratroopers had invaded Crete in WW2 and Stellio would tell us stories of his occupied childhood mixed with plenty of respect for the (failed) efforts of the British army to stop the surprise air invasion in its tracks.

Stellio had visited Britain on a number of occasions and I felt he secretly harboured dreams of Englishness. He'd often ask his European work gang questions of the values of things in Britain as compared to Crete. This usually related to how much his house would be worth if for instance it was on the market in London, to which Rod would sarcastically reply: 'Around about twenty thousand Draks, Stellio.'

This comment would always raise a wry smile or two about the camp, even from Mark, and Stellio soon decided not to venture the values and comparisons of British verses Greek currencies anymore.

Stellio worked us hard day in day out, but all in all he was a fair man and could speak English very well. But those olives just kept on coming, sacks and sacks of them, the relentless whir of 'The Machines' continued unabated. Once a week, one of us took a trip to the processing factory in the village to fill up an empty two litre Coke bottle with pure, recently crushed oil for cooking purposes. The thick, unprocessed liquid looked much like snot in its base form, but we lived on the stuff, it tasted great and we all became really healthy in no time at all. Our breakfast would usually consist of tomatoes on fried bread as cooked in olive oil rinsed down with a shot of Metaxa in our coffee every morning which would set us up until lunchtime.

Olive trees are an amazing plant, you can cut them right down to a stump on the ground and they'll grow sprigs back within a season, followed by more olives soon after that. They are very tough and resilient trees indeed, some of them on the island and in Stellios' groves were over a thousand years old. This particular year he bought himself a new lightweight chainsaw which he could hold in one hand and cut back many of the overgrowing branches. It looked like there was going to be a lot of burning to do after this year's olive crop was in…

The tools for the olive job were as simple as they were prehistoric. Apart from the modern addition of 'The Machines' we, the 'Mat Scum' would use a thin, 'specially prepared' two-foot length of an olive branch to simply knock the olives off the freshly cut branches in a downward sliding action (as trained by Stellio) onto the mats, it was as easy as that. It rarely rained during those months, which in effect meant a day off. In all the time I worked for Stellio I only took a handful of days off (usually to get pissed in town) in nearly three months of second world hard labour.

But without a doubt the best day of all was when Stellio came running through his groves one morning when were picking in his own garden to invite us up to his house to watch the latest breaking news…

We eagerly made our way up to his villa to observe the joyous headline news on CNN… 'Thatcher resigns!' The six of us (including his mother) stood in his kitchen toasting the end of the Iron Lady with our Bosses home brewed, smooth Retsina as we watched the now famous footage of the blue-rinsed-bitch weeping and waving as she climbed into a black Jaguar and was swiftly sped off into history. I cheered and raised my glass as we watched a news clip of a couple of women popping a bottle of Champagne in Whitehall as the unmentionable woman in blue was finally trucked off, hopefully to an asylum.

Those images pretty much summed it all up for me that morning, and I knew in my heart that I'd played my part in her downfall and that (along with the Retsina) gave me a warm feeling inside.

39 – Trains, Thumbs and Autobahns

Sometime in the beginning of February '91 I felt the need to move on. The olive groves were all picked and we were now down to burning the seasons cut branches in a pit, this being yet another medieval labour task that was indeed functional, but seriously wore you out. This particular task would involve tying up the cut branches with a piece of rope, then dragging them behind you to the end of the groves and throwing them onto the ever burning pit. This toil was okay for the first few days, but soon enough you'd have to travel further and further along the groves to bundle up the loose branches, which meant you were gradually walking an increasing number of miles each day. Although I was now quite fit and strong after months of olive picking, I'd pretty much had enough of the mountain man life and second world farming techniques.

I decided to leave Crete and do a bit of tourist type travelling through Europe on route back to England, as it felt like I'd actually earned a bit of a holiday.

I spoke to Stellio about my imminent departure and we sat down with our notepads and worked out how much I was due, and better still, how much he owed me. The final figure was a princely 110,000 Drachmas, (about £450) which was considerably more than the £60 I turned up with on the island four months previously. He charged me 1,000 Drachmas for electricity usage which was fair enough, all bosses do this in Greece as that utility is an expensive commodity especially on Crete. He asked me to stay as there was plenty more work available, but although I'd grown to quite like him as he was a decent man, I'd made my mind up to leave and travel my way back to the now Thatcher-less Britain.

I'd heard plenty of stories about workers (usually English ones) who simply pissed all their hard earned cash away at the end of the season, thus becoming trapped on Crete once more without the 5,000 Draks required to get the ferry back to Athens and the European mainland. This entrapment was not going to happen to me; I packed my rucksack, said my goodbyes to the olive crew and set off back to Chania to see some more faces before moving on.

I hitched back to town one last time, had a meal, got drunk, played a bit of backgammon at the café and stayed a night in the same hotel that I might have painted had they still been in possession of my passport. Next morning I said my goodbyes to all the people I'd met on this enlightening journey, and thumbed a ride to the port of Chania in the late afternoon.

I'd met some great people on that trip, tough, seasoned travellers, experienced in working their way around the world, and had made their choices in life. A few others however were simply misplaced piss heads that'd probably never get off that island, and may well still be there to this day…

I decided to do at least a little sightseeing on the way back to Britain, and as I now actually had a bit of cash in my pocket to spend, why not I thought? I ended up on an overnight ferry to Bari in southern Italy arriving on a bright, sunny morning. Although the Gulf War was now in its last days, there was still a lot of paranoia in Italy regarding terrorism and the fading possibility of a stray chemical missile attack from Saddam's depleted and nearly defeated army far away in a troubled land.

On close inspection via a mirror in a public toilet, I concluded that I looked decidedly rough, just like real a traveller, I felt scruffy and somewhat dodgy looking when walking around the pretty city of Bari for a day. Being Italy and therefore the population were always turned out well, it appeared that everyone dresses stylishly just to pop out and buy a pint of milk, or at least in Bari it seemed that way.

I made the fateful decision to hitchhike out of Bari and make my way due north. I then spent a number of fruitless hours on a main road waiting for a lift that never came. Eventually a guy stopped in a small red Fiat and immediately asked if I was English?

'Yes, I'm English,' I replied with a smile.

He then added, 'You'll never get a lift in this town, people won't pick up hitchhikers, they're all paranoid, especially at the moment' he informed me in a very good English accent.'

'Ah, I see' I replied. 'That figures,' I added.

He turned out to be a school teacher; and offered me a short lift to the train station, which I promptly took.

I spent the next couple of days on trains travelling north through the lovely Italian countryside until I ended up in Rome. I just had to get out there and check out those historic Roman sites at least for a day. I really enjoyed the old city once the seat of a huge empire as it buzzed with stylishly attired good looking people riding brightly coloured shooters to park outside coffee bars and chat passionately in their beautiful language. Next stop was Milan, and sadly from what I saw, a bit of a dump. But I should've got off and seen Florence when the train pulled in late one night.

I continued my rail journey on through Italy in their delightful wood panelled carriages and then eventually we rose over the cool Alps, as the temperature started to fall. I continued on through an uneventful Austria until we came to a snowy halt in Munich.

So now I was in Germany? I reckoned it was time to get off.

As I walked out of the station and found the main road north, I decided to visit an old girlfriend now living in Hamburg and a former resident of Villa Road whom I'd been periodically exchanging letters with from Crete.

Standing by the road, thinking of my next move, I suddenly realised that it was very cold, a real German winter was going on here, and I wondered what fate would visit upon me next. I stuck my thumb out and within fifteen minutes a car slowed down and pulled over just in front of me. The (German) car contained three occupants, two women and a man all in their twenties, looking suitably scruffy dressed mostly in black clothes.

The window slid down and the female driver then asked me a question I couldn't understand in German,

I quickly replied that I 'Specken nein Deutsch, specken ze English bitter?' I quizzed.

She then asked me in excellent English, 'Are you English?'

'Ya,' I replied.

After a quick conference with her passengers she turned asked where I was going.

I answered assertively, 'Hamburg.'

Another pause as they discussed something between themselves.

'Do you know how far Hamburg is?' was the next question.

'Yes, the other end of Germany,' said I.

'Vot vill you do if you do not get a lift tonight? It iz minus zen degrees,' she enquired.

My reply was not so swift, or assured this time, 'Err, hum, I'll find somewhere to sleep I guess,' came my best reply.

More consultation inside the warm (German) car at this response, followed by, 'Get in ze car, we vill take you somewhere for ze night, okay?'

'Okay, dunkershern,' I replied, as smiling to myself I knew that I'd landed on my feet at the last minute once again.

I climbed in, momentarily bringing the cold Munich winter with me as I introduced myself to the occupants who relayed their respective names back to me. We then drove at a pace along dark lanes shrouded by those tall fir trees common in that country. I was soon informed that they jointly owned a pub and were taking me there for the night.

Shortly after we arrived, they showed me around their Bavarian style drinking house, to which I was suitably impressed. It was decked out in solid pine forest wood, it smelt rustic and comforting, and they had the whole place set up to cater for drinking on long straight tables, in the German style. This venue also included a stage out back in the beer garden to accommodate live music in the balmy summer months. Next up of course was my initiation into the world of German beer, we sat down on one of those thick, heavy pine tables, as the guy of the outfit cracked open four Hefeweizens. He then meticulously showed me how it should be poured, and it was of course very nice on the palette.

We started to talk about various things while swilling our beers; they of course had to accommodate my inability to speak German, to which I was somewhat ashamed, but their English was top quality. Soon enough, the current Gulf War made its way into the conversation, as it was presently the top global news item anyway. I had to be careful here, as these young people felt that Germany was not involved and that the US and Britain were ultimately responsible. I agreed with them of course, it wasn't my war either.

At that the female driver then blurted out, 'Dis time, it waz not uz zat started it!'

There was a slight pause before we all burst out into laughter, and I told them not to believe the jingoism of our red top British press as most of the population in the UK were just as pissed off about it as the rest of our 'European partners'. After that, things cooled off, they obviously realised that I wasn't yet another English moron with a passport, and a superior attitude.

The guy of the trio then lightened things up and told me that tomorrow as a special treat he'd show me his Harley Davidson in the garage out back.

'Yeah, right, that'll be cool,' I said, believing that he was obviously talking bollocks.

We all ended up a bit drunk on said beer, and a warm bed was eventually offered, and gratefully taken.

Next morning, after coffee and some breakfast, the guy proudly took me out back and showed me his black Harley parked in the garage – nice. I was then informed soon after that the other girl in the car the night before would call by in an hour to kindly drive me a few miles to the nearest pick up point to catch the autobahn heading north.

From that moment on, I started to feel totally differently about 'Germans' all the preconceptions I'd had (or been taught) were melting away in view of the hospitality that these people offered when they'd pulled over the previous freezing night and taken me into their care.

Within what seemed like minutes of being left at the pickup point by the pretty girl who'd dropped me off I was offered a lift by a businessman type bloke driving a flashy, cream coloured, leather lined Jenson. This is the score regarding hitch hiking in Germany, it's the best country on the planet to do this, and they have fixed points to pick up travellers on the Autobahns. All very well established and organised, in that typically efficient German fashion.

I was also about to find out just how quickly one could travel the length of Germany… This guy was either in a hurry, late, or he usually drove like there was no tomorrow. With no speed limits on the Autobahns people can drive at the speeds they're comfortable with, and in this guy's case, it was about 150 mph. We were weaving between lanes and I thought after all the luck I'd had recently on my travels, it was about to run out. He was going so fast that he passed the point where he should've dropped me, so he then swung around a roundabout and went back (also at 150mph) to leave me at the right stop. I said my thanks and went to the café at this point and waited for the next maniac with a sports car and a heavy right foot to take me further up the road, or possibly to my messy and untimely road death.

I waited once more at a roadside café for another lift north and it wasn't too long in coming, such is the reliability of the unique German system, and the generosity of the hitch hiking ideal.

I was taken another fifty miles or so further up the autobahn by a truck driver, who then dropped me by an all night German equivalent of a motorway services station. The same soulless venue as you'd expect on the M1, only cleaner and considerably cheaper.

I bought a coffee, wandered the bland building for a few hours, bought more coffee, sat down periodically and gazed out of the expansive windows, awaiting my next road trip adventure…

40 – Horsebox Hotel

After a few tedious hours, a Turkish lady (as I soon found out) who was also taking a break in the same venue as myself, asked me in passing if I needed a lift.

Quite taken aback by this I replied, 'Yes please, if you're heading north?'

'Yes, I'm heading towards Frankfurt, is that in your direction?' she enquired.

'It is thank you,' I replied

I quickly swallowed my ninth coffee, grabbed my bag and followed her outside as she took me away from that tedious, muzac filled motorway services café.

This is not what one would hear of in Britain; a woman offering a lift to a man at a twenty-four hour service station at night? But this was Germany and it seemed that she'd observed me from a distance, then used her intuition and decided that I could be trusted to share her car.

'Are you English?' was of course the first question.

'Yes,' I laughed 'Is it that obvious?'

After the initial introductions, we then talked about various cultural matters as she drove me northwards along the ordered, tree lined German road until she dropped me off at a motel further along the autobahn, and then raced off into the darkness. I wandered into this soulless three star building and asked the price of the cheapest, blandest room for the night, which turned out to be too bloody expensive for me anyway. I immediately made my excuses and slipped downstairs to the clinically lit toilets and contemplated a few hours sleeping on the loo. However, I knew I'd be sussed in no time and thrown out into the wind chill factor of a German winter, so an urgent re-think of my situation was now necessary.

I wandered back through the dull, thickly carpeted reception area and out through the swinging doors of the motel. The icy, freezing gale blew straight through me as I stood outside, hoping for a lift at this now late hour in the deserted car park. I waited, and waited some more, thinking hard and somewhat desperately of how to burn a few hours away until I could procure another ride northwards once again.

By now it was really cold with snow swishing through the air, and the chill factor was dropping the temperature to dangerously low levels. To contemplate sleeping outside on a night like this was not only madness but would probably guarantee a slow, stiff death too. Then as if appearing from nowhere, I suddenly noticed a metal horsebox with an advertising board attached to its side parked on a grass patch in front of the car park, facing the motel. Out of curiosity I wandered over to this grey metal tomb and placed my hand on the frozen latch, then with a reassuring 'click' the door just popped open. I was naturally expecting a sharp smell of horseshit to hit me, but no, it was clean inside, there was even a sprinkling of new hay laid out on the floor.

That was it, the answer to my dilemma, a bit zero star in quality, but fifty times better than dying under a bush outside a German motel on a quiet stretch of the autobahn.

After 'unpacking' I put on as many clothes as I could get over my body, including gloves, a scarf, three pairs of stinking socks and most importantly, a hat pulled down over the ears, as any wilderness survivor knows that 80% of human body heat leaves via the head. I then curled up in my sleeping bag and set the alarm clock for 8am. I hardly slept a wink at all, it was the coldest night out I've ever spent out in the elements; minus ten once in a lifetime is more than enough for anyone I think. I did eventually drop off and if it wasn't for the alarm clock bringing me back from the perils of frostbite; I may well have died in that metal coffin.

As soon as I got some circulation back in my hands and feet, my belongings were packed up in moments and out I stepped from my no star horsebox into the grey car park, just as a warm German saloon car was exiting the motel and driving slowly past as the wheels slipped and cracked on the thick layer of ice. The occupants (being a family) stared out of the steamy windows of their posh motor in part amusement and the rest horror, as they must have soon realised where I'd spent the night. I could almost hear the mother mouthing the words in German: 'Da Britishzen, he schlept ze nicht in ein horzebox!'

Perhaps that family have eventually worn that tale rather thin at dinner parties down the years to this day, who knows? But I did raise a smile and was tempted to wave cheerily at them as they slipped around the corner and off on their journey still watching with craned necks as I strode confidently towards the motel. I calmly walked through the reception area at about fifty miles an hour and went straight downstairs to the mega lit, recently polished and highly slippery floored toilets.

I then washed, shaved and hurriedly changed into slightly less grubby clothes than I arrived in the previous night. There were storks of hay sticking out of my hair, clothes and pockets; I looked like a bloody scarecrow. I cleaned myself up as much as possible, which isn't always easy when you're on the road. Then it was off to the restaurant for buffet and some coffee, passing (at speed) the confused looking receptionist on the way.

I kept my head down a bit in the buffet bar; I had the impression that people were furtively looking and muttering in my direction as I chomped into the German style breakfast. I can only imagine what they would've thought on seeing a crazy Englishman emerge from a horsebox after a freezing night like that. In fact I was rather proud of my ability and instinct to survive in such abject conditions. Had I slept out in the open anywhere else that night and I'd have be done for and frozen stiff like a meat locker ham, I'm certain of that.

After my German breakfast and a litre of coffee I 'booked out' and made ready for the next stage of thumbing a lift to Hamburg. The original occupants of said motel gave me a wide berth and looked elsewhere as they crunched past me in their comfortable Deutsch motors; can't really blame them can you? But when I did get a lift after an hour, I happened to glance up at a bridge crossing the autobahn the moment I climbed into the heated car just in time to see my horsebox squat being towed behind a 4x4 Jeep on its way to god knows where in an easterly direction.

    I was suddenly stuck with thoughts of being marooned inside that shed on wheels for hours upon end, banging hopelessly on that cold metal shell while the toasty warm driver drove on obliviously mile after mile following the signposts to Poland.

41 – Der Deutsche Squat

I was then offered a ride by a big truck driver… huh huh? I guess I must've looked 'cute, ya'. I thought ominously to myself as I climbed aboard.

Sitting high up in his cab, I watched the tall trees go by hour after hour as we listened to Lederhosen muzac rhythmically booming away as we drank up the kilometres towards my preferred destination, Hamburg.

The timeless Bavarian knee slapping um par par, um par par, um par par played away on the cab radio as the long straight road ebbed by beneath his truck. I didn't mind his taste in music of course as I was after all getting a free ride all the way and though neither of us could understand one another, it was part of German culture I found his general demeanour friendly as he tapped to the rhythm of his chosen musical style on the big steering wheel. Lederhosen trucker guy dropped me off at a motorway service station on the outskirts of Hamburg, where I thanked him and walked into the nearest metro station to find my old girlfriend, Ira, at an address I had in my pocket. We were neighbours in Villa Road and had become friends before she decided to return to Germany and start a new life after the fall of the Berlin Wall at the end of the eighties. She worked in a toy shop called Die Drukerie based somewhere in the middle of Hamburg.

She was somewhat surprised to see me when I walked into the shop, which was rather quaint and sold traditional, handmade, painted wooden toys from what now seemed a bygone era in the now age of mass produced plastics.

I'd turned up out of the blue, but she welcomed me and took me along to her flat nearby. We talked the old stories over coffee of Villa Road which she still missed somewhat and of my experiences on Crete. It was good to meet her again, but there was a drawback, she had a new boyfriend whose name escapes me, but a real arsehole I deduced within moments of meeting him. He was one of those unforgiving Germans, he positively hated the English, spoke only in German to me, was aggressive and intimidating. But I was mildly amused by this guy, as he was currently reading the complete works of Shakespeare, in German, which meant that at the very least he admired a form of literature that is quintessentially English.

I couldn't for the life of me figure out why Ira was hitched herself to this creep, she was a Jewish German for a start and his anti Englishness made her and I somewhat nervous when we occupied the same room for more than a few minutes. I only stayed in her spare room for a couple of nights before deciding to move on to a large communal squat that I'd been directed to in the area by her.

When I wandered into an area consisting of small squares of rundown buildings on either side of the entrance I asked three guys in my pigeon German who were peering down an open manhole if there was any space in the complex. They looked up from their frozen shit blocked drain and pointed me towards a ground floor building then they collectively returned to that old squatter's task, clearing up other people's shit. I entered what immediately seemed like a communal bar / club room. This is more like it I thought. It was centrally heated and fitted out in that colourful squat style, with a bar; tables and general self-build nail jobs throughout. There was nobody about but evidence of at least one person sleeping there, so I made a coffee and waited for the occupant to return to discuss available space in this German squat city.

A couple of hours later the door opened and in stepped the other occupant, he looked directly at me and announced in a perfect Liverpudlian accent, "Are you looking for somewhere to stay then mate?"

"Yes if there's any room," I replied

"Well you're in the right place, nobody else is living in the bar, it's been out of action for some time, no one uses this place at the moment, so you can stay here a while."

We exchanged names, his I cannot remember only that he was from Merseyside, had a sense of humour and was taking advantage of free accommodation while it was going.

After a very warm and comfortable night's sleep, the following morning he invited me to go 'shopping' locally for supplies. My new English friend offered to show me the right places to get all manner of provisions and all 'for free' he enthusiastically informed me.

This I had to see…

The first advice he gave me was to only shoplift from German stores, never the Turkish shops, it was an unspoken rule to be followed at all times. Shoplifting as a profession was a dying art in Britain by then as there were too many over enthusiastic store detectives and CCTV coverage everywhere by the end of the previous decade. People just didn't do it unless you were a desperate smack head, or perhaps from a northwest region of England?

Although I was running short of cash, the prospect of being nicked for shoplifting in Hamburg didn't much appeal. I'd been giving serious thought to trying to find work and stay in Hamburg for a couple of months or maybe more, to see how I liked it.

I bought a pan for the self contained kitchen we could use along with and a few other general bits and pieces also needed. I then followed my new scouse friend from one shop to another and watched him effortlessly help himself at will to canned foods, packets of pasta, plates and anything else he could stuff under his large coat. I was surprised at how easy (and appealing) he made it all look, and soon enough I realised that shoplifting in Germany was a piece of piss for the traveller on a budget.

Within two days I accepted my fate and we decided to work together as a team, I would act as the decoy by asking the helpful and efficient shop assistants for something on the top shelf while my Merseyside accomplice furtively slipped various culinary goods under his roomy winter jacket.

We kept to the rules, only take from Germans and it was like taking candy from a child.

Due to the trusting nature of the average German shopper, it seemed that there was little call for security in general stores in Hamburg. So, with such a low percentage of thievery going on in this town we took full advantage of the 'free goods' on offer on a daily basis.

We sat down at the end of our day's 'shopping' and usually had ourselves a feast of cooked hams, olives, coffee, bacon, eggs and even large loaves of French bread somehow ended up on our dinner table. Fuck knows which orifice my northern low rent crime partner found to store *that* in during our 'grocery runs' I just laughed when he produced a stick one supper time like a rabbit from a hat.

I will of course admit that stealing is wrong, but when it comes to food then I think it's a different matter, I didn't have any idea of the state of my Merseyside friend's funds, but I also knew that despite reports regarding the well documented, so called criminality of Liverpudlian people; I could trust him with my few possessions while we shared the grubby bar house. He was a nice enough bloke, who enjoyed light-heartedly taking the piss out of 'Ze Germans' and scraping out an existence in a foreign city. Bent or not, thieves we were, but we were only taking from those who wouldn't miss the odd sausage or two anyway.

Our exploits very soon attracted the attention of some of our neighbours in the commune. We'd seen a couple of crusty types peering through the snowed up bar window one evening while we tucked into our nightly banquet, washed down with a nice bottle of red, as opened with a stolen corkscrew and drunk via thieved glasses. One evening a few tough looking guys came into the bar and 'enquired' if there was any beer, to which we jointly answered no. After a brief and uncomfortable pause, we offered the three lads a share of our stolen booty which immediately neutralized the threat of aggression that may have materialized moments later.

Word got around and we were soon asked by a few people when we were opening the bar up as we were occupying the place and sort of expected to run it too. There was a certain level of cooperation going on in this commune, that German sense of organisation and delegation of duties was evident here and we were supposed to join in for the good of all. This is a fair comment and I agreed with the idea and was willing to get involved, however, my Liverpudlian friend and I were without the finances needed to stock the bar in the first place. Perhaps these people thought that as we seemed to live on good food and fine wine, we therefore must be well off while freeloading our accommodation in a centrally heated (empty) bar in the midst of a German winter. This was obviously a complete misunderstanding but I don't think they believed us when we tried to explain to a few of their number in our pigeon German of the situation, so unfortunately the bar remained closed.

I then met an oddball American man residing in the commune too; he was leaning under the bonnet of someone's car in the freezing snow one afternoon. He was Afro Caribbean, ex military, from Texas and a petrol-head mechanic busy repairing another's car. We got to chatting and exchanging the usual travellers checks on each other, he was living among 'The Germs' whom he quietly referred to them while he shifted his gaze about before blaspheming the whole German race. He seemed like a nice enough, friendly bloke, but it wasn't until I visited his room in the block opposite that

I soon realised he was also bonkers-bonkers. He occupied a single room in a miserable, dirty, hovel up a couple of flights of stairs, and his only conversation topic revolved entirely around the motor vehicle. He spoke, ate and no doubt shat the automobile; he lovingly showed me his boxed, mint condition collection of various Matchbox Motors. When he reached down to delicately pick up one of his prized toy cars and play with it in wide eyed wonder much like a child would with a new present on Christmas Day I realised that I was already edging backwards towards his rickety door...

After a couple of weeks I ran into Ira again in the street, she was pleased to hear I was happily living among the German squat community. She invited me over one evening as she and her prick of a boyfriend had tickets for some horse racing at the Hamburg track. She also mentioned that there was another woman accompanying them too, so would I like to make up a foursome? I accepted the night out despite the presence of the Shakespeare reading dickhead and went along to the evening races as invited.

    I soon discovered that betting is pretty much the same everywhere, meaning people get into debt because of gambling regardless of location, culture or the odds. This was plainly and painfully true of Iras' man who subsequently made a total prat of himself (in public) as he began to lose more and more money and therefore become ever more obnoxious and animated with each passing race. He had a couple of winners (as did I) but then pissed it all away on the next race, like a fool.

    However, what made German horse racing rather different to the English variety is that the jockey's don't ride on the back of their mounts; they straddle inside little two wheeled carts attached behind the horse. With the jockey sitting with each leg astride of the mare and about twelve inches directly in eye line of the said horses arse. It looked uncomfortable, comical and in my opinion, completely the wrong way to race a horse. Sitting in a saddle high up on its back is surely the way to ride and race a damn horse isn't it? And not in some half cocked chariot type contraption bouncing along behind its butt?

The betting system in Germany was different too, one didn't write out the race and horse on a slip, one filled in blocks on a pre-printed card stating your bet which was then passed through a punched card type machine. This was another example of that German efficiency once again I thought to myself as I placed another small, but calculated flutter.

Yet again, had I been a bit braver I could've won some decent Deutschmarks for my night out, as I'd backed two winners that evening, but my funds were now low and I needed to keep enough cash aside to get the ferry back to Britain sooner or later.

In the last race on the evening's card, as the lights were dimmed once again in the restaurant area, our idiot companion had put his lot on a nag and having filled up on booze was now becoming ever louder and more embarrassing and was generating plenty of attention among the other (also losing) punters in our surrounding area. It was reassuring to know that my impressions of this total wanker were not entirely without good cause, as I could hear the general mutterings (in German) of others around us regarding the obnoxious behaviour of this creep. He duly lost his money, and I was deeply glad for him too.

After that charade, we ended up in bar close to Ira's place, and the four of us sat at a table while he mused and sulked over his subsequent (and hopefully, substantial) evening's losses. I'd made the effort to make polite conversation with Ira and her friend during the evening and thanked them for inviting me. But this arsehole hadn't finished with me yet; he then kicked off about the war and started to ask about my impressions of Churchill in his now familiar, loud and animated posturing. This once again drew the attention of other Germans seated near us, as they plucked up their ears in our general direction, possibly awaiting the reply of an

Englishman?

At this point I could stand no more of this fucking idiot, so I stood up and said, "I don't like your obnoxious attitude and you're not going to embarrass me or yourself anymore, I've got nothing more to say to you, goodbye."

At that I shook hands with Ira and her friend, who accepted my apologies and I left ignoring that total wanker. I saw Ira briefly for an hour before I left to catch the ferry from Hamburg port, she apologised for her boyfriend and we said our goodbyes.

I can only hope that she soon found herself a decent man, German or otherwise.

I then spent a night and half the following day on a big Scandinavian ferry as it traversed the North Sea and delivered me back to an England no longer ruled by the iron bitch.

42 – No Hats in Brixton

Back in the previous decade, central (Conservative, that is) government had proposed a white paper regarding a new housing 'idea' onto the residents of Lambeth, a selection of other London boroughs, a district of Sunderland and some other estates in north east England. These 'new housing policies' were adventurously named 'Housing Action Trusts' or 'HATS' for short.

The adopted new scheme required various English councils to hand over control some of their 'problem estates' to these HATS for 'about five years', and to gauge how well these organisations dealt with the day to day running of these estates. This was to be done with a view to then offering the residents the choice of opting out and returning to local authority control or to be run permanently in the future by these Housing Action Trusts. However, these organisations would now be in a position to sell off these estates to the highest bidder, also known as private landlords. Basically, this was yet another get rich quick deal that as usual involved those who were already minted during the decade of the get richer quicker, if of course you already were…

This 'scheme' as set up by the clueless, greedy, interfering Tories, was another example of their ludicrous policies by brushing inner city problems under the carpet in preference of profit. It's one thing to offer residents on a shitty estate the option of a possible move into a housing association accommodation, but many in the country by then had wised up as regards just how Thatcher's government thought and operated.

It was almost a certainty that after a few years of bad management, leading to the obvious debts, that these trusts would be promptly sold off to the highest bidders. Everyone knew that the highest bidding winners would come from the private sector, who'd buy up whole estates lock, stock, and then after some meagre 'improvements' they'd inevitably commence to hike up rents at their convenience, just as most private landlords do.

It didn't take a particularly high IQ to work out what would happen after those private landlords were free to evict at their convenience; more homelessness people which would now include families with children who'd be offered no rent protection or legal support.

Why not just have done with it all and bring back Victorian workhouses and debtors prisons?

Considering that Lambeth at during this time was a grotty, poor and badly run borough, whose council corridors whiffed of long term internal corruption, and were operated by a traditionally large majority of Labour councillors in comfortable, safe seats. However, some of Lambeth's blindfolded residents had voted a few Tory councillors into office in more recent local elections and that is where the trouble soon began.

The housing figures banded about during this time were stating that 43% of people were council tenants; 24% owner occupied; which goes some way to explaining how the Tories arrived in Lambeth Council. But more so was the fact that many of these homeowners in SW9 and surrounds were Jamaicans who'd arrived during the Windrush era in the 1950s. Many had found it seriously difficult to find anywhere to live in south London due to institutional racism being far more commonplace back then.

Hence, our new 'British Citizens' often had no choice but to buy property (whatever the going price) and become homeowners, who'd then have to work all hours usually in the low paid public sector to make the mortgage payments every month. Ironically half a century later many of our British Jamaican citizens were now sitting pretty on quality prime property in sort after locations around south London's fashionable zone two. This many felt was a well earned payback for a lifetime of working in hospitals, on the underground, driving buses and hard toil in the building industry.

After that came a mere 8% of the population who were housing association tenants, followed by 23% privately rented. The final figure of 'about 3%' was classed as 'other public sector' which basically meant us, the squatters, which must've added up to quite a large, unwashed crowd of people at that time.
    It didn't matter how much hot air came out of Lambeth town hall, nobody believed a word of it, and demonstrations in all the proposed areas were soon organised by those who'd be affected with widespread support from local people and unions. It was going to be a bit of a battle to win this one, as hundreds of millions had been allocated to HATS in Lambeth & Sunderland, which meant that 'they' had a serious sum of money at their disposal to 'persuade' tenants into submission.
    But we in squatsville and in the local estates were just not having any of it; we could see a steaming pile of bullshit from a mile off after eleven long years of steaming piles of bullshit. Thatcher might be gone and the grey geezer John Major in charge now, but it was still yet more Tory nonsense.

Gigs were rapidly organised in Max Roach, Kennington and Brockwell Parks and also in the car parks of the local estates earmarked for 'Action'. Barbecues were lit, and estates became 'no go areas' during the lovely sunny weekends of 1991.
    Reggae gods Aswad came to Brixton and played their own variety of tunes to support the local cause, as did various other musical entities of the day. But it was mainly union people, civil servants and even DHSS staff who staged flash strikes and made every effort to slow the whole unpleasant process down.

Some nice anti HAT artwork was creatively produced around town too; the best of the bunch were paste-up A5 posters emblazoned with the large words 'No Hats In Brixton' painted in bright anarchist red, and daubed between a black bowler hat of the type that city bankers wear. A most fitting and arty piece of symbolism to represent the urban struggle and counter offensive against the ridged structure of a right wing political system, who had held all the aces in Britain for over a decade.

Within a few months, the council wrangling, the spineless indecision and an ever increasing level of mutinous objections from the residents (or rebels) of Angel Town and Loughborough estates (who were situated right next to us in Villa Road) a public ballot was finally offered to those who'd be affected most by these Housing Action Trusts.

This meant in layman's terms that we could now actually vote for or against the motion…

Soon after the final death knell of Housing Action Trusts in Lambeth and elsewhere in England's pleasant land was rung immediately with a resounding 'No!' as the multi hair styled voters ensured their right to democracy be brutally apparent.

It was a relief to know that the people of Brixton still had the spirit and fight to stave off the ever increasing 'me, me, me' culture of the Tories as they tried to spread their deadly influence in a southerly direction from the halls of Westminster.

It was also a warning to our cricket loving, Brixton born Prime Minister John Major not to venture south of the river again, unless it was to watch England get thrashed at The Oval, usually by our former colonial 'partners' of Australia, The West Indies, India and others.

43 – Victim Value

As things progressed in Villa Road, no sooner had we buried HATS, when the next housing 'offer' came to our round table at number 29. An 'Agreement' had been struck up with Family Housing Association who were to undergo some basic work on our place, next door, and a few other houses that were also in a bad way in our street.

We were all to get fire resistant doors, some 'proper' rewiring, a gas boiler, 'real' plumbing, roof repairs and a sort of 'fitted kitchen'. This was no doubt going to be a cheap job, a quote of around £25k per house was mentioned, which is 'bargain price' when considering the six week timeframe as promised in which to finish the building and in some instances, structural jobs.

The residents in the chosen houses agreed to strip back large areas of flaky old Victorian plaster mostly in the landings and hallways as part of the arrangement and to keep costs down prior to the start of works. I made my objections to what I and others in Villa Road termed as a 'back door takeover' of our street by Family Housing, as this would mean our rights of ownership would be subsequently erased.

As the date neared, all of us at 29 then drifted off to our temporary accommodation we'd arranged elsewhere. Dean went to stay in a neighbour's house in the street, Ian stayed with a friend locally as did Jim and Marlene, and I was offered use of a now vacant ground floor room in number 9 Villa Road. I had my suspicions (as did others) that this build was going to take considerably longer than six weeks, bearing in mind what we'd already ripped out in prep and the mammoth task that was to be completed in such a short time. However, I took the room just along the street, grubby though it was, but also because it was local and wouldn't involve too much stress having to move my gear very far.

On being shown 'Victor's room' at number 9 I instantly wondered if I could've done better elsewhere; it was a real miserable shithole, furnished with a single rancid armchair, complete with tired brown curtains hanging off a broken rail, a dull cracked mirror, your standard issue squatters' carpet (that being in a light patterned blue) and to round it all off, several years' worth of dust decorating every visible surface.

In short, this was the sort of room to top yourself in.

Victor's 'apartment' had been vacated some months previously when the old guy lost it completely and had to be carried away kicking and screaming by the men in square, black rimmed glasses and clean white coats. He was pushing seventy-five and apparently had 'a number of health problems'.

He'd lived in the street for many years, but was now seen as an eccentric, slightly crazy old man who really needed home help or 'secure accommodation', rather than to be squatting in a rundown house as his age. Rumours were floating around the street of old Vic's strange behaviour, and then all of a sudden he was gone.

Even if it was in a bit of a state, his abode was a better temporary option to living outside Brixton station or in the park so I took it.

Besides the dank and distressed décor, there was also an odd and not pleasant smell in the air in old Vic's room, though I couldn't locate where it was coming from. I gave the place a quick wipe down, blue-tacked a few posters over the rough areas, placed a few pot plants by the windows to install an element of cheeriness into the room. I carted my hi-fi the short trip down the street, along with the now well travelled portable telly to keep me company in stinky old guys' room a while.

Ian came over one evening when he was in the area, and I invited him into my 'temporary new accommodation'.
 He sat down in the formerly mentioned mankey armchair and quickly scanned the miserable, uninspiring room before his eyes as he pulled some rizlas out to build a welcome spliff.
 When his eyes had finished surveying the dreariness before him, he turned to me with a big grin spreading across his face as he sarcastically announced, 'Hmmmm, nice room!'
 Upon this observation, we burst out laughing in the musty smelling atmosphere and immediately decided to go to the pub for a pint and smoke the spliff on the way.

One afternoon soon after, my curiosity prompted me to take a look in the floor cupboards which I hadn't investigated since arriving. Maybe Villa Road's eldest resident had left some goodies behind before he was carted off to the land of soft white walls and hard white pills?
 I knelt down and pulled on a hinge-less cupboard door in one corner of the room (which wasn't connected anyway) placed it to one side and then peered into the darkness beyond. As my eyes adjusted to the low light before me, all I could see in the dimness were rows and rows of those two litre plastic Coca Cola bottles each filled to the brim or near to with a light coloured and cloudy substance that certainly didn't appear to be 'The Real Thing'.
 I reached in and took one out, looked closely at the 'off yellow' fluid inside, then gingerly unscrewed the red cap. Immediately my suspicions of the contents of these bottles were soon confirmed as the riotous smell of old man's piss hit me like a train. My eyes streamed with tears as the deadly release of noxious urine gases wafted into the already stuffy room. I barked out and wretched noisily in the rapidly poisoning atmosphere while still down on my knees during this nauseous discovery. I couldn't help but to splutter out a laugh too, as this

was yet another squat event that should've been shared with another at that moment. I quickly screwed the bright red cap straight back onto the offending bottle making sure not to lose my grip and drop a full two litres of elderly guy piss onto the nasty carpet below.

Now it seemed that I'd found the answer as to what was causing the ghastly aroma in Vic's room? The next unpleasant task would be to dispose of the old boy's well fermented piss, and fuckin' gallons of it there were too.

One identical bottle after another was then returned into the daylight from the dark recesses of that deep cupboard. Several minutes into the grim task I glanced over my shoulder at the other identical floor cupboard on the opposite side of the fireplace, and knew almost instinctively that there would be yet more nice neat rows of ye olde bottled pissy duly awaiting discovery. Sure enough upon inspection, there they all were brewing away in the musty darkness; another thirty or so assorted bottles tinged in cloudy shades of grey and yellow, fermenting away in their various stages of 'production'.

My stinky afternoon discovery was then followed by a grizzly sixty minutes involving many trips to the toilet to hurriedly teem the said contents down the loo. I filled two bin bags with the 'empties' alone, as the bubbling, warm bottles were poured away one by one. The vicious and feisty aroma constantly reminded me (as did the tears streaming down my laughing, retching face) of just how sweet my room was going to smell after this nasty task had been completed.

Incense sticks were lit and placed all around the ground floor to encourage that smell of a male public urinal to go away.

The stinky afternoon was brought to a close with a nice hot bath, a cup of tea, a spliff and the common feeling of another nasty squat job going smoothly, like shit off a shiny shovel. Only this time I didn't have to bury anything manmade.

I also pondered upon a feeling of sadness for poor old Victor; why had it come to this? Maybe people could've cared a bit more about that old boy; after all we were a community looking out for each other were we not?

Life in the city can be a lonely existence for anyone, let alone the aged. I also wondered amusingly to myself if he'd used a small funnel for accuracy when 'bottling' his waste product or if he'd simply allowed for the occasional dribble to splash upon the nice (but nasty) carpet?

44 – Fire and Underpants

As the months progressed, the nation adjusted to life without Thatcher, despite the fact that the new PM John Major was still a Tory. He had an unassuming personality, clearly enjoyed his cricket more than running the country but at least he didn't carry a mandate of hatred among the general population, who on the whole were more than happy to see the arse end of the Iron Lady.

The Tories had been in power for eleven years and had certainly made their mark on the people of Britain during the previous decade. There would be a General Election in 1992 and it was almost unimaginable to think of a record fourth term in office for the bloody Conservatives.

Meanwhile, we moved back to our place after the refit and got on with our lives and we now had a new member of the household, a baby boy to Dean and Dawn followed some months later by another boy to another couple who'd moved in earlier the previous year. Donkey Paul moved in permanently as well.

There were now ten of us living in number 29 and although we had better facilities, a functional communal kitchen, a non leaking roof and standardised electricity, we were basically still squatting.

It was on one of those warm midsummer's nights in which it never really gets completely dark until the last couple of hours before dawn, when the next shit storm of trouble came to call upon us once again.

It was still humid in the late hours past midnight; I was finding it difficult to sleep as I laid in my bed listening to the silence. Just as I was drifting off, a sudden high pitched warbling scream of a smoke detector going off somewhere nearby brought me back from my dozing. I remember thinking as I became fully awake that the piercing alarm sounding off so very loudly in the quiet must've been quite close by; perhaps it could be a neighbour's house?

I got up to investigate, opened my door to reveal smoke filling the landing which then confirmed that it wasn't next door on fire, it was our place.

I banged hard on my neighbours room on our landing, and told them to wake Ian in the attic above as they were now rising from their slumber as well. I then raced downstairs and followed the smoke trail to Paul's room in the basement, on glancing through the door I saw that his 'new music centre' (as found on a skip two days before) was being engulfed by three foot high flames which were now lurching from the melting knobs and turntable and reaching eagerly for the ceiling.

Paul was nowhere in sight, so I ran upstairs to our new and recently 'fitted kitchen' to find both he and Dean had already swung into action as they busied themselves by filling up Slippery's tin water bowl and a small saucepan with water from the sparkling, just installed taps. This was of course in preparation to heroically extinguish the raging inferno rapidly developing under our bare feet, as we stood in the dark in our underwear. I joined the end of the queue, snatched the mop bucket stationed by the recently fitted sink and asserted the fact in my head that we could extinguish it ourselves in no time whatsoever.

We in the water queue could now hear the trample of footsteps descending the smoke filled stairways as people hurriedly made their way out.

Ian poked his head around the door and told us to forget about being heroes and get out as well, which was promptly answered in unison by the three of us who exclaimed that, 'We can deal with it, it won't take a minute!'

So there we were; three guys dressed only in our underpants about to tackle a 'small localised fire' without a second thought of our own personal safety. It seemed to take an eternal number of seconds to fill up each of our pathetic water carriers, as we patiently waited for one another to be armed and ready with what was in effect little more than a few pints of water to throw upon the gathering blaze below. We bravely edged our way downstairs slopping water in the now choking corridor, with Paul taking the lead (it was after all his possessions on fire) Dean went next with Slip's bowl, then me making up the rear with half a pail of old mop water.

As we descended the last few stairs which were situated next to the wall adjoining Paul's room, we really began to feel the heat that was now emitting from that wall due to the fire on the other side. In just those few minutes it had taken to fill a couple of containers, the flames had got a hold of everything combustible and the heat was already unbearable. Things were getting decidedly dangerous, especially to bare skin. Paul gingerly pushed the door open slightly as we peered into his room which was now a complete inferno.

Long, red flames were now furiously melting what was left of Paul's 'new music centre' licking the ceiling above and searching for more food. His wooden bed frame to our right (as constructed with his carpentry skills only the week before) was comfortably imploding in the heat as were the curiously quaint pasted-up magazine advertising posters that had decorated that room for a number of years.

The fire realised that the door had been opened wider as it fed itself on a fresh supply of oxygen entering what was left of Paul's new room and rushed headlong towards the three now brown-panted heroes via the quickest route; across the ceiling. At this frightening sight, we simultaneously threw our water containers into the room as Paul just about managed to shut the door in time before we lost most of our body hair and we ran from the house in nanoseconds.

Of course and in hindsight, with this being an electrical fire, water was the very last thing one should throw on a blazing (skip found) music centre in the first instance anyway. But in the moments you have to assess the situation when confronted by it, one automatically thinks water versus fire in those initial shocked seconds.

    We all gathered in the street outside wondering what the fuck to do now. I ran a few doors down to a neighbour's house and banged on the window shouting for the fire brigade, who'd already been alerted by someone anyway. We then awaited their quick arrival as our squatter associates appeared in dribs and drabs to watch our house burn down too. A bottle of whiskey was generously passed around and we all took a slug to ease the gathering reality of our situation. It took on a surreal feeling a bit like bonfire night but in the middle of summer, all we needed now was a few spuds to throw into the raging inferno and maybe we could all dance around in our pants and have a sing song.

So there we were; eight adults, two babies and Slippery the dog standing out in the mild early morning waiting for the big red trucks to speed to our rescue. All of the inhabitants of our now burning home were attired in various and differing styles of undergarments; the women holding the babies stood watching the house in their bras and knickers, Ian had his dark green summer shorts on backwards so that the rear pocket was now facing the front. Meanwhile, Dean modelled his shiny and slinky black Y fronts, and then there was me; adorned in the tightest pair of black and white leopard skin cotton panties, bought in Brixton market on a sad, bad underwear afternoon and still an uneasy source of embarrassment to this day.

    I'll never, ever live that one down. Everyone who was standing outside number 29 watching our possessions burn will always be on hand to remind me of my choice of underwear (in public) on that fateful night. Friends of friends of friends have heard the tales of those underpants, and wish to know if I still have them stored in the back of a drawer to this very day…

Paul on the other hand, proudly wore his amply packed boxers on that occasion; but then again he certainly wasn't nicknamed 'Donkey Paul' just due to the fact that he was born in Doncaster, this being a medium sized town situated in the East Midlands…

'Where's Jazz? Did he get out?' I asked.

This question was out of real anxiety for our house cat, but also partly to distract the gathering assembly of neighbours from the attention my hot pants were making.

I was assured by a grinning neighbour that cats always find an exit unless completely trapped, and as our house was full of holes, there were plenty of escape choices for him to opt for.

It seemed like an age before the blue flashing lights arrived, and as the firemen stepped from their truck we could see that they were already covered in muck and dirt and had been summoned to our location having just extinguished another similar blaze somewhere else nearby. They were late due to the fact that they'd been filling someone else's place up with water and foam before arriving to do the same to ours.

Ian showed one big burly fire-fighter up to the open front window on the ground floor, as he climbed in he stopped momentarily and turned to Ian to say, 'Oh you've got a pool table, that's cool.'

'Yeah,' replied Ian. 'You should pop over for a few games sometime.'

I then showed another equally large fireman the route through our neighbours' house and over the garden wall to our back door. I wonder what he made of my leopard Y fronts as he followed my tiny arse through their hallway. But this was no fashion show as he vaulted over the garden wall in one heroic leap, charged up the flight of concrete steps and in a single motion kicked the flimsy, cheap and newly re-fitted back door in, completely splitting it in half just under the handle.

'It's okay mate, it's unlocked,' I interjected.

I laughed as he apologised and subsequently used the knob to open what was left of our back door; it then flapped stupidly behind him as he disappeared inside.

As we waited patiently for the firemen to do their work, we collectively resigned ourselves to the fact that at least half of our house would be destroyed. Paul's room would be gutted of course, the 'new kitchen' above it would be a torched out disaster area, and the whole place would smell like an extinguished bonfire for months afterwards.

We realised in all probability that our musical equipment which included my lovely drum kit, the PA, all the amps and everyone's guitars in the rehearsal room next to Paul's place would also be burned to a crisp in this unfolding tragedy.

The firemen dutifully hosed the house down for around twenty minutes, then they ripped up some the smouldering new floorboards in the kitchen and eventually let us back in to view the miserable wreckage after all had cooled down sufficiently and been made safe.

On closer inspection we found that we'd in fact been very lucky; for a start Paul's dog Sid (stupid as he was) had woken him up as soon as the fire had started, Paul then punched the smoke alarm outside his room which in turn set the other two alarms off which had been linked to each other on the landings upstairs, which in turn had alerted us all.

But Paul's room was completely gutted, along with most of my record collection which I'd loaned to him just the day before to play on his 'new music centre'. His passport (or rather half of it) was located in the debris, but apart from that he didn't have anything left bar a few clothes, a pair of boots and his amply packed boxer shorts.

Because Paul had the foresight to close his door as we ran for it, this had greatly restricted the oxygen supply to the blaze, which in turn had prevented absolute destruction. The rehearsal room next door although blackened a bit across the ceiling, was virtually undamaged. Our valuable and loved instruments were covered in a layer of sticky black dust but all were saved. Despite the downstairs walls being coated in charred shit and the place now smelt like Guy Fawkes Night, we'd definitely been very lucky to have sustained zero casualties and to still have a house left at all.

Jazz turned up next morning wanting his breakfast, was probably first out of the house and had watched the blaze from a safe distance the night before.

We were all somewhat depressed and fucked off with the reality of yet more building work to do on 'our house' so Paul, Ian, Dean and I decided a trip to the pub in the afternoon was in order to down a few beers and review our good fortune of still being alive. Although Paul had nothing left to salvage as all had been properly torched, he was pretty philosophical about it. I was very glad that my drums were saved as was Ian and the other musicians whose equipment was also in the rehearsal room that night.

I think that if our musical gear had been ruined it would've really knocked the spirit out of us, as if we didn't have enough to cope with let alone losing our only possessions of any real importance. After a number of beers and a good laugh about it all, we returned to the mess, destruction and that awful burned smell as we set ourselves an impossible task... finding a 16th of spliff lost in the fire the night before, in Paul's room of course... A pointless thing to do you'd say under the circumstances, but almost immediately Ian found it under a broken floorboard in middle of the floor in what was left of Paul's cellar apartment.

We then retired to the pool room to get more stoned and drunk, knock some balls around and count our lucky stars.

45 – A Squat with a View

Over the following weeks we cleaned out the charred parts, kept windows open to drag the smell of burnt house away and then set about doing a quick paint job on the landings and stairwells. It didn't take too long a time to bring the house back to normality.

The street was still officially recognised as a squat by Lambeth Council, we were now required to pay a small donation each week to the housing association that'd overseen and paid for the work completed on some of the houses in Villa Road. This was a debate that now split opinions on our long term status in the street. While some of the newer residents were keen on the help being offered by the housing association, other longer term squatters in the street saw this as a legal issue regarding their right to ownership of their homes some of which had occupied them, repaired and maintained them at their own expense and in some instances for considerably more than twelve years.

Legally speaking, if nobody contested a claim to a squatted property for a minimum period of twelve years and one could show proof of occupation for that time, the law in the UK meant that you could then make a claim on it as the owner, and if legally proven and you qualified, one could then sell your squat on the open market if you so desired.

It was not a cut and dried path in which to pick sides on, I'd always gone with the resistance standpoint and said we should not invite a large organisation in via the charitable back door only for us to soon find out our right to claim a large, valuable townhouse in central London would be impossible after we'd agreed to allow thousands of pounds worth of work on 'our property' by a housing association.

A number of others in the street held my views on this too, these houses, despite the general state of many were valuable all the same, and we knew a developer would not have a problem spending hundreds of thousands if not millions on renovating this street, as the inevitable price on the open market would make it very worth their while. Opinions were divided and it did lead to a rift among the once solidly united residents of Villa Road.

In the autumn of 1991, Neil, who lived at number 11 offered me his rooms in their house, he was moving out to set up home with his partner.

He told me that he was only going to offer his space to single guy as there was no chance of ever being re-housed by Lambeth (or any other) Council, and being a squat mate and single he kindly gave me first refusal.

Neil occupied two rooms on the third floor at number 11 and had lived there for years. The 'flat' consisted of a small bedroom at the rear entered via a quaint self-made arch knocked through the adjoining wall, and a spacious living room with a great high view overlooking the park below. All the utilities were legally sorted long ago, the only drawbacks being that the bathroom was situated two floors downstairs, and the tiny kitchen was another floor below that.

Mikey and Janice (who lived in the flat below me) were at the time away in California, and had been for some months, while Mark on the ground floor (also a drummer) mostly stayed at his girlfriend's place. Then there was Kev who occupied the attic room above Neil's place.

I'd always had a natural affinity with the occupants of number 11; they all shared the same distrust as I over the fact that control of our street was gradually being ebbed away by some of the liberal moderates who mostly ran the Villa Road Co-op. We wanted to keep the Villa Road fund going for the sort of emergency repair work that we had used for our roof and to pay into that instead of Family Housing. But it appeared we had been somewhat by-passed in the signature signing process by some of the less radically minded squatters in the street.

With the emergency repairs now completed on the houses in most dire need, Family Housing Association were now seeking to claw their investment back, and more to the point, they were talking of the 'next round' of repairs on some of the other houses in the street.

It was fair enough that the serious structural work could only be carried out by trade professionals, and those types of repairs would always cost money. But the reality of the situation was that in order for this work to be carried out, the main protagonists in Villa Road Coop had by now signed away all rights to ownership and possession in the future not just for themselves but also it appeared for everyone else in Villa Road as well.

This simply meant that the occupants of the houses that had been (or were due) to be re-fitted, would now lose the right to claim their properties as their own in respect of the twelve year unbroken occupation rule. This was a serious blow for many in Villa Road who were split in their opinions of the needs of the now and their potential ownership rights in the future.

One would occasionally hear stories of flaky old hippies who'd been sitting pretty on prime locations that they'd squatted for twenty years. They could then sell the property for hundreds of thousands to developers, just on the strength of a bank statement named, dated and addressed to that property twelve or more years previously.

Squatters considered this as a reward for preventing a house from falling down due to neglect on behalf of their 'legal' owners, be it council or privately owned. If you left a place to fall down and couldn't care about squatters, then with the reality of the housing crisis in the capital, you really didn't deserve to keep 'your property' anyway. This was also a long term option to help squatters to get out of their unpredictable and continuous housing problems and possibly change one's life and future.

This situation included the occupants of number 11, who'd collectively been living there for over ten years, and could prove it too. They came to street meetings when these issues were at the forefront of discussions and finally announced that they did not wish to be a part of the Association deal and would continue to remain independent, and to keep the option of full legal rights of occupancy. But by all accounts, it was already too late.

Mikey was by trade a builder, and had designed a curious kitchen extension and the back of his flat, to which he was quick to demonstrate its sturdiness by jumping up and down on the floor as it gently swayed from side to side. His kitchen design had passed that particular 'safety test', or at least good enough in his opinion. Therefore, he and Janice were totally self sufficient (toilet included) and occupied the whole second floor in the house.

He'd undertaken a lot of repairs on that house down the years, usually out of his own pocket, and he wasn't about to let any surveyors armed with clipboards and hard hats to pass through the front door to nose about in what he now regarded as 'his house'. I don't blame him for his stance, and he had the backing of the rest of the occupants in that house, along with a number of other misinformed residents in Villa Road.

Although number 29 and next door were seriously in need of major building work, my objections to losing our squatters' rights were overruled and out voted by everyone else in the house. I could understand my housemates for going with the option of having a kitchen fitted, hot running water, a new roof and various other life essentials added to our house. We had all lived in pretty abject conditions for years and there were now two young babies barely up on their feet to consider as well. I decided to take up Neil's offer and move to my own space while the opportunity was still there.

Mikey and Janice were still away in America when I moved in, so they didn't really have a say in my arrival, there were only three of us living there until they returned months later. In the meantime, I cleaned the place up and went at the disgusting kitchen with the usual gusto that I'd tasked myself with on many occasions in the past. I even found a pint of milk in the scummy fridge, which was now so off that the carton had blackened and was sagging around the middle with a dense mould. That horror find was subsequently poured into the bin at arm's length as the contents gradually succumbed to the forces of gravity and slipped out in one large, foul smelling, sloppy lump.

I gave my new room a quick lick of paint and a general shift around as one usually does when moving into a new/old squat/accommodation. I pushed the tatty furniture about until it looked about right, cleaned the windows, tacked up the usual anarchist and pop art posters and within a matter of days all was looking like a proper upper middle class squat. One thing that really appealed about this place was the superb, elevated view down onto Max Roach Park, along with the morning sunshine that poured in and warmed the front of the house during the day.

I now found that I had plenty of space, with two adjoining rooms and the house was quiet too, I didn't have to concern myself with communal living anymore, though it had always been well organised and convivial at number 29. I did miss the people and camaraderie of my former digs along the street, the pool table, and the many solid hours of musical creation in our rehearsal room were good days and nights in my memory. I still spent time with my friends at that incredible house, only now I could now return home to my mini apartment on an evening and began to appreciate living on my own again.

For the first few months after moving into number 11, I usually had the place to myself. Kev upstairs in the attic stayed with his girlfriend more often than not, as did Mike downstairs. Whereas Carl (who occupied the rear ground floor (and always rather chilly) room only slept there occasionally. He mostly used the place to drink Stella, smoke spliff and strum his guitar during lunch hours to escape his dreary desk job at the Council.

But Kev however was often on hand to liven up the house more than most; we shared similar tastes in music, he liked to play a few instruments and was a regular pool player, musician and general entertainer at number 29 too. We'd known him pretty much from our start in Villa Road, he was an enterprising bloke, well connected and established in the street, and he made me cry with laughter on loads of occasions with his well-delivered hilarious tales on life in our squatted street.

He was friendly and fun but also not someone to make an enemy of should you choose to do so, as someone once did in Brixton. Sadly for him, things escalated on one particular occasion, leading to violence and some heavy gangster type shit in SW9. I don't know the reasons why all this low rent mobster stuff kicked off, but he moved soon after and I've not seen or heard from him since.

Mikey and Janice eventually returned, and found the house in a better condition than when they'd left it. Jo commented that she'd expected to see that downstairs kitchen 'moving under the weight of roaches'. This of course wasn't the case and they accepted me as a new tenant in number 11 soon enough. Mikey paid me to paint the hallways at one point and this further brightened up the interior landings and allowed the sunshine to pour in through our cool antique front door. I occasionally did a few days' work with Mikey which usually involved unblocking restaurant drainage systems in the west end. Kind of a shitty job, but then again well suited to dirty squatters such as he and I.

Mike, the other drummer moved out soon after Mikey returned, they never did get on anyway. This was especially due to the fact that Mike had constructed a raised bed using lengths of 2 by 4 in his small front room to create much needed storage space underneath this build. However, he had neglected to allow for the fact that his bed was now mounted only a couple of feet under Mikey and Jo's bed in the floor directly above. Therefore, the noisy sex sessions with his girlfriend would keep poor Mikey awake at night seething and turning in his bed above now literally only a matter of inches away. The solution he eventually arrived at was to rip up his floorboards and fill them up with those terrible polystyrene packing chips, to deaden the sounds of the squelching intimacies going on night after night just under his right, or left ear.

With Kev gone as well, this left number 11 a little under occupied, so next in line for rent free accommodation at the house were big Dez and his son Mike. Dez was a friend of Mikey and being six foot six, Jamaican and a former heavyweight boxer he was (and still is) a real gentle giant who could carry a cooker single-handedly up three flights of stairs with a minimal need for the slightest leak of perspiration. Dez took Mike's old room on the ground floor, while Michael who was around sixteen years old took the attic room above me.

    It was all change once again, but I instantly liked Dez and Michael, they were welcome as far as I was concerned, really friendly guys, easy going and fun to have around the house.

46 – The Pig's Head

Alan, and old friend, bass player and formerly a member of a band I was once in, decided one day that he needed some decent bones for his next generation of weird sculptures. He had a flair for designing oddities out of plaster and latex, including shrunken heads and unfriendly looking aliens. We were around Brixton market one sunny afternoon and came across a meat stall selling all the awful animal parts that you really shouldn't eat; trotters, oxtails, hearts, lungs, tongues and pig heads.

Alan could see the aesthetic properties of the bones in a pig's skull, and after a quick market side discussion by the body parts stall, I offered our unused back garden at my place to intern a pig's head in. This burial would be until the necessary time had passed when the skin and gristle were sufficiently decayed enough to dig up the grinning skull for him to procure the creative and grizzly purpose he so deemed it was fit for.

Alan selected the grimmest looking head, which included a pair of unsightly staring blue eyes, a full set of yellow teeth and hairy, pointy ears. The pig's head vendor man viewed the pair of us with some confusion as he slid the chosen head inside two of those thin, blue striped carrier bags in exchange for money. We walked back to Villa Road while the occasional drip of blood seeped from the doubled up bags, as little piggy made his way to a new, dark but temporary home.

After a brief ground survey we found a nice spot then furtively buried the head a couple of feet down in my back garden like a couple of nervous serial killers, and left a marker to remember where piggy was located. Then it was back in for a nice cup of tea and forget about the bloody purchase until the bones had been picked clean in worm world below the surface.

About five months later, Alan was hanging at my place once more, and it was decided that it was time for piggy to re-surface. We dug down carefully until soon enough we hit skull. However, this little piggy was not quite 'bone clean' which meant that some 'scraping' would have to be carried out in order to arrive at that brilliant 'whiter than white' look. I filled a bucket with hot water and bleach products then stood a way back in my kitchen retching and barking up as Alan went about the most unpleasant of tasks on the steps by the back door.

    If the smell of shit from our broken drain that time at number 29 wasn't bad enough, closely followed by a whiff of old Vic's fermented piss, then the smell of death beats all bad odours by a country mile.

    You hear stories of dead pensioners rotting away in a council flat for weeks on end in the height of the summer, whilst the next door neighbours simply fill their flats up with air freshener to get rid of that 'terrible smell', and wonder why they've been using a job lot of fly repellent too?

    If a pig's head could smell that bad after being buried for a few months one can only imagine the stink that a human body would make while gradually decaying in front of the still switched on telly week after week, as the bills and junk mail piled up on the doormat. People? They simply forgot about old Bob next door who hasn't been seen 'in weeks' and 'What is that awful smell everywhere?'

Eventually, after a lot of barfing and weeping eyeballs, the deed was done, and a piece of shiny work piggy looked too. The bright, gleaming clean skull was carefully bagged up and taken away to Alan's workshop to be turned into a piece of art and expensively sold at his stall in Camden Market.

Dirty Squatters

47 – The Drum Shack

Part of the attraction in my decision to move along the street to number 11 was that the house also had a small, windowless room in the basement similar to the rehearsal room set up at number 29. This space was another ideal location for a drum practice studio; it was well sealed up, unused and I could store my kit down there instead of having to block the hallways or to lug them four flights up to my flat.

I converted this room into my very own drum shack, and with a music centre set up next to me I could now practise along to tapes of bands through headphones. As any drummer will tell you, having somewhere to practise alone is usually very difficult, after all, who wants to live next door, below or above a drummer, even if that person were a good stickman, or unfortunately not. The set up I created was convenient, very local and wouldn't disturb anyone nearby. I would only practise in the afternoons and muffled the kit down to take the edge off the shattering noise, but enough to be able to discern what was coming down the headphones matched by the sound bouncing back from my kit.

After a few months of hard practising, I felt I'd raised my level sufficiently to start on the hunt to find some musician types who were doing musical stuff.

I had an idea of what I was looking for and having driven my drums in a clapped out van to many backwater rehearsal rooms down the years, I'd often been disappointed when meeting a bunch of guys with expensive equipment, nice cars and zero in the 'give it some bollocks' department. Fuck that, I decided it was time to create head nodding noise with other like minded people that would make people grin the moment you stepped on stage, rather than wince at the first few notes, knowing that they'd have to endure a further forty-five minutes of drivel thereafter.

I would usually get to an audition a bit early, allowing time to drag my gear in and wait around whilst another drummer was giving it some on the other side of the padded wall/cell.

Then it would be my turn in the armpit sweaty 'studio' to meet 'the guys' and assemble my kit, quickly.

Sometimes the nervous excitement of an audition would be ruined before one had even set up the hi hat and sat down on the drum stool with the following enquiry...

The often asked question to a drummer at an audition:
'Can you play to a click track mate?'

The often answered question of said drummer:
'Do I look like a fucking robot to you geezer?'

I knew I wasn't the only muso who'd been brought up on Bowie, T-Rex, The Sweet, Alice Cooper and Zeppelin before punk came along to give bored teenagers something to really relieve the monotony of life and the dire selection of 'popular music' in Britain in the grey mid seventies?

It often felt as if Punk, new wave, 2 Tone and all the other diverse directions that came out of the late seventies and beyond had never happened when it came to band auditions. I always kept the faith and searched for a group of individuals who didn't necessarily need to be blessed with musical excellence or the ability to play fucking hammer cords. Please, just have something lyrical to say, hopefully with some volume, inside four minutes, and as so often the case, the usual four or five cords will do nicely in a songwriting sense, thank you.

There were occasions when something different and exciting was actually happening behind the 'soundproofed' wall, and I knew instantly that these people were playing good stuff and possibly desperate squatters as well; and therefore lived, ate, breathed and shat music in the same manner as I.

However, the downside to this scenario would often be that they were currently auditioning Keith Moon behind the wobbly wall; therefore the rest of the 'also showed up' drummers (like me) didn't really need to bother attending. There has always been plenty of competition for drummers, you usually had to be on the beat every time, and play pretty much like Moon, Copeland, Budgie or Bonham (or an fucking Android) just to make the shortlist.

There were many excellent drummers about during that time to which truthfully speaking I wasn't in the same league with, despite the fact I was in a position to be able to practice as and when I wished. I was now in my mid thirties and unexpectedly had to take nearly a year off after a rather embarrassing and painful drumming related testicle accident. I lost time and a certain level of skill during his break as my left one expanded to the size of a tennis ball for months. I wasn't convinced that I'd be able to regain a level of ability that was now much required to make the grade, or for that matter to actually wear tight jeans again.

The other factor that lingered in my conscience was how much more disappointment and muso poverty I was prepared to put myself through?

There will be chances that every musician would have during their career, even for those with natural talent it will take dedication and effort to arrive at an opportunity to possibly find a level of success that may last and provide a living income, or better should you attain something more lasting than Nano Glory.

Music is a place where a moment's creativity can completely change an individual's or a group's life direction at a stroke. Then there is the added bonus of so many hearing your sound the world over, this being in much the same manner as with all the arts. You never know until you turn an amp on, pick up a brush, a chisel or take a deep breath just before you push down on the pedal of a potter's wheel.

48 – End of an Era

As the 'building management process' moved on at an ever increasing rate in Villa Road, it was now 1998 and time for Family Housing Association to finally put their money where their mouth was and make good on the promises made to all the squatters in the street.

We, the signed up co-op members would all now be 'eligible for re-housing' and offered various alternatives when the builders arrived to start work on the selected houses next in line to bring them up to the legal requirements for proper human inhabitation. Alterations on our shabby houses would now have to include fire resistant inner doors, certificated internal wiring (as not installed by the Villa Road 'electricians') and also escape exits for each floor, which would be via iron spiral staircases leading into the back gardens. In the case of number 29 this would involve removing half a buried motorbike, and possibly flattening out a large mound (of buried, human shit) situated in the middle of the now weed ridden garden.

The options that FHA brought to the table were pretty accommodating under the circumstances; some of the houses were going to be left alone anyway, so those residents were sitting pretty, at least for the time being. This included number 11 where I'd now lived for a few years.

If your house was due for the refit, you were given the option to move out and be housed temporarily until your flat was finished and then you'd be able to return.

Similarly, after completion you could move back into the street and be re-housed in a different flat or house depending on your particular needs.

Finally, the last option was to move out of Villa Road entirely, and be offered an Assured Tenancy in another area in Lambeth where FHA owned housing stock. This was available to all Villa Road residents and was the option I went for; after fifteen years of squatting since moving to London, it now appeared that I was to be offered something that was traditionally impossible for a single man in good health living in this city; that being a one bedroomed, centrally heated flat, in roughly the same area, and at a reasonable rent as offered by all housing associations.

This was a far better an offer than a council flat on an estate; I knew I'd get something decent and probably a flat in a converted house in a nice street. Anyone who was interested in this option also had to be on Lambeth Council's housing waiting list, to which I had been for over twelve years.

As soon as the documents came through my door, I signed up immediately to finally escape the squat life without a second thought. I was excited at the prospect of what I might be offered in this new twist in my future accommodation fate.

I'd heard the rumour around the street that quite a few of our number had decided to go the same way as myself; out of the squat life once and for all. Soon enough, an appointment to view the first of my two choices arrived in the mail; I looked for the address in the A-Z and found it was very near to Villa Road.

I met the man waiting outside a nice looking house in a quiet, tree lined, street that I'd probably wandered down at some point in the past. We shook hands as he opened the front door, leading into a hall and then proceeded to another entrance on the ground floor. I wasn't really expecting much and was relatively neutral as he showed me the living room first. The whole place had recently been painted in the usual eggshell tint throughout; the front room was of a good size with large sash windows, Edwardian architrave and a curved wall on one side. I liked it straight away.

He then showed me the bedroom which had a door leading to a path onto a back garden, nice. Along the hallway was a small bathroom, then finally a spacious kitchen which was already fitted with cupboards and tops. This was the room that swung it for me; I simply knew that I'd never be offered anything better than this no matter how many choices I'd be given. The added bonus of the kitchen was that the back door opened straight onto the medium sized, Victorian walled garden.

I asked about the garden and my new housing officer said that I'd be sharing it with the family upstairs. Though on observation, and the general overgrown state of it, it seemed that it wasn't currently being used. I could already visualize balmy evening summer parties and barbeques out there; it was just the right dimensions to comfortably accommodate about twenty-five chilled people.

Not only was the flat clean, decorated, and completely fitted out for human inhabitation, it was centrally heated with radiators and a back boiler behind the toasty gas fire in the living room. I nosed about looking in cupboards as you invariably do when viewing a property, only this time without the need of a jimmy bar, a peg over my nose and a mate to hold a candle.

We stopped at a door in the passageway between front room and kitchen that didn't have a handle attached, so I was unable at that point to satisfy my further curiosity.

I asked my soon-to-be housing officer, 'What's behind this door?'

'I don't know, I haven't seen this flat myself before, probably another cupboard,' he replied.

'Okay,' I responded, 'I like the flat and I'll take it if it's available, how much is the rent?' I further ventured

'£49.50 a week,' he replied.

On hearing just what I'd be getting for the money, I could hardly believe my luck. All this and a back garden for less than £50 a week in central London? Fuckin' marvellous I thought.

'When can I move in?'

'In a couple of weeks, once the contract has been signed.'

I had a good feeling about this place and was relieved at my final good fortune regarding my long term housing 'difficulties'.

Dez and Michael helped me to move all my squat furniture into the flat soon after, the mystery door revealed stairs down to a small basement area which could be used for storage or growing weed as one friend suggested immediately upon viewing. The three of us somehow manhandled my old piano down several flights of stairs in number 11 Villa Road, got it through the door at my new place and shoved the thing up against one of the living room walls where it's sat ever since. I've never been able to bring myself to get rid of it besides the fact I can't play a note, but it's great when friends who can actually play come over and knock out a few tunes on the ageing keys.

So, here ends the story of my life as a dirty squatter? Fifteen years with a 'short break' of some twenty months in the middle whilst I resided in grim, serial killer Bedshitland, which I count as practically squatting anyway.

What did I learn from these experiences? I learned to be self sufficient and know that you didn't have to live outside a tube station or under a bridge just because you were 'homeless'. There were empty properties aplenty all over London, at least at that time, so we opened them, occupied them, fixed them up and lived in them.

I made lasting friendships with those I'd struggled with during the dark Thatcher years. We became a strong, unified collection of people who would live in appalling conditions and make the most of it. Anything was and is better than living on the streets as we took control of our situation, understood our legal rights and acted upon them.

We learned how to install plumbing, without the leaks, eventually. We learned how to rewire, without getting electrocuted, eventually. We learned how to hot wire a fuse box, usually by candle light while standing in rubber soled boots. We toiled to unblock sinks full of rice and maggots, and usually both. We climbed seventy feet onto a wobbly, windy, smashed roof to stop the rain from filling our house up with water (and pigeons) during the winter months. We learned how to break into practically anywhere, at any time.

If London councils failed to give an empty flat to someone in need, then we'll maintain it until they'd made up their minds what to do with it.

We also learned how to paint; boy, did we learn that one too? We could decorate a squat in a day and then sit back while it was still drying to muse upon our ability to help ourselves in a dire situation.

I believe that after a decade and a half of hard living in sometimes pitiful conditions, I was finally rewarded for my efforts on behalf of London's housing crisis, by being given a flat which was the envy of many who came to visit me, and of course I looked after the place like it was my own.

Dirty Squatters? Well, for so many especially in 70s and 80s London it was just a question of a highly important priority in this world…

…And that was somewhere to live which was usually procured by a hook, a crook, a hacksaw and a jimmy bar.

The End

Appendix

Baby Belling – A small, easily transportable, all-in-one, twin ringed oven sometimes fitted with a grill. A popular kitchen addition sought by squatters on a budget who are in need of an alternative cooking solution other than an electric bar fire turned on its side.
Bailiff – Short necked, thug-like representatives of British councils, contractually employed to forcibly remove squatters, their pitiful belongings and their non exotic pets from illegally occupied buildings.
Bedsit (Bedshitland) – Grim, uninspiring, cheaply converted townhouses, often located in Streatham, London; a marginally better housing alternative to living in a cardboard box under the motorway or in a buckled shopping trolley with a fucked wheel.
Black Monday (1987) – A bad day for yuppies, stock brokers, property developers and venture capitalists.
Blagger – A person who possesses the ability to gain entry into a club, gig or festival by pretending to know someone in a band on the bill or an organiser of influence at said event. 'I'm on the guest list mate, honest, check again.'
Bollock Bowl – An aged, plastic handled, aluminium cooking vessel as kept in the bathroom. Most commonly used to procure a 'Gentleman's Wash'.
Botch Job – A quick fix repair solution for the squatter short on tools and budget.
Brown Bread – A London (or Cockney) rhyming slang term for the dead. 'I'm tellin' ya, he was well and truly brown bread.'
Broadmoor – An infamous, highly secure, psychiatric hospital in England that houses the criminally insane.
B.T. – Formerly known as British Telecom, the primary supplier of telephone connection lines in the UK (until priva-

tisation) which also included service to squat homes, provided you could cover relevant identification and the installation fee.

CND – Campaign for Nuclear Disarmament; the general public's global, angry voiced opinions against the nuclear arms race as delivered via megaphone from the 1950s to the current day. Gerald Holtom's 'Peace' symbol is the worldwide recognised logo for campaigners against Mutually Assured Destruction.

Crustafarian – Caucasian persons who wear their hair in the dreadlock style, have a fondness for loud dub reggae and are often spotted lying down in city parks during the summer months.

DHSS – Formerly the Department of Health & Social Security, a government department primarily concerned with all matters in relation to the sick, the 'Non Employed' or a combination of both.

Dive Bombing – The act of furtively picking up half smoked cigarette butts at bus stops. A 'first smoke of the day' find for the homeless nicotine addict.

Dolia – The Greek expression for 'work', more commonly known in other western nations as hard manual labour.

Donkey Jacket – A black coloured, heavy duty 'workman's coat', often worn by site workers.

Dossing – The act of casually sleeping rough on a friend's settee; 'You're welcome to doss on my sofa tonight mate.'

Drachma – Formerly the currency of Greece, as used in payment for employment served under mostly medieval working conditions.

D.S.S. – Department of Social Security, as newly known when the 'H' for 'Health' branch was outsourced.

Dyno Rod – A twenty-four-hour emergency plumbing organisation, who *do not* offer a shit bailing service prior to unblocking six months of your own effluent jammed in your own sewerage drain.

Essex – A Home County in southern England, predominantly occupied by the middle Classes.

Evening Standard – Formerly 'London's Newspaper' sold daily outside tube stations, until its demise, subsequently followed its resurrection.

Fag – An Anglo Saxon slang term for a cigarette, a hit of tobacco. Cockney Adj; 'Can you spare me an Oily Rag?'

Gentleman's Wash – The act of cleansing one's genitalia in an especially reserved bowl or old saucepan. See 'Bollock Bowl'.

Giro – A white, green and purple coloured government issued cashier's cheque. A sum of money confirming your eligibility to be classified as not employed in any capacity in the previous two weeks by the state.

Glastonbury Festival – A collection of muddy fields sited in Wiltshire that annually plays host to thousands of stoned music lovers who wish to spend three days and nights living like hobos in the burning sunshine, or more likely, the pouring rain.

Greenham Common – A popular camping destination in eastern England; primarily occupied by non married ladies who wished to air their grievances over the US/Russian cold war arms race in the 1980s.

Iron Lady – Thatcher, Margaret Hilda, Ruler of Britain: May 1979 – November 1990.

Labour Party – The 'Socialist' or left wing arm of the British political system.

L.E.B. – London Electricity Board, formerly London's one and only electricity utility supplier to those who were legally connected, and to those who were not.

Legal Notice – An A4 sized document explaining your legal right to occupy a property. A warning of prosecution for trespassing should someone desperate enough decide to break into your squat and steal nothing of any value.

Lift (Elevator) – A graffiti covered, rubbish strewn, urinal smelling metal container used to convey residents and squatters alike to their high rise accommodation on council estates.

Loadsamoney – Referring to the Yuppie culture during the 1980s; those who made a fortune in property speculation, venture capitalism or stock broking and enjoyed all the financial benefits of Thatcher's Britain.

London A-Z – The quintessential cartography map book listing the roads, streets, lanes and avenues in the Greater London area.

Loot – A cheap, colour coded, thrice weekly classified ads paper. Most often purchased by those in need of shabby second hand furniture, to hire a person with a light van, to locate fellow musicians or to leave brief voice messages (charged at premium rate) to potential suitors in the ' Lonely Singles' section.

Mankey – Squalid, dirty, cheap and semi broken. A term commonly used to describe an old sofa found in the street and subsequently impounded by a squatter for use as 'furniture'.

Mary Whitehouse (Deceased) – Formerly Britain's premier anti porn and sleaze campaigner who was duly rewarded for her hard work when a top selling pornographic magazine named their publication after her.

Melody Maker (1926 – 2000) – British music news, record reviews, interviews, gig listings and a classified section where cash struck musicians can trade thrashed amps, faulty wah wah pedals, hammered drum kits, buzzy guitar pick ups and nearly broken microphone stands.

Merrydown – A popular brand of inexpensive bottled cider consumed in vast quantities during the nineteen eighties by Punk Rockers, Goths, Crustafarians, sociopaths and the band Peter and the Test Tube Babies.

Middle Arse – A slang term for The Middle Classes, who reside in a place called 'Middle England'.

Mine Sweeping – The act of finishing other people's drinks in a bar or club after they've left, or at the end of the night. A low budget method enabling one to become inebriated for free. Especially popular among winos, dole scum, losers, desperados and students.

Mobile Phone – A multi buttoned hard plastic communication device approximately the size and weight of a house brick, and fitted with a hazardous two foot long extendable aerial. As used by Yuppies to converse loudly with stock brokers and sports car dealers whilst in public environments such as rail stations, restaurants and art galleries.

Mole Grips – A very sturdy, locking, portable vice grip, the essential all-in-one tool used by the soon-not-to-be homeless to gain semi legal entry into an unoccupied property.

Monkey – Commonly known in betting circles as the sum of Five Hundred Pounds (Sterling). The going price to purchase a medium sized living primate on the black market. Adjective; 'That's going to cost you a monkey.'

Nano Glory – A level of success attained in 'The Arts', be it only for a minute, or less.

National Grid – A network of large pylons, thick cabling and grey junction boxes stationed throughout the country which deliver an electricity supply to the population. Final costs of this commodity are sometimes extracted via a rectangular shaped switching unit with spinning wheels enclosed inside a windowed mathematical panel. This instrument is commonly known as a 'Meter'.

National Trust – A long running British institution claiming to protect buildings of historical importance from the public, squatters and property developers alike.

NME (New Musical Express) – British music press and chief rival to the Melody Maker. Weekly news of the music industry and often purchased by musicians seeking musicians or by drummers seeking a job.

Pikeys – A collection of travelling people who usually reside in caravans and trailers on wasteland areas; Known especially for their adept and persuasive skills when selling broken down cars as 'runners'.

Poll Tax – A 'living space levy' originally conceived in the year AD 1381 which subsequently led to the Peasants' Revolt in England and Wales. The Poll Tax Act was passed into law by the Conservative Government in the United Kingdom immediately after the second and also failed revolution commencing from April 1st 1990 (AD).

Poll Tax Riot (31st March 1990) – See 'failed revolution' above.

Pot Noodles – Snack based dried food in a plastic cup, supplied in various exotic flavours. An instant hit among the long term unemployed, the elderly, the classless, the tasteless and students.

R.A.B.I.E.S. Party – An independent political party based in Lambeth who also failed to unhinge the Conservative Party from power in the 1987 UK General Election.

Red Top – A British national newspaper ideologically angled at and for readership by the working classes.

Retsina – A Greek alcoholic beverage sometimes referred to as floor polish. Occasionally mellowed over time and usually drunk very quickly. This act is generally followed by throwing a perfectly decent shot glass into an open fire.

Scouse – An endearing term given to the accent belonging to those who were born in or around the city of Liverpool in England.

Scuzzy – Untidy in appearance, the look of the unwashed.

Spliff – The act of rolling and then smoking a hashish joint, as usually mixed with tobacco.

Squatters Advisor – A person who claims to know much about squatting and will occasionally accompany squatters on accommodation sorties. The outcome of this often results in the arrest of one or all parties at any moment during the evening.

Tories – The Conservative Party, the right wing occupancy of British politics.

Torch – An alternative description for a flashlight; 'Pass the torch would ya? I can't see shit in here.'

Totting – The practice of hurriedly ripping out the copper fittings from empty properties with a view to selling the valuable metal commodity onto a local scrap merchant for quick, hard cash.

The Barrier Block – A monolithic, public housing building located on Coldharbour Lane in Brixton, London. Now an established part of 'Architectural Planning disasters in England and Wales during the 1970s.'

The Black Death – Also known as 'The Plague', as spread by fleas attached to black rats. A deadly pandemic that ravaged Asia and Europe during the Dark Ages, fatal in approximately 100% of those infected regardless of class, wealth, gender, or if you already carried syphilis anyway.

The Dole – A small, twice monthly sum of Government money paid to unemployment benefit claimants; these benefit claimers are commonly known as 'Dole Scum'.

The Bosse – Occasionally a term used to describe a Greek employer who supplies endless hard labour in the melting Mediterranean sunshine, in return for a small Drachma fee and an even smaller can of beer.

White Paper – A political idea scribbled on a napkin by a member of the cabinet over an all expenses paid lunch, and subsequently fast tracked through Parliament into law.

U.B.O. – Unemployment Benefit Office; where one visits to receive unearned money from the state.

UB40 – Formerly the official job seekers benefit card and proof of identity when claiming unemployment benefits on a twice monthly rota. This design was then used in pictorial reference on the album cover on the release of their multi million selling first album 'Signing Off' by the British reggae band UB40 in 1980.

Yellow Pages – The business telephone directory, delivered free of charge c/o British Telecom to every home in the UK once a year. Weighing over four pounds the manual could be used as a door wedge, a deadly weapon or a highly combustible method to start a roaring fire in your Victorian squat.

www.ingramcontent.com/pod-product-compliance
Lightning Source LLC
Chambersburg PA
CBHW061634040426
42446CB00010B/1415